"If you want to know what led up to the epic clash described in Mark Bowden's *Black Hawk Down*, read [this book.]"
—DANIEL P. BOLGER
Author of *Savage Peace* and *Death Ground*

"Marty Stanton is a great soldier and American hero. He has given us a superb view of the Somalia intervention from the perspective of the grunts on the ground.... This is a must read for those who want to get a real sense of how these strange new missions of peacekeeping and humanitarian assistance are handled by our troops."
—GEN. ANTHONY C. ZINNI, USMA (Ret.)

"Sophisticated and contextualized observations are rife in this field memoir, one of the few to come out of the conflict [in Somalia] and certainly in a class by itself in terms of the quality of the writing . . . . It is certainly one of the finest books of its kind."
—*Publishers Weekly*

"A sort of unofficial prequel to Mark Bowden's *Black Hawk Down*, this eye-opening chronicle of Operation Restore Hope lets us see the turmoil in Somalia through a soldier's eyes . . . . For fans of military nonfiction, this is a must-read."
—*Booklist*

Books published by The Random House Publishing Group
are available at quantity discounts on bulk purchases for
premium, educational, fund-raising, and special sales use.
For details, please call 1-800-733-3000.

SOMALIA
ON $5 A DAY

A Soldier's Story

Martin Stanton

PRESIDIO
PRESS

BALLANTINE BOOKS • NEW YORK

A Presidio Press Book
Published by The Random House Publishing Group
Copyright © 2001 by Martin N. Stanton

All rights reserved under International and Pan-American Copyright Conventions. Published in the United States by The Random House Publishing Group, a division of Random House, Inc., New York, and simultaneously in Canada by Random House of Canada Limited, Toronto. Originally published by Presidio Press, an imprint of The Random House Publishing Group, a division of Random House, Inc., in 2001.

Presidio Press and colophon are trademarks of Random House, Inc.

www.ballantinebooks.com

ISBN 0-89141-822-9

Manufactured in the United States of America

All photos from author's collection

First Mass Market Edition: August 2003

OPM   10   9   8   7   6   5   4   3   2   1

ents

Contents

Prologue

Hostile fire or imminent danger pay for U.S. armed forces personnel is $150 per month. It works out to about $5 a day.

Kismayu (February 1993)

The crowd on the street scattered at the shots from the gunman, and two people went down with bullet wounds. We chased the gunman but he disappeared into one of the numerous alleyways, and the crowd soon returned to the street, screaming and chanting. A few of them looked at the two men on the ground, but most took up where they left off, throwing rocks down the street at the other faction. I watched the rioters swarm past us, bent on pursuing their adversaries. I didn't know if they were supporters of Jess or Morgan. It really didn't make much difference. We were supposed to keep the opposing sides apart, but how could we? Two under-strength rifle battalions couldn't keep a city full of Hatfields and McCoys from immolating one another. We were like the security guards at a fever pitch college football game trying to keep the crowd from pouring onto the field to tear down the goalposts after the final gun. Only these people weren't celebrating; they were murdering one another. Whole communities had taken to the streets—men, women, and children—all hurling rocks and throttling their neighbors. Gunmen from both sides used the crowds as cover to spray the other side with assault rifle fire or grenades.

It was blazingly hot. Kismayu sits right on the equator.

Sweat ran off me in rivulets. My uniform was soaked underneath my flak jacket. I looked at my watch, nine o'clock. Today's riot had been going on for two hours and showed no sign of abating. The previous day's riot had petered out around four o'clock. But all that meant was the factions had drawn apart to regroup and prepare for the next day's riot. This was the third day of rioting and mayhem in Kismayu. I wondered how long it would last.

I looked at the men with me. All were tired and sweating profusely under their body armor. None of us had gotten a good night's sleep for three days. There were six of us in TAC-2, the battalion's alternate command post. Lieutenant Colonel Sikes was about a quarter mile away in TAC-1. Between us we were supposed to control our companies trying to contain the rioting. At the moment, however, I didn't feel as though we had control of anything. The general uselessness of trying to keep all the rioters apart had long since become evident, and the directions from brigade and JTF (joint task force) Kismayu headquarters were to concentrate on the capture or neutralization of gunmen. I supposed the rationale behind this was to keep down the number of fatalities. Considering that the Somalis were bludgeoning, stabbing, and stoning one another to death with reckless abandon, focusing on gunmen seemed pretty futile. Still, there it was.

We had begun the operation four days ago, searching for weapons, trying to disarm the major factions in Kismayu. It was like trying to disarm the National Rifle Association. The combined American and Belgian search found weapons everywhere—in wells, in fresh graves, in the beds of wounded people, in every hiding place imaginable. After a day's worth of effort we had captured more than a hundred weapons, but this was only a fraction of what was in Kismayu. The rioting between factions had begun on the second day of the search. Hundreds and then thousands of people from the two factions took to the streets and began attacking one another, the crowds providing cover for their armed gunmen. We started by trying to keep the two sides separate. Imagine a bunch of Japanese businessmen trying to settle a gang dispute in South Central Los Angeles and you will begin to understand what it was like. Now we were just trying to keep down the casualties by taking out the best-armed members of the factions. Somewhere a negotiator and the Special Forces guys were trying to arrange a truce, but that wasn't part of our world right now.

A platoon from Alpha Company moved past us to disperse the rioters. The troops carried as little equipment as possible in order to compensate for the heat and strenuous activity. Most soldiers wore only their body armor and helmet and carried a two-quart canteen on a strap. They carried their rifles with bayonets fixed and extra magazines in their body armor pockets. This allowed them to better chase the fleet gunmen; it also deprived rioters of individual load-bearing harness straps to grab. I watched the soldiers slam into the rear of the rioters and start to disperse them. Most of the rioters merely squirted down alleyways into new fights in other streets. A few of the dumber ones tried to fight the Alpha Company troopers and got thumped for their troubles. A rock pinged off my helmet and I whirled to see several young boys and women disappear around the corner. No use going after them.

Bravo Company reported on the radio that they'd just found another victim of the riot. Another dumb peckerhead who was out throwing rocks and got pummeled to death. It was an oft-told story in the past three days. The two factions would advance and retreat up an avenue, throwing rocks at one another with slings. They would rarely come to blows in a stand-up fight. The rocks thrown by slings would raise a huge welt and even break bones. If a person was hit on the head and knocked down, he could be seriously hurt. Worse, if his side happened to be retreating he'd be left on the street. If the other side advanced over him, he (or she) would literally be torn limb from limb. The Tactical Operations Center (TOC) acknowledged the transmission, just another fact to report. I wondered how many people had been killed in the riot. No one was keeping a running total. We and the Belgians were finding more bodies all the time, some of whom had been tortured gruesomely.

Having cleared the street, Alpha platoon moved to the side into cover. No point in deliberately making yourself a target. A couple of grenade explosions a few streets over signaled a shift in the action, and the platoon moved toward the contact. We weren't making any useful contribution to command and control where we were, so I moved TAC-2 to link up with the Alpha Company headquarters. Somalis darted out of our way as we drove cautiously down the street, lined with stucco and cinderblock buildings, our weapons facing out, with each man in the truck taking a different sector of observation. We passed a few wounded people, including a man holding a bloody rag to his head. A twelve-year-old boy and his mother were sitting on the side of the road looking at his bloody leg. People began coming out of alleyways into our street in greater numbers. When they saw us, they stopped and watched but made no threatening gestures. They looked at us like children bent on mischief, just waiting for the teacher to pass. A few didn't even bother to hide their machetes and spears. They had no guns visible, so we just moved through them, like tourists driving through Lion Country Safari in Florida.

I decided to stop in a shady spot and watch the street. It looked as though a good crowd was beginning to form and we'd probably have fighting again here soon. The radio was a constant stream of reports and incidents. The Belgians had a man wounded and had shot a gunman. Several more Somalis had been killed by the grenade explosions, and Bravo Company had just been in another firefight and captured two gunmen. I reported my position to Lieutenant Colonel Sikes and told him that we had another group of rioters forming near where I was. He acknowledged but said no one was available to break them up right now. I sat in the shade and watched the crowd grow as I listened to the sporadic shots and explosions ring through the town around me. I took a long drink of warm water and looked at my watch. God, it wasn't even ten o'clock. This was going to be a long day.

Introduction

Operation Restore Hope and the Somalia intervention of 1992–95 will probably fade to a footnote in American military history. It's easy to understand why; the Somalia intervention was a failure. Not a heroic-battle-against-the-odds failure, such as Bataan in World War II, nor a spectacular nation-rending failure, such as Vietnam. No, Somalia was a squalid and puzzling little failure. We went there to save the starving and left sixteen months later with our weapons facing out as the last helicopter took off and the last Marine amtrac left the beach. Then we had to go back a year after that to ensure that all the allies we'd left behind got out too. Such events do not produce epic poetry.

Somalia was important, however. It was the first intervention of the "new world order." Had it succeeded, the history of many other parts of the world might have been different. Why it didn't succeed is worth studying.

Though the operation was a failure, the army and the services in Somalia performed magnificently. The tactics, techniques, and procedures applied in Somalia became the cornerstone for the army's doctrine in operations other than war (OOTW). The soldiers, sailors, Marines, and airmen did all that was asked of them. More's the pity the policymakers were not asking for the right things.

Somalia was like Vietnam in one respect. Where you were and when you were there dictated what kind of action you saw. A soldier fighting in Vietnam's Ia Drang Valley in 1965 saw a different war than one who served in Khe Sanh in 1968, the Mekong Delta in 1969, or the Cambodian invasion of 1970. The same was true of Somalia. Troops deployed at the beginning of the intervention saw a significantly different picture than those deployed toward the end. Units in Mogadishu saw a different conflict than those in the hinterlands. There was no one "Somalia experience"; rather, Somalia was a kaleidoscope of different experiences.

This book is both a history and a remembrance. It is a history because I can reasonably reproduce in sequential order the events that happened to Task Force 2-87 infantry in its deployment. It is a remembrance because I can recall how I felt at the time about Somalia and what was happening there. It is also a reflection, because one who participated in the Somalia mission must think about it and wonder how it went wrong. Beyond that, this book is also a tribute to the officers and men of Task Force 2-87 infantry, 10th Mountain Division, in Somalia, a small offering of affection from one who knew them well and is proud to have soldiered with them.

I have tried to capture the battalion's experience from the point of view of the battalion operations officer, the position I served in during the operation. I did this mainly through amateur expedience—my own point of view is the one I can express the best—but there were more than five hundred points of view in the task force. I have done my best in this narrative to also represent the thoughts and impressions of my comrades in arms. I hope I have done them justice.

Preface

Saudi Arabia, Eastern Province (April 1991)

The 2d Brigade of the Saudi National Guard drove south from Khafji in a flurry of national flags. Each one of their hundreds of V-150 armored cars flew at least one large Saudi flag, with a sword on a green field and Arabic script proclaiming the greatness of God. They drove south from the oil fires that still burned in Kuwait and turned the sky black even at midday. South from the devastation and twilight, armored cars and trucks weaved in and out in a long, exceedingly happy, and rather unmilitary formation. Convoy procedures and speeds were not always adhered to, but they had an excuse. They were the 2d Brigade, the King Abdul Aziz Brigade, the victors of Khafji, and they were going home.

Among the convoys rode the few American advisors who had been with them during the war; I was one of them. The GMC Jimmys of the advisors showed the wear of the past eight months. We, too, had been happy when the brigade received its orders to return to its garrison in Al Hofuf. The war had been a tremendously exciting adventure, but the weeks stationed on the Saudi-Kuwait border after the war was over had drawn on interminably, every day spent clearing battlefield debris and looking at that black sky. Not tonight. Tonight we were going to sleep in real beds and have real showers. Tonight we would eat in the best restaurant in Al Hofuf. Tonight we would call our loved ones at home. The convoy moved south through Jubayl and Dammam. Saudis who had grown inured to the endless convoys of American troops went wild at the sight of a unit of "hometown" boys. Cars passed us honking and cheering. The Saudi guardsmen waved back, proud enough to burst. The convoy rolled on to Al Hofuf.

I was proud of them too. I was coming to the end of my two-year tour as an advisor, and to me the Saudi guardsmen had grown immeasurably during the war. They faced the Iraqi attack at Khafji and defeated it. They made the initial breaches in the earth berm and the minefields of the Iraqi defenses on the Kuwaiti border and passed the rest of the Eastern Coalition forces through it. They had soldiered well. The confidence they exhibited took me back to some of the training we had done before the war. I was proud that, in my own small way, I had helped them prepare for what they'd just accomplished.

For me, the end of this mission brought the inevitable question: Where would I go next? There is a stratified pattern of jobs that an infantry officer must hold before he can be promoted to the next grade. I had been a major for a little less than a year, and it was time for me to return to an American unit to be a battalion operations officer (S3) or executive officer (XO). I knew and accepted this. But where? Being newly married (four months) with our first child due in September (it *had* been an eventful year), I was curious as to where I would end up.

The brigade reached Al Hofuf, and we rolled in to an impressive welcome. It was a Saudi moment, so we advisors quickly faded into the background and went to our own quarters. The big house in which the advisors stayed had eight bedrooms. We cracked open the dusty doors and turned on the air-conditioning. I didn't try to be the first one on the phone or in the shower. I just went to the refrigerator and got one of the Cokes that I'd left there on 1 August 1990, before the insanity started. I went up to my favorite spot on the roof and watched the sunset. We were finally far enough south that not a trace of the oil fires could be seen. I took off my boots and socks and rolled up my pant legs. After wiping dust off the deck chair, I sat down to cool my feet and enjoy the end of the day.

A truck came from the headquarters of our advisory group in Riyadh and brought mail for us. There were letters from friends, from my mom and dad. The letters from Donna, my wife, I opened first. Along with some bills and a few pieces of junk mail there was an official envelope from MILPERCEN, which I opened last. MILPERCEN was the army's Military Personnel Center, and a letter from them is normally interesting because it often deals with your immediate future. The letter was a simple sheet of paper known as a pink slip, or RFO (request for orders), telling me that I was to report to Fort Drum, New York, for duty with the 10th Mountain Division.

The mosques were just beginning to sound evening prayers, and the song of the muezzin was loud and tinny over the loudspeakers. I looked out over Al Hofuf and wondered, *Fort Drum?* I didn't know anyone in the 10th Mountain. With the post–Cold War downsizing that the army was about to embark upon, the light infantry divisions such as the 10th Mountain would probably go away. But I rationalized that this wouldn't happen for a few years yet. And besides, Fort Drum would probably be a peaceful assignment, just the place to start a family. After all, who ever heard of people from Fort Drum deploying anywhere?

Part One
Fort Drum

Dear Soldier and Family Members:

Welcome to Fort Drum, New York, home of the 10th Mountain Division (Light Infantry) and the beautiful North Country. Your tour of duty here will be filled with adventure and challenges.

> In processing welcome
> on Fort Drum home page

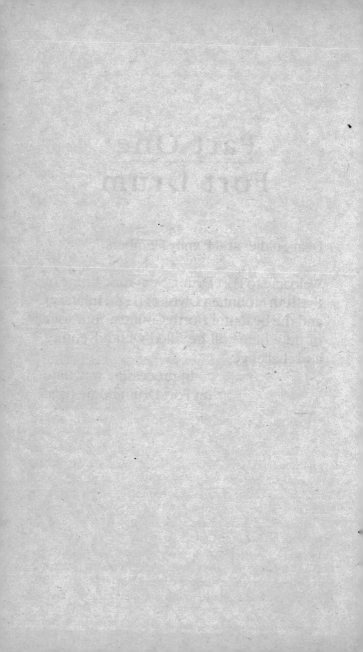

One

The 10th Mountain Division (July–September 1991)

Three months later I was driving through the incredible
greenness of summertime in upstate New York to report to
Fort Drum. After six years in the desert (four in Fort Irwin,
California, and two in Saudi Arabia), going back to a place
that had grass was something strange. Fort Drum was only a
few miles from the Canadian border, so I knew we would
often visit Donna's family in Toronto. Being so far along in
her pregnancy, she had flown on to visit her folks. I would
pick her up after I signed for quarters. The trees and lush
countryside were a feast for the eyes, and even though we had
been back from Saudi for almost a month, I could still take
simple pleasure in being in America. The miles rolled on, and
the sign for Fort Drum came up. With a sense of anticipation
and well-being, I turned off to report to my new duty station.

Fort Drum (previously Camp Drum, and before that, Pine
Camp) has a long history of army and National Guard use going back to before World War I. Camp Drum had served as a
key mobilization post during World War II. In fact, Pvt. Bill
Mauldin, the cartoonist, had served there, training with the
45th Division before shipping out overseas to Italy. Many of
the cartoons he drew of stateside training were based upon
his experiences at Pine Camp.

Camp Drum soldiered on as a National Guard mobilization and training post over the next four decades, becoming
Fort Drum somewhere along the line. Then in the early 1980s
the decision was made to activate a light infantry division

(the 10th Mountain) there. A massive construction effort transformed the sleepy little post with its World War II buildings into one of the most modern and well-laid-out posts in the U.S. Army. By the time I got there (July 1991), Fort Drum was the newest post I'd ever seen. I was pleasantly surprised as I drove around the troop areas and checked out some of the other modern facilities, such as the PX and commissary. It certainly wasn't some run-down post with inadequate housing in the middle of east overshoe. Not a bad place to begin family life, I thought as I drove up to the division headquarters and went to sign in.

The 10th Mountain Division was a J series TO+E (Table of Organization and Equipment) light division of the kind that first came into existence in the early 1980s. The army had been pulled in two directions then. We, of course, had to maintain heavy forces to face our potential adversaries in Europe and Korea. But we also had to have forces ready to deploy swiftly to conduct operations on the lower end of the spectrum of conflict. There was a real possibility of conflict in Central America plus contingency operations elsewhere in the world. The 10,000-man light division was the answer to these requirements. It was designed to fit inside 500 air force C-141 transports (although in practice this number grew to about 560). The division had no armor. Its combat power was made up of three brigades of three infantry battalions each. The division also had a Division Artillery (DIVARTY) consisting of three battalions made up of M102 105mm howitzers and a battery of M198 155mm howitzers. The 10th Mountain Division's aviation brigade had AH-1S attack helicopters both in the attack helicopter battalion and the 3-17th Light Cavalry Squadron. Its other aviation battalion was made up of UH-60 Black Hawks, for transporting troops and equipment. There were also engineer, signal, air defense, intelligence, and logistical support units that rounded out the division. It was a no-frills outfit. The ratio of supporters to combat troops was the lowest in any unit in the army. (In the vernacular, it had a high tooth-to-tail ratio.) In truth, in some cases there were too few supporters for sustained operations, so the division had to be augmented with assets from other army units. But whatever the shortcomings of the light division's organization, there could be no doubt that at least the primary design factor had been met. The 10th Mountain was indeed a rapidly deployable outfit. We could be anywhere in the world in a matter of days.

The teeth of the 10th Mountain Division were in its three infantry brigades; two of these were regular army and the third was the 27th Brigade of the New York National Guard (whose ancestors were the famous "fighting 69th" of World War I fame). The two active brigades would, of course, be the first to be deployed to a contingency, followed by the 27th Brigade after a period of post-mobilization training. Each brigade had three infantry battalions, making nine in all in the division. These battalions were the core of the division's combat power. It was my ambition to serve in one, either as the S3 or the XO.

The army had activated four light divisions (the 6th, the 7th, the 10th Mountain, and the 25th) during the mid-1980s. The 6th was already in the process of being deactivated as part of the post–Cold War/post–Gulf War drawdown. Another division (the 7th) would be chosen for deactivation while I was at Fort Drum. The 10th Mountain was thought to be a similar candidate in the summer and fall of 1991. We hadn't served in the Gulf War or in Panama, and although the division could look with pride to a short but illustrious battle history in World War II, it had nowhere near the historical lineage of the 7th or the 25th. In any event, I was keen to get into one of the infantry battalions before they were deactivated.

I was not surprised to learn, however, that my first assignment with the division was to be in the division headquarters G3, or operations and training section. This is a normal pattern of assignment, because once I served in a battalion and became "branch qualified in grade," I would be subject to reassignment. Hence the division wanted to get some other use out of me before I was sent to a battalion. Relatively few officers walk directly into a battalion. There was a whole crop of guys just leaving the G3 to go down to serve in units after a

year at division headquarters. I told myself philosophically
that I had to wait my turn like everyone else.

As it turned out, my stay at division headquarters was short-
lived but enjoyable. The G3, Lt. Col. Buster Hagenbeck, was
a good man to serve under, and the work, although interesting, was not particularly stressful. Donna and I spent a lot of
time getting to know our surroundings. The city near the post,
Watertown, was a midsized town that had most of the amenities of civilized living, and upstate New York was beautiful.
We spent our time off in these first few months alternately
furnishing our house, preparing for the baby's arrival, and ex-
ploring the environs around Watertown. We did most of the
tourist things and were only moderately inhibited by Donna's
ever-burgeoning size. The fact that we were within four hours'
drive of Donna's family in Toronto was also a considerable
help. Life soon developed into a comfortable routine of work,
property acquisition, housing setup, and gestation. Donna
would pick me up around half past six each night as it was
getting dark and we would drive home looking at the dozens
of rabbits that would edge out of the forest along the road to
munch the sweet grass. I was still itching to get to a battalion
but at the same time was reasonably content.

Then in a flash it all changed.

The officer who was holding the S3 slot in the 2d Battalion,
87th Infantry transferred to a combat service support branch
(a rare but not unheard-of occurrence). The 2-87 was scheduled to go to the National Training Center (NTC) at Fort Irwin in three months. I was asked if I would please go down
to 2d Brigade to be interviewed for the job by the brigade
commander.

Would I ever.

My interview with the brigade commander, Colonel Burnette (who would go on to command the division in later
years), went exceptionally well. I was told the next day that I
had been selected to be the S3 of the 2-87 Infantry and would
start work there the next Monday. Thus after less than two
months in division headquarters, I was going to do what I had
come to the 10th Mountain Division for.

The 2-87 Infantry (September 1991–June 1992)

The 2-87 Infantry (Mountain) was one of nine identical (six regular army and three National Guard) infantry battalions in the 10th Mountain Division. In the cold and bureaucratic designation of army organizations, the battalion was a Table of Organization and Equipment (TO+E) 07015L0 light infantry battalion. The mission of these types of battalions was stated tersely in the TO+E document; it was in part a classic restatement of the infantry's mission and had changed little throughout the centuries. A Civil War soldier would have instantly understood the first portion of the mission statement (once he'd gotten the computer printout). Mission: To close with the enemy by means of fire and maneuver in order to destroy or capture him, or repel his assault by fire, close combat, and counterattack.

The second part was a gray concession to the post–Cold War world. I can well imagine Lee or Grant scratching his head and asking for clarification: ". . . To conduct low intensity combat (LIC) and operations other than war in an internal defense and internal development environment." Basically, it was to do any other mission that the army could think of (but couldn't be called a war). Even if the definitions of internal defense and development were ambiguous, it was taken for granted that we'd sort it out on the ground. Policy formulation was not our thing. Policy implementation was.

When it came to the listing of capabilities, we were generally capable of just about anything short of fighting a Russian tank division in the desert or on the plains of Europe. The list given was generic and relatively meaningless, because the battalion never was meant to act in a vacuum. It would always (supposedly) be part of a larger whole. Nonetheless the army made the assumption that the light infantry battalion could more or less accomplish the following:

Capabilities—At level 1 (manning over 90 percent) this unit:

• Provides base of fire and maneuver elements
• Seizes and holds terrain

- Conducts independent operations on a limited scale
- Provides mortar fire support for organic and attached units
- Conducts long-range patrolling when properly equipped
- Participates in motorized and/or mechanized operations when provided with appropriate transportation assets
- Participates in airmobile and/or airborne operations when provided with appropriate air transport
- Maneuvers in all types of terrain under all climate conditions
- Participates in amphibious operations
- Participates in counterinsurgency operations as part of a brigade-sized force

To accomplish this, the battalion had four companies, one headquarters company, and three rifle companies. It was a unique organization for the highly mechanized U.S. Army in that the majority of its combat power came from foot mobile infantry. It was an organization that Willie and Joe (and their Vietnam veteran sons) would have recognized and felt right at home in. It was the U.S. Army's latest wrinkle on an ancient and necessary social skill—the ability to fight and defeat your enemy face-to-face at close range.

The 2-87 Infantry had a good reputation in the division headquarters. It was an outfit that had a history of strong performance on field exercises, and most of the people I knew on the division staff spoke highly of it. Being chosen to be the battalion S3 was an incredible stroke of luck. As I came to the battalion for the first day, I cautioned myself to make an objective evaluation of the unit and neither embrace nor reject what I saw until after a few weeks of observation.

As it turned out, the 2-87 was a moving train, and I really didn't get the time for introspection and the evaluation I would have liked. I did learn that the battalion staff and the companies were indeed strong and the battalion as a whole was very proficient. If there was one undercurrent within the battalion when I joined it in September 1991, it was that many of the soldiers and leaders were physically tired. The unit had been training hard throughout the summer, and everyone was worn a bit thin. They'd just finished a large live fire demonstration for the Chief of Staff of the Army that had gone well but had taken a lot of effort. Now they were hip deep into preparation to go to the NTC. When I joined them, they were just about to move back into the field for more platoon and company training. After a short break this would be followed by the battalion's last big exercise against an opposing force that would be controlled by Colonel Burnette. It would be the battalion's last training before deploying to Fort Irwin shortly before Thanksgiving. It was an ambitious (but not impossible) schedule. No rest for the weary, I thought.

The battalion commander, Lieutenant Colonel Eikenberry, was an exceptionally proficient soldier and somewhat of a perfectionist. He was a highly experienced infantry soldier with long years spent in both airborne and ranger units. He knew more about live fire training than any officer I had ever met. He was also unique in that he was fluent in Chinese and had spent time in China as the assistant defense attaché. He set such a blistering pace for the battalion's operations that we sometimes had to scramble to keep up. Somehow we always did. From this you could conclude that he knew just what we were capable of better than we ourselves did. What earned him respect was the fact that he drove himself harder than he drove any of us and spared himself nothing.

The last time I'd been in an American infantry battalion was six years before, as a company commander. Getting back into the swing of things after a six-year hiatus took a bit of effort. However, my four years as an exercise controller at the NTC prior to going to Saudi in 1989 gave me a good background in battalion-level tactical operations. I soon found myself growing comfortable with the job. Administration and training management would take longer, but fortunately we were thrust right into tactical operations, which had always been my strong suit. Soon after I joined the battalion, we went to the field for the battalion's platoon and company training in preparation for the NTC.

My wife, Donna, was already overdue with our first child at this point, but there was no reason not to go out, because I could always be called in. Sure enough, about six days into the exercise I got the call to come in from the field immediately. We must have broken the humvee land speed record getting in from the field. I raced home from the battalion headquarters to find Donna quite nonplussed but telling me definitely that "this is it."

After hastily showering and scrubbing off most of the camouflage paint (a little green still showed around my ears, a nurse told me later), I took Donna to the hospital in Watertown. It was a fairly difficult delivery (in which I incurred the wrath of my Mrs. by falling asleep on the floor by her bed; I hadn't slept for almost thirty-six hours by then, but try telling that to a woman in labor).

Presently, John Charles Stanton was born, a great kid in perfect condition. Donna was tired but exultant, and I was happy enough to burst. I left the hospital in bright sunshine. (It had been an all-nighter.) I called my father, Donna's parents, my sister, and everyone else I could think of. Then I called the battalion in the field, and Lieutenant Colonel Eikenberry graciously gave me time off, so I didn't have to go back out for the last four days of the field problem. October was spent in a blur of training and new parent duties. I didn't sleep much, and Donna slept even less.

By November we found ourselves back in the field on the last major exercise before the NTC. This was a force-on-force battalion operation against an opposing force of armor and infantry. We did all of the missions that we could expect to be given at the NTC. We came out of the field in the second week of November and were as ready as we'd ever be for the NTC. After an early Thanksgiving dinner, we departed for Fort Irwin on 24 November 1991.

The battalion had a highly successful NTC rotation. We won some battles and lost some but learned lessons in every one. Our defense in conjunction with 3d Brigade, 24th Division (just returned from the Gulf War) was particularly successful, with the controllers saying it was the worst beating the opposing force had taken in some time. The 24th Division commander, Major General McCaffery, complimented the battalion on its performance in the final battalion after-action review. We flew home feeling quite pleased with ourselves. Lieutenant Colonel Eikenberry was of course already working with me planning the next major training event.

It was almost Christmas when we got back to Fort Drum. Donna, John, and I went to Florida to see my folks, and the grandparents got to see John for the first time. My parents and baby John hit it off from the start, and we had two pleasant weeks with them. Then it was back to the snow and cold of Fort Drum.

After returning from the NTC, the battalion staff went through a lot of personnel changes. Our intelligence (S2) officer, Captain Conyer, was replaced by Cpt. Mike Klein, a brilliant young man who had been an infantry platoon leader in our division before being sent to Germany. He was a Gulf War veteran and a recent graduate of the Military Intelligence Officers' Advanced Course. He was incredibly smart and never at a loss for words, and he had a terrific sense of humor. I was to depend upon him a lot in the deployments ahead of us.

The biggest change was in the S3 shop. I lost my chemical officer, the dependable 1st Lt. Chuck Alverez, who could not get over his disappointment at having missed the Gulf War and figured that a career in the Chemical Corps was not for him. He was replaced by 2d Lt. Bill Haas, fresh out of Chemical Officers' Basic Course. I had concerns about taking a brand-new second lieutenant into the S3 shop, but they were quickly allayed. Bill was a former enlisted MP and had been around the block a few times. What he didn't know he learned quickly and became a real asset to the team. The biggest break officerwise was that I finally got an assistant S3. It is normal to take new captains to any unit and place them on staff jobs to wait their turn for the next company to open up. Lieutenant Colonel Eikenberry gave me Capt. Kelly Jordan, fresh from the Gulf War and the Infantry Officers' Advanced Course. Kelly was typical of what you'd find in a young infantry officer in 1992. He was smart as a whip and superbly trained and possessed of tremendous foresight and initiative.

Being surrounded by so many super-efficient young officers made me feel somewhat inadequate at times. Remembering myself at their age, I wondered how well I would have fared competing with this generation.

The biggest changes were in the S3 shop's noncommissioned officers (NCOs). All of my staff sergeants were replaced, as was my noncommissioned officer in charge (NCOIC). I was a little chagrined at this because of all the training we had just gone through, but there was nothing to be done about it. Retirement and natural rotation of people combined to hit us all at once. In the space of a few weeks, my old Tactical Operations Center (TOC) crew was gone. We would have to train the S3 shop from scratch. I wondered what kind of NCOs I'd be getting.

What I got was pure gold.

My two new assistant S3 NCOs, SSgt. Dale Brown and SSgt. Mark Magnant, were both pulled from the companies to fill the gaps. Normally, units use opportunities for taskings such as this to get rid of their awkward customers, but Lieutenant Colonel Eikenberry was adamant that the operations shop be given people who could do the important staff coordination. The battalion's senior NCO, Command Sergeant Major Key, assisted in the choice, and we couldn't have done better. Having two NCOs who had already spent more than a year in the unit meant that I didn't have to waste time orienting them about Fort Drum or teaching them the peculiarities of some of its training areas. In addition, they were both air assault qualified, and Staff Sergeant Brown was a Pathfinder (a soldier qualified to control airdrops and establish helicopter landing zones). Because a light infantry battalion does a lot of helicopter operations, having two NCOs with these skills assigned to my S3 shop was fortunate.

The two men couldn't have been more different. Staff Sergeant Brown was a man of few words and serious demeanor who was possessed of a sly, subtle sense of humor. Staff Sergeant Magnant was a perfect foil for him—a small, wiry, bull terrier of a man whose sense of humor and constant jokes did much to relieve the tension. "Beavis and Butthead"

were just coming onto television, and Staff Sergeant Magnant could imitate perfectly the "heh, heh, heh" of Beavis. In
the field, each would be a shift NCO in the TOC. In garrison,
they were responsible for coordinating training ranges (Brown)
and ammunition (Magnant) and a host of other tasks. They
never let the battalion down.

Best of all was my new S3 NCOIC, Sfc. Scott (Dusty)
Hardcastle. He was just what the doctor ordered: a senior E-7
on the promotion list for E-8 who had long experience working in operations staff sections. He was a commonsense troop
leader who brooked no nonsense from his subordinates but
always managed to get things done without having to be
harsh or autocratic. He also had a gift for organization and
soon had the S3 shop significantly better organized than it
had been in the previous three months that I had been there.
He was proactive in his work habits and would often initiate
the necessary movements or coordination steps for the battalion's next task, then report them to me. At first this made me
somewhat uncomfortable, but he clearly knew what he was
doing, and my two officers and I had more than enough work
to keep us busy. Empowering Sergeant First Class Hardcastle
to act for me was one of the smarter things I did as an S3, even
though I can honestly say it was a decision I made almost by
default as opposed to any brilliant managerial insight.

Unfortunately, Sergeant Hardcastle didn't have the best
living arrangements we could have hoped for. We tried and
failed to get him on-post housing. As a result he had to travel
more than twenty miles from the government-leased housing
in Gouvenor to the post. Despite that, even in the worst conditions he always made it in before most anyone else. He was at
all times rock-solid dependable. Looking back on my career,
it seems to me that whenever I have been placed in a demanding position, I have always been blessed with utterly superb
subordinates. But never had I been so blessed as the day I got
Sergeant First Class Hardcastle as my S3 NCOIC.

So this was my new team. We were to stay together through
the Hurricane Andrew relief effort and Somalia, and were
to become pretty tight. Like any good staff section that works

together frequently, we learned to play off one another's strengths and weaknesses. We developed a degree of teamwork that was among the finest I have seen in my time. We had a team of resourceful and proactive people, which was good because we needed all the resources and imagination we could find to execute the training schedule before us in the winter and spring of 1992.

Some of the most useful training we did after Fort Irwin came on the battalion's month-long deployment to Fort Pickett, Virginia, in March 1992. Fort Pickett had one of the best military-operations-in-urban-terrain (MOUT) training sites, or "combat in cities" to you old folks, in the army. We spent more than a month there, alternating the companies through a cycle of MOUT training, squad and platoon live fires, and force-on-force training with the multiple integrated laser engagement system (MILES). MILES is a kind of laser tag in which rifles and machine guns shooting blanks project laser beams that set off sensors on an opponent's body (the same system we'd used at the NTC). Lieutenant Colonel Eikenberry was especially concerned about the MOUT training, knowing that light infantry bears the brunt of fighting in cities. He was determined that the 2-87 would be trained for such missions, and he spent much of his time in the MOUT site observing, correcting, instructing, and exhorting the troops to greater effort. It was an easy sell, because everyone was into this challenging and fun training anyway. The defenders would barricade the stairs of buildings with derelict furniture. Booby traps were everywhere, and troops had to really pay attention. Squads practiced building-entry procedures, room clearing and marking, building search, casualty evacuation, and other skills until they knew them inside and out. It was the best kind of training, adequately resourced and not rushed. If a squad or platoon screwed something up, there were enough blanks and pyrotechnics to practice it again, and again after that if necessary. As the manager of the battalion's training ammunition, I was at first a bit concerned. At this rate of expenditure, the battalion would be out of most kinds of training ammunition by the end of the third quarter of the year. But Lieutenant Colonel Eikenberry explained to me that it was better to shoot your whole allocation by June and see what you could scrounge than try to fire off ammunition at the end of the year in unproductive "use it or lose it" training events. This MOUT rotation was our most productive exercise density of the year.

We also did squad live fire exercises, which involved skill on the part of the squad leaders, because the exercises were done on ranges that we designed and built ourselves. A squad leader had not only to direct the fire of his two fire teams but maneuver them and ensure that they were not endangered by each other's fire. Controllers watched the squad but interfered only in situations that were truly dangerous. Consequently, the live fires were a squad leader's dream, allowing him to maneuver and shoot with his fire teams with safety considerations that would apply only in combat. They were tremendous confidence builders.

It's hard to explain how gratifying this training period was at Fort Pickett. The battalion was clicking. Troops were doing what they joined the army for. All of it was spurred on by the relentless drive of Lieutenant Colonel Eikenberry, who was absolutely determined to get every last bit of training from the deployment. He succeeded. The 2-87 went to Pickett sharp and left a lot sharper. Some of the people in the battalion would rotate out before we went to Somalia, but not that many. Later, during the Somalia deployment, I asked the troops what training had best prepared them for Somalia. Their answer was almost always the same—the platoon live fires in November 1992 and the MOUT training at Fort Pickett.

After returning to Fort Drum, the battalion concentrated almost exclusively on platoon- and squad-level live fires and tactical training. As a result, at the lower level—independent squad, platoon, and company operation—the battalion was extremely proficient. This was complemented by the battalion headquarters' participation in the division Battle Command Training Program (BCTP) Warfighter exercise, in which the staff had to conduct command and control and generate orders as part of the overall division exercise. After this, we did another series of platoon and company field exercises that took us into May and a post-support tasking cycle.

Lieutenant Colonel Eikenberry was due to rotate out of command in late June. Battalion commanders get only two years of command, and his time was up. The previously designated replacement for him had to drop out for personal reasons, so an alternate replacement commander had to be chosen. Lieutenant Colonel Jim Sikes, the 2d Brigade XO, was chosen, making us all happy. We knew Lieutenant Colonel Sikes already, so there would not be the long feeling-out period that came with a new commander.

I did not see the change command ceremony. The battalion had been tasked to send a major and a captain to conduct the annual evaluation of the 3-172d Infantry Vermont National Guard, and I was the major. I wish I could have been at the ceremony.

Although Lieutenant Colonel Eikenberry did not come with us to any of our upcoming deployments, his presence was long felt in the training that we had all received under him. His insistence on tough live fire exercises, battle drills, and challenging maneuvers had turned us into a skilled infantry battalion, especially at the platoon and squad level, at which virtually all of our fights in Somalia would occur. He drove the battalion and he drove himself and at times could be demanding, but his methods paid off. He handed Lieutenant Colonel Sikes a sharp and shiny sword. There is no reward in the army for the guy who had the unit just prior to its deployment. Lieutenant Colonel Sikes took the battalion, kept it well trained, and fought it superbly. But Lieutenant Colonel Eikenberry deserves a mention because his training helped keep us alive. In Kismayu and other places, where I watched the troops of the 2-87 go through their building-clearing drills and watched them instinctively react to contact, I mentally blessed Lieutenant Colonel Eikenberry and the MOUT training we did at Fort Pickett.

Two

Personalities: The 2-87 Infantry (July 1992)

Each battalion has a unique identity given to it by the character of the leaders and men within it. A battalion is a living thing, an extended family or tribe. A battalion can be an autocracy, where the hierarchy leads from rigid authority and everyone sticks to his place in the hierarchy, or it can be a more congenial organization. It can be self-assured or skittish, professional or paranoid. The personality of a unit does not necessarily correlate with its performance. In the short term, a driven and fearful battalion can be quite productive. In the long term, however, the best battalions are those that are led.

The 2-87 Infantry in the summer and fall of 1992 was led; moreover, it was a happy battalion with an easy, confident atmosphere to it. The soldiers were motivated. The NCOs and officers were competent and professional and concerned for the welfare of their men. It was one of those units in which everything seemed to work with a minimum of effort. Personalities complemented one another, and everyone had a common sense of mission.

The Command Group

Although every battalion has only one commander, the command group consists of several people. In addition to the battalion commander (first Eikenberry, then Sikes), the command group consists of an executive officer (XO) and the battalion command sergeant major (CSM). The XO is the second in command of the battalion and is a major normally in his mid- to late thirties. The CSM is the battalion's senior enlisted soldier. This individual normally has more than twenty years of service and, although theoretically junior to the newest lieutenant, actually wields considerable power as the commander's enlisted advisor and primary contact with the soldiers of the battalion. There are also several drivers and radiomen in the command group.

The battalion is a collective effort. No single person is the difference between success and failure, victory or defeat. Everyone contributes and makes the whole greater than the sum of its parts. The commander sets the tone, though. In the case of the 2-87, this was Lt. Col. Jim Sikes.

He had been the commander for about six months when we went to Somalia. He commanded in an unhurried and confident manner, letting all know what was expected of them. He put people at ease, maintaining a command presence while at the same time not being threatening. He was a large but unimposing figure, about six foot three, with short black hair and wire-rim glasses. He and I were often mistaken for each other at a distance, because we were both about the same size, had about the same hair color, wore glasses, and were cursed with naturally bad posture. In garrison his uniforms were always crisp and pressed, but this only made him look presentable as opposed to sharp.

I've often thought about what made Lieutenant Colonel Sikes special. That he was absolutely competent at his profession there was no doubt. He had spent five straight years in infantry units as, in succession, battalion S3, battalion XO, brigade S3, and brigade XO. This made him somewhat more experienced than most, but all of the battalion commanders I'd ever worked for were accomplished soldiers. In fact, Lieutenant Colonel Eikenberry had been truly brilliant. All of them had been concerned with the welfare of the men and the training of the unit. All had been tough professionals with high standards. Sikes too was all of these things, but he also had a special quality, a kind of optimism. Sikes projected a self-assurance that no matter what, things would be all right.

It was not a cockeyed optimism, nor was it the uninformed optimism of someone who didn't know what was going on. Rather, it was the optimism of a leader who knew the tools in his hand and knew the abilities of the people who worked for him. Sikes radiated confidence. No matter what the difficulty encountered or its circumstances, he would look at a mess and give guidance to set it right. His response to mistakes on his subordinates' part was characteristically, "Okay, let's fix it and try not to do it again." He was the kind of leader you didn't want to fail.

Major Joe Occhuzzio, the executive officer (XO), was another superb influence on the battalion. A laconic but congenial individual, Joe never got excited about anything. Not that he couldn't move quickly or decisively when he had to. He'd just reached the point where he realized that screaming usually didn't do any good. He coordinated the activities of the staff with a sure hand, allowing the staff sections as much independence as possible but moving in decisively to resolve squabbles between them or put someone back on course. This he normally managed to do without getting anyone's nose out of joint.

Command Sergeant Major Hubert Key was the third member of the command group and the senior NCO in the battalion. Key was one of the few Vietnam veterans left in the battalion and had been in the army almost twenty-four years. He was a picture-book sergeant major, a distinguished, elder soldier of immense personal presence. He had a deep bass voice that sounded as though it was coming from the center of the earth. He had a wealth of knowledge that we leaned on heavily, both in the technical aspects of soldiering and in the more imprecise science that the army refers to as leadership. His imposing figure and demeanor hid a humorous, friendly, good-natured soul. His was the easy carriage of a person who was confident in his abilities and used to working with people.

The Primary Staff
To assist the battalion command group in commanding and administering the battalion, each infantry battalion had a

staff, suborganized into functional areas. These were S1 (personnel administration), S2 (intelligence), S3 (plans, operations, and training), and S4 (logistics). Each of these staffs was headed by an officer: the S1, S2, and S4, who were captains, and the S3, a major, who was the number-three man in the battalion. The responsibility for coordinating the actions of the staff rested with the XO, with the S3 assisting when the XO was occupied with other matters.

The S1 was responsible for all personnel administration in the battalion. This included schools, transfers, end time of service (or "ETS," soldiers leaving the army), actions, awards, punishments, new personnel requisitions, casualty reporting, finance actions and pay inquiries, assisting soldiers in preparing their files for promotion boards, assisting soldiers in registering their families in the army's dependent care system, coordinating chaplain services, and sundry other duties. To accomplish this, the S1 was authorized six personnel: one senior personnel services sergeant, who was the noncommissioned officer in charge of the S1 shop; personnel services sergeant; personnel administrative sergeant; legal specialist; personnel administrative specialist; and administrative clerk.

It was a tall order for one officer and six men to do all the personnel administration for a battalion of more than five hundred people. To add to the problem, few of the S1 shops in the division were up to full strength, and the 2-87's was no exception. To make up for shortages in the S1 shop, several infantrymen with typing and clerical skills were drawn up from the rifle companies. This had a negative effect on rifle strength, but the battalion commander was put in a no-win situation. He could either keep riflemen in the rifle squads, in which case soldiers' personnel actions would not be taken care of properly. (People would not get transfer orders in a timely manner, soldiers would not get points for promotion recomputed or would miss boards for promotion, soldiers' family members would not get registered, and so on) or he could take a few guys out of the companies to keep the S1 shop afloat and hope replacements for the S1 personnel would come in before we went to war.

The S1, 2d Lt. Bill Haas, was our battalion chemical officer and also the S1, due to a shortage of lieutenants and captains in the brigade. Battalion S1 is not normally the start-off position for a second lieutenant, but Bill was not your typical baby-faced new lieutenant. A former enlisted MP, he was wise beyond his years and not at all prone to panic. He was given the unique situation of handling a battalion's personnel actions and maintaining end strength on a combat deployment while still meeting all of the normal personnel rotation and peacetime garrison requirements. Bill faced this catch-22 situation with aplomb and never let it get to him.

The S2 shop was the intuitive side of the battalion's thinking brain. The S2 processed and analyzed intelligence and, from that, briefed the commander and the staff on probable enemy courses of action. From this analysis and prediction, the battalion's own plans were formulated. The S2 used intelligence provided from higher staff organizations (who sent down information from radio intercepts, side-looking airborne radar, thermal imagery satellites, and the whole network of intelligence-gathering assets). He also used patrols he directed to obtain information. Normally these patrols were from the battalion scout platoon but could be from the line companies as well. He also was responsible for debriefing soldiers after contacts with the enemy and for tagging captured equipment and personnel. In garrison the S2 was responsible for physical security (key control, classified document storage, arms room access, et cetera). This kept him more than fully engaged. With his small staff, staying trained on go-to-war tasks and still keeping on top of administrative duties was a challenge. To accomplish all this, the S2 shop had four persons: a military intelligence captain, two sergeants, and a radioman. The S2 is the kind of job in which it is easy to perform the minimum standard but hard to be excellent.

Fortunately for the 2-87, we had an excellent S2 in Capt. Mike Klein. A burly weight lifter from Pennsylvania, he was the typical Aryan German, with blond hair and pale blue eyes. He was also a tremendously funny person who kept us entertained. A former infantry officer and scout platoon leader, he was just the person to be planning the battalion's reconnaissance effort. At the time, he was going through some significant family troubles that would ultimately culminate in divorce. However, this never affected his duties. He was at all times even tempered and fair and was liked and respected by everyone in the headquarters. He and I got on exceptionally well.

The battalion S3 section was the senior staff element, being the largest and the one headed by a field grade officer. The S3 shop consisted of a major (the S3); a captain assistant S3; a lieutenant chemical officer; a senior NCO (by organization a master sergeant E-8 but in actual practice a senior E-7); two assistant operations sergeants; a nuclear, biological, and chemical (NBC) NCO; an operations specialist; an administrative specialist; two radiotelephone operators (RTOs); and a signal support specialist.

I was the major.

According to doctrine, I was responsible for planning, organizing the force, and coordinating the combat operations of the battalion and attached/operational control (OPCON) units, as well as coordinating with combat support units. I coordinated with the S2, the fire support officer (FSO), and other combat support planners in preparing the battalion task force order. My responsibilities also included integrating other combat support assets (such as indirect fires, engineers, air defense assets, close air support, electronic warfare, and army aviation) in task force operations. My place in a fight was forward, assisting the commander with current operations. Doctrine called for me to be co-located with the commander, but as often as not in practice I found myself employed separately from him. This was to increase the overall battalion span of control and to ensure that both of us weren't in the same place to be hit by the same enemy action. If the commander was hit, my job was to take over the battle until the battalion XO could come forward and relieve me.

My own tight little part of the battalion was my S3 shop. I would trade out assistant S3s in October when Kelly Jordan took Charlie Company. My new assistant S3, Frank Kirsop, was a solid individual and a Desert Storm veteran from, oddly enough, the same battalion as Kelly Jordan. Kirsop was yet another of the seemingly inexhaustible supply of smart, aggressive, young captains in the army. He was also a computer whiz. Like Kelly, he was a loyal subordinate and a joy to work with. This was important, because losing 2d Lt. Bill Haas, the chemical officer, to be the S1 cut my officer strength in the S3 shop virtually in half.

For NCOs I had the superb Sergeant First Class Hardcastle and Staff Sergeants Brown and Magnant, whom I mentioned before. I also had an NBC NCO, Staff Sergeant Issac, brand new to the battalion, whom I hadn't gotten to know yet but who seemed competent enough. The enlisted men in the shop included Terry Henry, my driver and radiotelephone operator, who was just the kind of person needed for this job in that he was highly intelligent and in superb physical condition. He was also blessed with considerable patience and a good sense of humor (both of which he would need when the major was undergoing one of his periodic bouts of disorganization). In the upcoming deployment he would be invaluable to me, always there when he was needed and calm under fire.

There was also Private First Class Hugley, who worked with Staff Sergeant Magnant in training resources. Hugley was a puzzle to me at first, because he was rail thin but could not pass the run on the PT (physical training) test. Push-ups and sit-ups? Sure, no problem. But make the two-mile run in time? No way. Sergeant First Class Hardcastle stayed after him, and I hung on him like a limpet during the run and got him across the line with about thirty seconds to spare. Other than that, he was a good, dependable soldier, if a little quiet. I never really got to judge his good qualities until the Somalia deployment, where he blossomed and turned out to be one of the most dependable people working in the TOC. His performance made me glad that I'd taken Hardcastle's advice and run with him on the PT test.

Private First Class Higgenbotham ("Hig") was another type. He'd joined during Desert Storm and was somewhat disgruntled that he'd missed the war. He was the archetypical Southerner from Mississippi with a slow drawl and a craving for adventure. He personified the words of novelist (and soldier) Josiah Bunting in his description of an enlisted man fighting in Vietnam: "The typical southern solid citizen, he knew more about war by instinct than anything that could be taught in books . . ."

Before Somalia, Hig came up to me and asked how he could join Special Forces. When I told him he had to be at least a sergeant, he was heartbroken. He told me he'd joined the army to see action and so far all he'd done was train at Fort Drum. As it turned out, Hig got his wish.

Private First Class Labonte, our third enlisted RTO, was a perfect foil for Higgenbotham—the slow-talking Southerner—and the quiet Hugley. Labonte was a New Englander who had enlisted for adventure and educational benefits. Like many of the first-term enlisted people in the battalion, he wasn't planning to make the military a career but was a wholly professional soldier just the same.

The battalion S4 section had a total of five personnel: the S4 himself (a captain); a senior supply sergeant, normally a sergeant first class (E-7); an assistant supply sergeant; and two supply specialists. The S4 was responsible for all battalion logistics activities, supervising all organizational and extraorganizational elements supporting the task force. He planned, coordinated, and supervised the logistical effort of the battalion. He was responsible for the service and support part of the battalion operations order. He was also responsible for the security, movement, and positioning of the battalion's logistical trains.

The 2-87 S4, Capt. Steve Michaels, was the type of quiet, dependable officer who was so efficient and conscientious that his performance might go unnoticed. That's often the way it is with logisticians (and communications officers): when everything is going well, no one notices. When there is a foul-up and something is late, everyone is baying for the S4. In Steve Michaels's case, this was a rare occasion indeed, because the S4 shop normally got everything done to a high standard. Steve had been the support platoon leader for the battalion prior to being promoted to captain. To have been given the specialty platoon was a key indicator that his performance as a lieutenant had been well regarded. He was another perpetual optimist, one whose Caribbean accent had a lilting, musical quality to it, especially over the radio.

The Special Staff

Attachments

In addition to the staff sections, the battalion had attachments from other units in the division without which we rarely went anywhere. These were the fire support element (FSE), an engineer platoon, and an air defense platoon.

The FSE was made up of the fire support officer (FSO), a small staff, and his forward observers. The FSE normally came from the brigade's direct support (DS) artillery battalion. In our case this was the 2d Battalion, 7th Field Artillery. The FSO was normally a captain, and his FSE section also contained an SFC and two other sergeants as well as a driver. The company forward observers were normally artillery lieutenants who accompanied the company commanders. There were also supposed to be sergeants as platoon forward observers, but the FSE never had enough for each platoon in the battalion. The battalion FSO worked directly with the commander and S3 and was responsible for coordinating all fire support for battalion operations. In addition to planning and recommending methods of employing fire support, he was also a key player in the positioning of the battalion mortar platoon and the employment of its fires. Captain Tom Hollis was the battalion FSO, taking over from Tim Husman soon after we left the NTC. Hollis had a mainly heavy force background, and he had just come from Germany. His FSE section had been with us for a while and was made up of solid veterans of numerous training exercises. The men fit into our TOC smoothly and were a fully integrated part of the battalion team.

The engineer platoon came from the divisional engineer battalion, in our case the 41st Engineers. The platoon was similar to one of our infantry platoons except that it had a single humvee, which carried tool kits and other specialist engineering equipment. The engineers were used for a variety of specialist tasks, from the highly dangerous (breaching minefields under fire) to the mundane (fixing roofs, digging culverts, and filling holes in the road). They all had specialist training that allowed them to utilize labor from the infantry battalion to create obstacles or improve mobility. They were also demolition specialists. This was a skill that was to be of considerable use in Somalia.

The battalion normally had an air defense section attached to it. This was a section of twelve men making up five Stinger missile teams in six humvees. They were normally attached out one per rifle company and two per Headquarters and Headquarters Company (HHC). Because the Somalis had no air force, the Stinger racks were taken off the vehicles and used as additional transportation. The highly trained air defense soldiers were excellent at land navigation and radio procedures and were a welcome addition to the battalion.

Normally, there was also a ground surveillance radar (GSR) team attached to the battalion. This was an asset from the division's military intelligence battalion that allowed the battalion to see movement far beyond the range of its night sights. Each GSR team came with two radar sets, each carried by a humvee.

The battalion would have other specialist attachments in Somalia with which we had no habitual relationship. Psychological operations (PSYOPS) units and civil affairs (CA) units were foremost among them. The PSYOPS guys had humvees with loudspeakers mounted on them to broadcast approved messages to try to win the cooperation of the local populace. They were pretty good at it. The one maddening thing about them was their absolute unwillingness to deviate from the script without saying "mother may I?" to the senior PSYOPS representative in country, no matter how far from the scene he might be. Once we got this nonsense sorted out, they did just fine. The CA guys were an even more unusual bunch. Headed by a major, they were used to working with local populations to help restore order and get people back on their feet. My Gulf War experience had not brought home to me the problems associated with refugees and the devastation of government and services that war brings. Yes, Kuwait had been trashed, but there seemed to be a massive effort to put it right (fueled by the promise of petrodollars). I didn't give it any more thought than that. In Kuwait, CA operations seemed to be a natural consequence of combat operations. In Somalia, CA at times drove operations and was always a major consideration.

The Rifle Companies

The majority of the battalion's combat power was in the three rifle companies. These were each organized in turn into three rifle platoons, a mortar section, an antitank section, and a headquarters section. Except for the breakdown of squads into fire teams, it was the same organization of combat power that the 10th Mountain Division had employed in its last combat assignment, fighting in the Italian mountains forty-eight years before.

The rifle companies were commanded by captains who were between twenty-six and twenty-nine years old, who were assisted by first lieutenant XOs of about three years of service and a first sergeant with between sixteen and twenty years in uniform. The rifle platoons were led by first or second lieutenants with one to three years of service (although some of them had prior service as enlisted men). The average age of the platoon leaders was twenty-four. They were assisted by platoon sergeants with between ten and fifteen years of service. The squad leaders within the platoons were sergeants or staff sergeants with five to ten years in uniform; most of them were in their late twenties to early thirties. The troops themselves ran the full range of ages, from eighteen year olds newly enlisted out of high school to men who had enlisted later in life for a variety of reasons. The average age of the soldiers was about twenty-two.

Each rifle platoon possessed three squads of nine men each, two machine-gun teams, a platoon leader, a platoon sergeant, an RTO, and an attached medic from the battalion's medical platoon. The platoons sometimes had field artillery forward observer teams (FIST) attached to them from the field artillery battalion supporting the infantry. These soldiers would accompany the platoon leader and direct artillery fires based upon his instructions. There were never enough FISTs to place one in every platoon, and the battalion commander usually allocated them to those elements with missions most likely to need them. All together, the rifle platoon had a full strength of thirty-six persons. However, even before the post–Cold War/post–Gulf War drawdown really hit, full strength was rarely, if ever, achieved.

The rifle platoon was organized in a manner similar to that of its World War II ancestor, but its capability to inflict violence was many times greater. Each platoon had two machine guns, six squad automatic weapons (SAWs), and six grenade launchers. Every other man in the platoon carried an M16A2 assault rifle. In addition, disposable antitank rockets such as LAWs or AT-4s could be carried as necessary. The firepower possessed by a platoon was easily as great as that of a World War II company.

The platoon's three rifle squads were each made up of two fire teams of four men each and a squad leader. Each fire team had a SAW, an M203 grenade launcher, and two M16s. The squad leaders also carried M16s. If a squad was understrength by one or two men (and most of them were), the rifles would be the first weapons to be left unmanned.

Each rifle company also had a thirteen-man antitank (AT) section with six Dragon antitank missile systems. The Dragon was one of those bad bargains in weapons systems that the army gets saddled with from time to time. An antitank missile with only a thousand-meter range, the Dragon system was a man-killing 45.6 pounds to carry (25.3 pounds for a single missile, 6.6 pounds for the SU-36 day sight, and 13.75 pounds for the AN/TAS-5 night sight). This last piece of equipment was the system's only redeeming feature; it was a thermal night sight with a superior night acquisition capability.

Unfortunately, the Dragon missile system was an exceptionally hard system to train on. Actual missiles were much too expensive to fire in large numbers, so there was a heavy reliance on unrealistic simulators. As a result, in actual live fires almost invariably many of the missiles failed to hit their targets. This did little for troop confidence in the system. In addition to the Dragon system, the antitank section's thirteen soldiers each carried an M16, and each two-man team had a squad AN/PRC-126 radio. In an environment that didn't contain an armored threat (such as Somalia), the antitank section could be used as an additional rifle squad, a reconnaissance element, or an augmentation to the mortar section.

In addition to the antitank section, each rifle company had a six-man mortar section with two M224 60mm mortars. The M224s were beautiful little weapons with a surprisingly long range for so small a caliber (3,489 meters for high explosive and 1,000 meters for illumination). They could be fired conventionally from a base plate and bipod, or hand held using an ingenious bubble level device on the tube carrying handle. They were the company commander's "hip pocket artillery" and were a key part of the company's combat power. Unfortunately, the mortar section was undermanned. Six men were simply inadequate to carry all the equipment required. The mortar section would either carry a single mortar tube or would travel with a rifle platoon and spread the weight of the mortar equipment and ammunition among the platoon's infantrymen. The rifle company also had a headquarters section, to which the company XO, first sergeant, supply and communications specialists, and a company clerk were assigned.

Each soldier in the battalion was outfitted with a Kevlar body armor vest, commonly (if inaccurately) referred to as a "flak jacket." The vests issued to Task Force 2-87 were an improvement over the older body armor worn by troops in Vietnam. They featured Kevlar plates that had improved stopping power in comparison to the older Vietnam-era body armor. They were also lighter, although in the equatorial heat of Somalia they seemed quite heavy. They were not, however, the best body armor available. The special operations community was at that time fielding the "Ranger" version, which was to save the lives of many soldiers in the 3 October 1993 battle. The armor worn by the soldiers of Task Force 2-87, on the other hand, could still be penetrated by high-powered rifle or machine-gun bullets. Our flak vest did have one important advantage over the Ranger body armor, however, in that it included shoulder plates and a neck protector. This, combined with the Kevlar helmet, gave the soldiers of the 10th Mountain the equivalent of football pads when engaged in hand-to-hand combat during riot control. The shoulder plates allowed troops to take repeated blows without injury.

The rifle company commanders were a mixed bag of vastly dissimilar personalities, but all were dedicated young professional soldiers. They were all within about two years of one another in age (twenty-eight to thirty), they had all been officers for six to seven years, and they were all married. I was to spend a lot of time working with them and came to appreciate or compensate for each one's individual strengths or quirks (as they became comfortable with my own).

Captain Gordy Flowers was the Alpha commander. He was a dynamo—small in stature but built like a miniature version of the Incredible Hulk. He had none of the little man's disease of needing to prove himself. He knew exactly how good he was and carried himself with an air of alert, mischievous confidence. He was adept tactically and sanely aggressive. He was also a natural leader whose troops had complete faith and confidence in him. He was our strongest rifle company commander.

Captain Wes Bickford, a quiet, studious officer, was new as Bravo Company commander. He was doing the best he could with a reshuffled company. Bravo had been through a rough period with problem NCOs and officers, and of all the companies in the battalion, it was still the most skittish and unsure of itself when it deployed. Not that Bravo Company was a basket case. It was just the weakest of the three. A new influx of NCO leadership gave Wes an opportunity to start afresh, which he was in the process of doing when we deployed. Bravo would find itself in the thick of some of the worst fighting we saw in Somalia and would always acquit itself well.

Kelly Jordan was the Charlie Company commander, taking over from Capt. Tom Webb at the end of the Hurricane Andrew deployment. Kelly was my old assistant S3 and something of an intellectual. His goal was to be a professor at West Point. He was also a tough, imaginative soldier. He'd taken over a solid company and he kept it that way.

So those were the battalion's three main warfighters: the hard-charging Gordy Flowers, quiet Wes Bickford, and professorial Kelly Jordan. Together they were a good team, although fate was to separate us at the outset of the Somalia deployment.

Headquarters Company

The battalion Headquarters Company consisted of six separate platoons plus the staff sections of the battalion headquarters and the command group. Two of the platoons were specialist combat units; the others were support units. Kirk Haschak, the HHC commander, was the number-four man in the battalion. He had been the previous Alpha Company commander and had been chosen for HHC because of his outstanding performance. It was easy to see why; Kirk was one of those rare, gifted individuals upon whom the mantle of command fell quite naturally. He and I butted heads initially but after a while formed a tight working bond and became fast friends. He was humorous, imaginative, and tough. These attributes were to stand us in good stead in Somalia.

The combat platoons in HHC each had a special function. The battalion reconnaissance platoon was the battalion commander's dedicated intelligence collection asset. It consisted of three reconnaissance squads of five men each, a platoon leader, a platoon sergeant, and an RTO. The members of the scout squads had M16s or M203s and were well equipped with observer's telescopes, night vision devices, and other surveillance equipment germane to their specialist reconnaissance function. The squads of the platoon could operate independently of the battalion for several days. They were equipped with PRC-77 radios (as opposed to the shorter-range PRC-126s of the line platoon infantry squads), thus extending the range over which they could communicate. The scout platoon of any battalion was considered elite. Its soldiers were chosen for their field craft, communications skills, and physical stamina. Thus, assignment to the scout platoon was much sought after by the soldiers of the battalion. With only eighteen slots, competition was keen. First Lieutenant Osteen was the archetypical scout platoon leader, a super-athletic, brainy individual who could think on his feet and operate independently. He was the youngest-looking lieutenant in the battalion, although in fact he had six years of enlisted time and was pushing thirty. His judgment was absolutely sound, and the fact that he'd been chosen to lead the scout platoon was a reflection of Lieutenant Colonel Sikes's confidence in him.

The heavy mortar platoon consisted of four 81mm M252 mortars and thirty-two men. This platoon held the longest-range weapons of the battalion. The M252 81mm mortar had a reach of 5,608 meters for high-explosive (HE) mortar rounds and 5,050 meters for illumination rounds. Each mortar had a five-man squad and its own humvee to transport it, although the mortars could be broken down and carried by their squad members in places the humvee couldn't go. When this occurred, the mortar platoon would give its ammunition (9.4-pound rounds) to a rifle company to be carried. The mortar platoon also had a Fire Direction Center section, consisting of soldiers with plotting boards and computers who would actually compute the fire missions and send to the mortars the data regarding azimuth, elevation, and propellant charge per round. The mortar platoon could operate as one four-mortar platoon or a "split section" with two mortars each.

The mortar men were a different breed from the scouts. Mortars are ungainly and unlovely weapons, but they are among the most versatile and effective in the infantry. The soldiers, or "Eleven Charlies," as they are known in a slang usage of their military occupational specialty (MOS) number, showed the same lonely dedication to their weapons displayed by a tuba player in a marching band. Theirs was a higher calling, appreciated in peacetime only by those who were within the brotherhood and in wartime by everyone for whom they shot fire missions. They considered themselves a breed apart.

The heavy mortar platoon was led by 1st Lt. Stan Genega, a superaggressive young officer who had his sights set firmly on being in a Ranger battalion. This led to a talking to by me when he brought in a plan to take the mortar platoon on rubber boat training when they were supposed to be shooting. My point was that the mortar platoon wasn't too likely to be doing rubber boat operations anytime soon, but they would more than likely be called upon to shoot, and our priority should be putting steel on target. Genega took it gracefully. His platoon sergeant, Sergeant First Class Carpenter, was a rock-solid 11C who exerted a calming influence on young Stan.

The rest of HHC was made up of three specialty combat support and combat service support elements: the signal platoon, the medical platoon, and the support platoon.

The signal platoon was responsible for the battalion's communications equipment. Unlike many of the higher-priority units in the army, the 10th Mountain Division had not yet transitioned to the newer family of radios called SINCGARS (single channel ground airborne radio system). We deployed and communicated with basically the same 1970s-generation communications equipment that I had first used as a lieutenant, fifteen years before. So our stuff was old, and some of it broke down frequently. Doctrinally the battalion was supposed to be able to communicate over distances of about twenty kilometers. In Somalia we surpassed this on an almost continuous basis by the placement of retransmission stations and pushing each system to its limit. First Lieutenant Kenneth Call was our communications platoon leader and the battalion's token liberal. (Most officers in infantry battalions are politically to the right of Louis XIV.) Call was also blessed with the absolutely necessary personality trait of being calm in a crisis. Most of a communications platoon leader's life is spent fixing things, normally with impatient senior officers leaning over his shoulder. Ken Call had the ability to work through the worst communications failures at the most inopportune times and keep his head. No matter the frustration or difficulties encountered, he would work a problem nonstop until commo was back up. He was further challenged in that the communications platoon was seriously understrength, missing about a quarter of its authorized personnel.

The support platoon included the battalion's wheeled transportation section, consisting of five-ton trucks and cargo humvees. These trucks were probably the most overused group of vehicles in the army, because they were kept continuously on either supply runs or transporting troops for operations. The bare-bones design of the light infantry division was never so apparent as in the dearth of organic transportation available. We could have easily used twice as many vehicles as we had. They were kept going only by the superhuman efforts of their drivers and the attached maintenance section from the brigade motor pool. This last was yet another nifty little personnel saving in the light division. None of the rifle battalions had its own mechanics; rather they were all consolidated at brigade. As a result, you seldom got the same mechanics twice on any given deployment or field problem. It was another one of those things that lessened the overall efficiency and sustainability of the J-series light TO+E. The support platoon leader was 1st Lt. Bob Van Hoesen, a congenial giant of a man from upstate New York. He was the battalion's weight lifter, standing about six foot three and weighing 240 pounds, none of which was fat. In a battalion full of people with a droll sense of humor, he had the reputation as one of the funniest people around. He was also an excellent leader who was revered by the troops in HHC. He and his platoon sergeant (Staff Sergeant Cronin) ran a tight, happy ship, and the support platoon never failed to perform superbly.

The medical platoon consisted of company aid teams, a medical evacuation section, and a battalion aid station. The platoon was led by a Medical Service Corps lieutenant. In peacetime, normally the senior qualified medic in the battalion was a warrant officer physicians' assistant (PA). On active deployments, the PA would be augmented by a surgeon attached for the deployment. The 2-87, in fact, received a doctor a few days before deployment, and he stayed with us throughout the battalion's time in Somalia. On the negative side, we were short medics in the company teams and the aid station. This shortage was made up partially in the line companies by training "combat lifesavers." These infantry soldiers received a special medical crash course involving detailed training in treating shock and gunshot and shrapnel wounds. Each squad carried a medical aid bag; at least three or four of the squad's members had gone through combat lifesaver training. Lieutenant Colonel Sikes was a big believer in this training, and it was a great confidence builder. The battalion aid station was small and served mainly as a place where casualties would be triaged and stabilized while waiting for transportation back to the nearest field hospital. Like the other specialty platoons in the battalion, the medical platoon was well trained and highly motivated. They had won the most Expert Field Medical Badges (EFMB) in the brigade during the last EFMB test period, and they would perform well in Somalia.

Our medical establishment for the Somalia deployment had three officers. First Lieutenant Guy Lavellie, the medical platoon leader, was a smart, dependable youngster who was planning to leave the service when his initial obligation was complete. Next was our physicians' assistant, Warrant Officer First Class (WO1) Sandhammer. He was a former Special Forces medic who was absolutely superb at trauma and field medicine. He had spent more than ten years as an enlisted medic deploying to numerous third world locations in Africa and South America before being commissioned. He brought much more to the battalion than a brand new warrant officer PA normally would. His presence gave a lot of confidence to the battalion, and knowing that Doc Sandhammer was close by during operations was a morale boost. Lastly there was Captain Alexander, the battalion surgeon. He was attached to us for the Somalia deployment from a garrison hospital on some other post. He looked for all the world like Wally Cox. His manner at first was diffident, his field equipment didn't fit, and he seemed at sea in the strange, new milieu of an infantry battalion. Here's a fish out of water, I thought. But Doc Alexander rose to the occasion and became a real field surgeon. He and Chief Sandhammer were to have a lot of business during the deployment, and they always served us well.

E (Echo) Company, 87th Infantry
Antitank Company (Provisional)

Light infantry battalions normally have only one heavy anti-tank (TOW) platoon. The 2-87 was unique in that it had the two other antitank platoons of the brigade (one from the 2-14 Infantry and another from the 3-14 Infantry) attached as part of a provisional Echo Company. This company was created as a test to see whether or not the TOWs of the brigade were most effectively utilized under brigade control and allocated to whichever battalion needed them the most. The experiment also authorized a company headquarters and supply section. Each antitank platoon consisted of four TOW missile systems, for a total of twelve TOW systems. The TOW system could be employed either from a humvee or from a ground mount stored on the humvee. If it was employed in a dismounted mode, the four-man crew could carry only the basic components of the system and one missile (fifty-four pounds). Once again the burden of cross-loading ammunition would be given to the infantry companies. As a result, the TOW was rarely employed off its humvee carrier. It had a range of 3,750 meters and was a tremendously accurate weapon. Besides its primary employment against tanks and other armored vehicles, it could also be used in MOUT operations to target specific windows or buildings. It could also be used against bunkers, because the missile's twenty-five-pound warhead carried quite a punch. There was a total of six humvees in each TOW platoon: four for the TOW systems, one for the platoon sergeant (a flatbed cargo vehicle carrying extra missiles), and a hard-shell command humvee for the platoon leader. The TOW squads consisted of four men each. In addition, the platoon leader and platoon sergeant each had a driver. In an environment where there was no armored threat, the humvees could also mount machine guns and Mark-19 automatic grenade launchers in lieu of the TOW missile system. It was in this last configuration that the TOW platoons found their best use in Somalia as convoy escorts.

When the order came for 2-87 to deploy to Somalia, the decision was made to take not only our own AT platoon but the other two and the Echo Company headquarters (HQ) as well. Although there was no real armor threat to speak of in Somalia, the TOW vehicles could perform useful functions as mounted reconnaissance and convoy escort vehicles. The TOW systems themselves were dismounted from the vehicles, and the humvees were re-armed with Mark-19 automatic grenade launchers and M60 machine guns. The Echo Company concept worked like a champ in Somalia. The extra company HQ and the extra TOW platoons were to be a godsend on numerous operations, providing mobility and firepower, able to quickly form one side of a cordon in cordon and search operations. Echo Company was also critical in conducting security patrols on the main supply roads and in the daily grind of convoy escort.

Captain Tom Wilk was the Echo Company commander, chosen because of his previous experience as a TOW platoon leader. He was a cheerful and happy-go-lucky sort who had earned the wrath of Lieutenant Colonel Eikenberry on a few occasions. He and Lieutenant Colonel Sikes seemed to get along better, and Echo Company was an effective organization. Successful at the NTC in December 1991, the troops were eager to prove the brigade antitank company concept in a LIC environment at the Joint Readiness Training Center (JRTC) in April 1993. They were fated to do it "for record" sooner than that.

Training: July–August 1992

Immediately upon my return from Camp Ethan Allen, I was greeted by Lieutenant Colonel Sikes, who welcomed me like a long-lost brother. I had known him before as the brigade S3 and then as brigade XO and had always been on good terms with him. The effusiveness of his welcome was a pleasant surprise. He immediately wanted to go over the battalion's annual training plan. Looking at it briefly, he pursed his lips and told me to meet him on Saturday morning. He apologized to me for the loss of weekend time but pointed out that it was the only time we could work undisturbed.

That Saturday we set up two years' worth of desk blotter–sized calendars on the tables in the battalion classroom. We went over the training requirements for the battalion and what had already been scheduled. Sikes's formula was simplicity itself: look at what you were required to do to meet the training standards for the battalion; look at the time available; and fit it in at no more than one major event per week.

This led to our reshuffling some of the training already scheduled and even canceling some of it. Sikes wanted to train at a sustainable pace. He had made his appraisal of the unit and found that it needed a breather. He was secure enough in his ability as a commander that he could do something fairly rare for commanders (then or now): go to his higher commanders and sell them on a decrease of the unit's training pace. To their credit, both Colonel Ward (the new brigade commander) and Major General Arnold, the division commander, let Sikes set his priorities.

There was a distinct method to Lieutenant Colonel Sikes's madness. That he'd made the appraisal about the battalion needing a breather was true enough, but he was also concerned about the upcoming rotation that the 2d Brigade would undergo in the JRTC at Fort Polk, Louisiana, in April. The JRTC is for light infantry what the NTC at Fort Irwin is for armor. It is a fully instrumented and controlled training battlefield, with an exceptionally proficient opposing force (OPFOR). Sikes had seen many units that drove their soldiers too hard in preparing for the JRTC and as a result arrived at the training center burned out. He was determined this was not going to happen to us. We would train and train hard, but we were not going to run from one event to the next for eight months.

The next week, Sikes told me to set up our battalion's TOC outside of the battalion headquarters. He, Sergeant First Class Hardcastle, and I then took a look at what we had. I knew that our TOC was too big, and we had added too many computers and gadgets over the years. Now in one fell swoop the boss announced a radical departure from the past. We were going to strip down and move almost opposite to the rest of the army. We were to become a low-tech TOC. We did away with the Xerox copiers and full workstation computers, working from laptops instead. We mimeographed copies off an ancient hand-cranked AB Dick copier that was impervious to punishment. The resultant decrease of electrical load on the generators meant that we could run the whole TOC off a single Honda generator. Ultimately, if we had to, we could operate without generators at all, using vehicle power to run the radios, battery power for the laptops, and storm lanterns to light the TOC.

As important to the TOC as cutting down on the excess power requirements was the way we reorganized it. The standard light infantry battalion TOC has an S2/S3 vehicle and an FSO vehicle. The S4, according to doctrine, co-locates with the HHC commander in the Administrative Logistics Operations Center (ALOC), located in the battalion supply trains. Lieutenant Colonel Sikes correctly saw that one of the things that was killing a light infantry battalion's ability to conduct sustained operations in the TOC was insufficient people. Divided up, neither the TOC nor the trains had enough people to conduct sustained operations for weeks or months on end.

So he made the decision to include the ALOC into the TOC, combining both functions. This made coordination easier and almost doubled the amount of personnel available to pull shift work. It was a decision that had its risks. Doctrinally, for example, the ALOC is supposed to act as the battalion alternate command post (CP) if the TOC is taken out. But the risk was more than offset by the ability it gave us to conduct sustained operations. The combined TOC/ALOC was an unconventional and gutsy command decision by a new battalion commander. Lieutenant Colonel Sikes, however, had an impeccable background of almost five straight years of previous troop experience before he took the battalion. The new brigade commander, Colonel Ward, wisely gave him the leeway to experiment with the new organization.

The battalion received yet another training opportunity in the training cycle we held for the National Guard in the summer of 1992 under the army's Bold Shift program. In this, the 2-87 set up the training lanes for the 3-108th Infantry, New York National Guard. The training consisted of a series of squad and platoon training lanes and live fires. In addition to providing opposing forces for the National Guard, Lieutenant Colonel Sikes made sure that all the companies of the 2-87 got to go through the training as well, thus obtaining even more practice. It was fun training. The guardsmen learned a lot and became sharper each time they went through the lanes. The 2-87 soldiers got excellent training by being the opposing force or by going through the lanes themselves whenever there was downtime in the guard's training cycle. While all of this was going on, we had the battalion's TOC in the field and became proficient at tearing down our standard integrated command post system (SICPS) tents, storing everything, and displacing to new sites. We did it at least once a day and usually more often. We did it day and night, in the rain, and became very quick. We operated and communicated while the TOC was being taken up or torn down around us, working at it until it became second nature. All the while, Sergeant First Class Hardcastle and the other NCOs continued to make improvements in the design of the TOC and the internal layouts of our TOC humvees.

At the beginning of August 1992, the 2-87 was an extremely well trained battalion. The staff and commanders had been in place for a sufficient amount of time. We all knew one another and worked well together. Tactically we were good. The troops could react to contact well and shoot straight. Although we had no idea that we would be going to Somalia, the training that we had conducted up to August 1992 could not have been better suited toward the type of firefights and small-unit actions we would encounter there.

As we finished Bold Shift, Lieutenant Colonel Sikes and I reviewed the training milestones that would get us ready for our upcoming JRTC rotation. August would see squad and platoon training, and there would be additional exercises in September, October, and November. Sikes didn't believe in three-week-long exercises. We would train for eleven or twelve days, then come in, stand down, and get ready for the next training. I was feeling pretty good about what we had planned. We had ranges and training areas laid on and ammunition and training aids properly forecasted. We would spend Christmas in garrison as the division ready force battalion (DRF-1), then go south of the snow line to Fort Pickett again in January and February 1993. After this we would go on a final brigade exercise in March.

The personnel shortages were starting to bite into the battalion. I was not crazy about losing Bill Haas to the S1 shop, and some of the squads were going down to seven people, but on the whole the battalion was in good shape and looking forward to JRTC. We were tight and had been through a lot together. We knew we'd acquit ourselves well against the JRTC OPFOR. We had a good train-up plan and knew we'd hit JRTC at the top of our form.

Then a hurricane hit Florida and everything changed.

Three

Hurricane Andrew (August–October 1992)

Scarcely had we returned from Bold Shift than Hurricane Andrew slammed into Florida and the whole 10th Mountain Division was alerted for disaster relief. As Division Ready Force-4 (DRF-4), the fourth battalion out of six in line to deploy, we were not among the first units designated to go. The 1st Brigade would go before us, followed by the Division Artillery and other support units, and then the 2d Brigade (which would include us). Prior to movement, the battalion was directed to send its assessment team along with the one from the 2-14 Infantry and Brigade. The teams consisted of battalion commanders and their vehicles, company commanders, S3s, and communications personnel. Their purpose was to assess the damage and do preliminary work in drawing up plans for the main body to follow in a few days. Although as the S3 I should have gone with the advance party, Lieutenant Colonel Sikes decided to take Joe Occhuzzio instead. This was because Joe's last assignment had been as an ROTC instructor in Florida and he owned a house in Homestead. He had had no word on the status of his property (which he was renting out). Sikes knew that Joe would never ask to go first but was desperate to find out about his house. I sent Kelly Jordan (who was then still my assistant S3) with the team and stayed behind to organize the main body for movement.

The advance detachment left and disappeared into a black hole. No phone contact, no daily updates, nothing. It was inconceivable to me that they wouldn't call, and I wondered what they were doing down there. We were all completely un-aware of the extent of devastation. There was literally no tele-phone infrastructure left, and the tactical satellite (TACSAT) communications available were being used by higher eche-lons of command. Meanwhile, back in Fort Drum, we contin-ued to organize for deployment. No guidance was received as to what to bring on the mission or what indeed the "mission" would be. There was a vague, overall mission statement: "It's a real mess down there so bring all your stuff for, you know, disaster relief." This situation did not get any clearer even when contact with advance parties was finally established by phone. This was mainly because most of them had not yet been informed of what exactly they were supposed to be do-ing. As a result, a great deal of confusion ensued and a "bring what you think you'll need" attitude prevailed. Unfortunately this led to some vital equipment being left behind. For exam-ple, the TOW platoons of two battalions did not bring their gun humvees even though there was a critical need for vehi-cles with radio configurations for command and control/liai-son duties. This was a grievous error; in fact, a good rule of thumb for a mission such as Hurricane Andrew relief should be, "If it rolls, bring it." Poor communications from the agen-cies on the scene and a lack of definition of what the units in-volved in this relief were supposed to be doing prevented units from optimizing vehicle and aircraft space by taking only vital equipment. A clarification of the mission (such as refuse disposal, building repair, search and rescue) would have helped planners decide what to bring when aircraft space was limited. This lack of guidance threw commanders back on what they thought best to bring. Not the most ideal solution.

There was also a lot of confusion about what weapons to bring and what the rules of engagement were. On the one hand, martial law had not been declared, and the National Guard and local law enforcement were charged with keeping law and order. However, there were a large number of news reports about armed gang members looting and getting into confrontations with unarmed soldiers. We had to assume that martial law was going to be declared, so I eventually decided to bring basic small arms but no heavy weapons. As it turned out, all of this was unnecessary. It was my first experience in 1992 with erroneous and overblown news stories. (Unfortunately it would not be my last.) We were completely over-armed for what we ended up doing. We did, however, manage to get in some target practice at the police range in Homestead while we were waiting to go back to Fort Drum, so bringing small arms wasn't a total waste.

Our preparation to move continued apace, and I would meet twice a day with the elements of Task Force 2-87 and give them updates. The troops fell to preparations with a will; everyone knew the urgency of the situation and everyone was eager to help. The troops and the junior leaders did all that could be desired. The division headquarters was energized and pushing troops out as fast as they could get them down there. However, missions were still being sorted out. The joint task force headquarters was so overwhelmed with the scale of the disaster that it took a little while before individual unit missions could be assigned.

Our turn to move finally came five days after the advance party deployed. We flew to Miami International on chartered airliners and boarded buses for Homestead. All the way south, the wreckage grew worse. By the time we got to Homestead, the men on my bus were speaking in subdued tones. The area looked a lot worse than Kuwait did after the Gulf War. There the devastation was localized in a few places, and Kuwait City merely looked a bit worse for wear. Homestead was almost flattened. The expanse of debris and shattered buildings was almost numbing. What was inconceivable was that fewer than a hundred people had been killed. Flying over the worst hit areas the next day for an orientation to the extent of the damage, I could scarcely credit what I was seeing. If I'd been told then that 10,000 people had perished in the hurricane, I would have believed it.

The battalion was made responsible for a refugee tent city set up on a high school football field. We were also given our sector of the town to assist in cleanup. We set up our command post in a corner of the athletic field and began to take stock of the situation. Sergeant First Class Hardcastle and the TOC crew, along with Mike Klein, began posting maps of the town showing our different areas of responsibility. Lieutenant Colonel Sikes, Joe Occhuzzio, and I set out to do a quick reconnoiter to familiarize me with the area. While we were settling in, Colonel Ward and 2d Brigade headquarters established themselves in the recreation center of a retirement community that had mercifully survived most of the damage. General Arnold and the division headquarters were emplaced in the basement of Homestead City Hall.

The major task, in terms of planning and command and control, was in coordinating our efforts with the other active-duty military, Florida National Guard, local law enforcement, health services, utilities, other public officials, and the numerous nongovernmental organizations (NGOs) that had shown up to lend a hand. In the initial days everyone was working hard but in an uncoordinated manner. As the relief effort developed, we became much more organized in who did what, and much of the duplication of effort was eliminated.

As it turned out, we had nothing to do with enforcing martial law or acting as a backup to the police. The activated Florida National Guard did that. Instead we worked mainly in helping to clear debris, restore refuse disposal, and set up relief sites. It was hard work for the soldiers, because it seemed as though there was no end to the debris. Strangely and depressingly, many of the residents of our area of operation were doing little to pick up the mess themselves. This was discouraging to the soldiers who would load up truck after truck of clutter, only to see healthy young men sitting on the porches of their wrecked houses drinking. On one occasion I watched a squad of troops give chase after a few punks who had the bad judgment to throw beer bottles at the soldiers. I quickly told my driver to leave the area. Some things are better not seen by officers. I was informed later that the squad caught them and "persuaded" them that throwing beer bottles at soldiers was a bad idea.

In the first days, many small NGOs set up independent efforts in the 2-87 area of operations. One of the most successful was a feeding and relief supplies distribution center run by the NAACP in the playground of an elementary school. Charlie Company was given the responsibility for this part of the 2-87 area of responsibility (AOR) and set up in the schoolyard adjacent to the NAACP site. The soldiers gave welcome help to the NGOs and contributed immeasurably to the orderly distribution of supplies. One of the first and most positive things Charlie Company did was help put a stop to large-scale hoarding of relief supplies and ensuring that those people who were coming to get certain types of relief supplies (such as baby food and diapers) actually needed them. Charlie Company also assisted county health services in setting up a clinic in the school. At the same time, navy construction engineers (Seabees) fixed the school roof. The neighborhood children especially were fascinated by the soldiers, their uniforms, and their equipment. The soldiers organized ball games for the kids, and it was touching and rather sad the way the children hung around the soldiers. No doubt for many of them these were the first positive male role models they'd ever had.

While some of the companies sent out their details to help clear away the rubble, others took turns in improving and administering the tent city we had set up on the football field. There were cots to be set up and refuse to be disposed of, water points to administrate and general camp cleanliness to tend to. Nothing can contribute to disease quicker than a poorly administrated and unsanitary bivouac area, and we were determined not to let this happen in our camp. Finding excrement outside a few of the refugees' tents from people who were too lazy to walk the twenty meters to the Port-o-Lets confirmed our suspicions that such measures were necessary. A pointed conversation between a few senior NCOs and these miscreants was normally all it took. If things had gotten bad, there were always federal marshals available, but at least in our camp it never came to that.

Our mess teams were operating at full tilt and feeding upward of 2,500 to 3,000 people daily (consider that a battalion mess section normally feeds 600). The cooks and KPs kept up a blistering routine, and as long as there were people to be fed we never turned anyone away. I'm sure, however, that the T-ration meals we served shattered a lot of people's illusions about how well the army eats in the field.

I was responsible for planning our operations based on the commander's guidance, coordinating our efforts with the other agencies in our sector, and controlling their execution. Battle tracking for the TOC staff was a little different and took some getting used to. Instead of combat power, and friendly and enemy situations, the TOC tracked a wide variety of information dealing mainly with the logistical support of the relief effort, such as:

- Number of Dumpsters at each site and when they were last emptied
- Number of Port-o-Lets at each site and when they were last pumped
- Location of all civil relief agencies and their functions
- Engineer equipment in sector and priorities of work
- Number of meals served at military mobile kitchen trailer (MKT) by type of person (military, civil relief worker, refugee)
- Status of waste disposal and power grid
- Locations of major destruction or unsafe buildings
- Population density locations
- Law enforcement activities (by type and purpose)
- Adjacent military units (regular and National Guard) and their functions
- Locations of invalid personnel and people with medical disabilities in sector
- Locations of medical facilities and fire departments in sector

This information was updated daily on our operations maps. We tracked much of it on a series of matrix reports similar to the way combat power is tracked, with Dumpsters and Port-o-Lets replacing tanks and rifle squads. We also had overlays for relief agency locations, debris clearing operations, power grid, et cetera. Disaster relief is just like any other military operation. There has to be a plan, command and control, and logistical support. The soldiers from the companies on the work details got to actually see and help people, but the rest of the battalion worked just as hard controlling and supporting the operation.

Eventually the Federal Emergency Management Agency (FEMA) and other government agencies got a good grip on relief services, and the smaller NGOs who had set up shop were phased out. This was an emotional issue at the NAACP site at the elementary school, which had done such fine work in the early days of the disaster. The large organizations of government had taken some time to respond to the disaster. In that period of time, the smaller and more impromptu relief organizations had filled the gap. Now, however, the smaller organizations were actually impeding the more organized relief effort that was kicking into high gear. It was with no small emotion that we assisted the NAACP in closing their distribution center at the elementary school. They had done a superb job of helping their neighborhood, and all the people who participated in that effort had every right to be proud.

Our camp continued to improve. We got in some portable shower trailers and engineers to put floors in the tents. We established a recreation tent, which was a big hit with the camp's population. The camp administration was handled by volunteers headed by a nice little white-haired old lady who was superorganized, patient, and stern at the same time. She registered the camp's population and with an iron hand dealt with individuals who could not follow the camp's rules. She must have been every bit of seventy but seemed inexhaustible. Many volunteers were elderly people. They were a striking contrast to many men in their twenties who were content to sit around the stricken neighborhood and do nothing.

After about a month it became evident that we were victims of our success. Many refugees were helped by the numerous camps set up by the army, navy, and Marine Corps. Some

liked it so well they didn't want to leave—a view that made
perfect sense. Three meals a day free in a place that was
clean, supervised, and safe from crime. Why should anyone
leave that? There were even people who would leave one
camp for another because the amenities of the newer camp
were "nicer." The washing machines in the Marine's camp
were a big draw.

Eventually we were ordered to hand over our camp at the
football field to the division's air defense battalion, the 3-62
ADA. I conducted the reconnaissance for a new base camp
site and found a dandy one by a lake. Lieutenant Colonel
Sikes looked at it and concurred, so we moved the battalion
there.

We had been at the site only a few days when I was ordered
back to Fort Drum for a week to assist the 3-14 Infantry in
getting ready for their NTC rotation. Donna and John met me
at the airfield. The next morning I went to the field with the
3-14, one of two infantry battalions the division had left back
from the Hurricane Andrew relief mission. They really didn't
need me. The S3, Maj. Joe Patykula, couldn't have been
sharper, and there were no major deficiencies in their TOC
operation that needed correction. I offered some tips on tactics, techniques, and procedures that had worked for me. So I
spent a pleasant few days in the field with the 3-14, watching
them doing real soldier stuff and enjoying the cool autumn air
of upstate New York, then flew back to Florida and more disaster relief.

Our new base camp was an airy and pleasant site. There
was a school next to our camp that was not too badly dam-
aged and soon put to right by us. Cleanup continued, with
details going out every day. However, the opening of bars
and restaurants, the general restoration of utilities, and the
ubiquitous presence of girls in string bikinis selling hot dogs
on the side of the road (with always a few green humvees
parked nearby) clearly gave the impression that the crisis
phase of this whole thing was over. We were starting to be
limited as to what we could actually do without taking work
away from the contractors.

It finally got to the point where we began to run out of things to do. We coordinated to get a police range and managed over a period of four days to conduct twenty-five-meter rifle qualification for all of our soldiers—not much, but better than nothing. Lieutenant Colonel Sikes lived by the adage, "Never pass up a chance to shoot." We also conducted PT more frequently while waiting for the word to go home. The school right next to our site was back in session, and the children would come up to the fence during recess and stare at the giant soldiers in their camp. You could always see somebody at the fence talking to the kids (or chatting with the cute teachers) whenever they were out.

The city of Miami set up a thank-you day at one of the waterside malls/stadiums. The troops had an excellent time listening to music or just walking around and looking at the girls. Most of the restaurants were immediately filled with troops. Soon afterward we were ordered back to Fort Drum. Before we moved out, the battalion held a party for schoolchildren in the adjacent school that we had helped return to serviceability. The children were jumping up and down and excited to see the giant men in their camouflage uniforms. The display of some of the battalion's equipment and a scout helicopter we'd arranged to land in the playground were a big hit, as was camouflage face painting. The children gave us a small concert, and their songs were enough to affect even the most cynical of us. That single event made all the frustrations seem worthwhile. A few days later, we broke down our camp and marshaled our vehicles for railhead. Buses took us to Homestead Air Force Base, which was looking better but not much. There we boarded a chartered 747 that took us home. I watched the area around Homestead recede beneath me. There was still a lot of wreckage and years' worth of work left to do, but I like to think we helped them get through the worst of it.

The Hurricane Andrew mission had been a great education for me, not only in terms of learning how to work disaster relief but in human nature as well. I learned that people in a disaster situation do not always react nobly and unselfishly. I learned that this was true not only of the victims of disaster but of some of their rescuers. Many lessons learned were directly applicable to us in Somalia, and in that it was a priceless dress rehearsal.

Some of the United States specific lessons learned were as follows.

1. Find out who the players are and what their boundaries and missions are.

Many relief agencies answered to separate civilian and governmental agencies and did not coordinate with the military (or one another). These agencies operated alongside the military and in the same areas. The basis of assigning their area of responsibility was often different from that of a military unit's division of sectors in an urban combat environment. Civilian agencies such as police, fire department, emergency medical services, and utilities could have their boundaries dictated by municipal borders, power grids, sewer lines, contractual arrangements, or any number of things that had nothing to do with a military's way of doing business. Units must ensure that they actively search for civilian agencies working in their area. Find out who controls them, then visit them to coordinate your efforts. Find out what their purpose there is; explore possibilities of combining efforts, exchange phone numbers, and give out graphics (have extra maps available) to explain the military division of the area and the military units, with what, where, and how to get hold of each unit. Develop a database of phone lists and addresses for these players.

2. Expect things to be disorganized.

Provide a single point of contact for all civilian agencies to work through (usually the TOC), and guard against end runs. Find out who the leaders of organizations are, and develop relationships with them.

The civilian agencies working with the battalion were a mixed bag of formally organized volunteers (for example, the Red Cross) and more unstructured contributors (such as the NAACP). All were trying to do the right thing; however, many were working at cross purposes (for example, the NAACP was trying to keep its distribution site open while the army, Red Cross, and FEMA were trying to consolidate distribution sites). There was also a tendency in some of the relief agencies to fight for "credit" as opposed to subordinating themselves for the common good. Additionally, it was difficult at times to find out exactly who was in charge at a civilian relief site. This was due to a constant turnover of volunteer workers and the lack of an established command and control structure. Often the person who spoke the loudest and had the most commanding presence was taken for the site manager when in fact this was not the case. This was compounded by the fact that the various civilian relief workers and organizations all felt free to come and ask for support from the army but would not coordinate internally. As a result, three different people would ask for the same thing at different times of the day, resulting in the army personnel having to do an audit trail on the requests to find out whether or not the need had been filled.

Find out early who the power brokers are at each site. Ensure that they understand who in the military structure they should deal with. Explain to them how we work and what we can help them with. Make daily contact with them. Ensure that they tell you who their designated replacement will be when they leave.

3. Go light on weapons but bring everything else.
The chances of federal martial law being declared are rare in a natural disaster. Local police, state troopers, and maybe the National Guard will most likely have the law enforcement roles. Regular troops won't. (It's best left to them anyway; they're much better trained for it.) Other than taking advantage of a police firing range, bringing our weapons was a waste.

On the other hand, almost everything else an infantry

battalion has is useful for disaster relief. This is especially true of vehicles such as humvees. Even weapons carriers (such as scout or TOW humvees) can be pressed into service carrying relief supplies or acting as command and control vehicles.

One lesson I learned was that the amount of office supplies normally brought to the field for the battalion's operations center needed to be seriously beefed up. The requirement to produce written orders expands in disaster relief operations. Everyone you coordinate with will want hard copy. Also you'll be making a lot more map overlays than you think. (We went through a month's worth of map acetate in a week.) Virtually every time you meet someone new, you have to inform him of your sector and capabilities. This usually means the current operations order (OPORD) with task organization and map overlay. If your field-purchasing officer can swing it, buy about two hundred local street maps. Distribute them down to squad leader level, but also keep some to hand out during coordination (some of the well-meaning people you will be working with won't have simple things such as maps). Have your TOC crew preprint the principal relief sectors and their headquarters' locations on each handout map along with pertinent phone numbers. The more information you can give out during coordination in the form of take-away maps and documents, the more successful your coordination meetings are likely to be. Another tip: don't be afraid to explain to people how to read that map you've just given them.

4. Tips for dealing with the local populace.
Units dealing with a massive disaster in a populated area such as south Florida must be prepared for an extremely varied response to their presence, ranging from overjoyed welcome to sullen noncooperation. As uniformed authority figures, soldiers will be approached with many questions from the populace, such as where are emergency medical services, how do we resolve refuse disposal problems,

where are food distribution sites, how do we apply for federal disaster relief, and a whole host of other problems. Each leader down to squad leader should carry with him a map of the area (a street map) and a notebook or series of note cards containing the answers to the most frequently asked questions. It is unreasonable to expect the small-unit leaders to be able to answer every question or solve every problem in detail; however, all should at least be able to point people in the proper direction. Junior leaders should also be prepared to take note of people's problems and pass these notes through their chain of command for action by the appropriate relief authorities. If possible, the same unit should stay in the same neighborhood as long as possible to foster recognition, trust, and cooperation.

A problem specific to south Florida was the large number of illegal immigrants who were afraid to seek aid for fear of being deported. These people would endure injuries and unsanitary conditions that bred disease rather than call attention to themselves. Units must take pains to ensure that these people are found and assisted prior to their becoming a health hazard.

Another problem faced by various units involved in Hurricane Andrew relief was dealing with the various criminal elements that lived in the neighborhoods. The soldiers themselves were in little physical danger from gang members and criminals. With all the old people and women around to prey on, no criminal in his right mind would want to take on a squad of healthy men in their early twenties. There was, however, a constant effort on the part of criminals and gang members to steal or illegally obtain relief supplies. Criminals were also active in attempting to extort relief supplies from the truly needy. Although soldiers were not authorized to make arrests or intervene in anything but stopping cases of violent crime, they did work closely with the police and National Guard elements as sort of an additional "neighborhood watch" by reporting suspicious activities such as break-ins. Units deploying to disaster relief operations should go through the same type of rules of engagement scenarios ("What do you do if you see . . . ?" training) that units deploying to low-intensity combat go through.

It is a sad fact of life that some of the people affected by disaster will do nothing to improve their lot. These people would rather sit in squalor, wreckage, and garbage than clean up the refuse. Often they were drunk and verbally abusive to the soldiers working on the streets. Having to work around people such as this is not something that most soldiers are used to. Leaders must be on their guard against soldiers becoming angry and demoralized over incidents involving people such as this. It is important that troops be told the importance of the work they are doing. It is also important that the unit (brigade, battalion, whatever) foster good relations with the community leaders. In the case of Hurricane Andrew relief, incidents such as the one described were fortunately in the minority, and troop discipline was universally good. The lesson to take, though, is that disaster relief operations are not all sweetness and light, and leaders should be on their guard against negative influences in the community.

Fort Drum (November 1992)

After coming back from Hurricane Andrew, we took a long weekend and then went back to training. The battalion was still scheduled for its rotation at the Joint Readiness Training Center in April, so we wanted to be at our best. Lieutenant Colonel Sikes was a great believer in live fires, and he directed that we do a series of platoon movement-to-contact live fires (both day and night) in November. So we came right off our weekend and scrambled to get the live fires set up. This was excellent training that took up almost the whole month and got us back into the sharp tactical mind-set we needed after more than two months in south Florida.

The live fires went well. The platoons got back into the

groove, and the company commanders conducted after-action reviews after each interaction to drive home the lessons learned. Lieutenant Colonel Sikes or I would always attend these. The support side of the operation ran like a Swiss watch. Trucks showed up on time, chow was never late, maintenance teams were where they were supposed to be. The battalion was clicking. Everyone was looking forward to JRTC.

After the live fires, the battalion was designated as Division Ready Force-1 (DRF-1). This meant that we would be the first battalion to deploy in case of a contingency and had to be prepared to do so within eighteen hours of notification. The preparation for DRF-1 involved preloading vehicles and equipment and preparing the battalion for air movement. Training was generally limited to the local area. Two of the rifle companies would conduct squad training and individual skills training at Fort Drum. Charlie Company and the scout platoon would be sent farther afield to Fort Chaffee, in Arkansas, for training. There they would augment the OPFOR at the JRTC for three weeks as part of the opposing force. The troops would get to fight in the same exercise that we were going on in April, but on the other side. It would be good training for them in preparation for our own JRTC rotation.

Lieutenant Colonel Sikes had been uneasy about this, but it was a tasking that had come down from division. We reasoned that with notification we could get Charlie Company and the scouts back in time. All of the company's go-to-war equipment was already palletized (other than individual and hand-carried equipment that they'd had with them). The first plane in the battalion's airflow didn't have to be wheels up until eighteen hours after notification. We could fly them back and still get the whole battalion out on time. Charlie Company and the scouts would just be the last element in the airflow. It was a calculated risk (one I advised Lieutenant Colonel Sikes to take when he asked me for my opinion), but a company from the battalion stood to get some excellent training. Besides which, I rationalized to myself, if something happens we can always get them back in time. Little did we know that this would not be the case. In retrospect I certainly would have advised the commander differently, but at the time it seemed like a good bet. I could see nothing happening in the world that could possibly cause the commitment of U.S. troops. None of us could have guessed that we were at the dawn of a new age.

Part Two
Somalia

If you have the yen to see a beautiful land of camels, sand, thorn scrub, endless beaches and interesting villages completely unspoiled by tourism, this is the place to head for.
—*The Lonely Planet Guide to Africa,*
comment on Somalia

Four

The Big Picture: Background to
Operation RESTORE HOPE

Somalia is and always has been an out-of-the-way, pastoral, no-account kind of place. In many ways the Somalis are the Irish of East Africa. Culturally homogenous, speaking one language, tribal, proud, and violent. They have a great oral tradition of stories and folklore, and they are conscious of their ancestry. They are fierce warriors who (until they ran the United States and the UN out of town) have never won a war. They also have waged ferocious, internecine wars between tribes and clans in which all members of the other side are fair game, including women and children. They have a problem with central government, they are stiff-necked and brave, and they don't like strangers telling them what to do.

Somalis believe that they are descendents of Muslim saints and the family of the prophet. Two of the main clans, the Darood and the Issaq, trace their lineage back to the eleventh and thirteenth centuries. Others are slightly more modern. The clan that a Somali belongs to is the central fact of his or her life. All political loyalties come from clan membership, and there are subclans within subclans like the layers of an onion. Clans tend to be geographically located (for example, the Issaq are mainly in the north); however, nomadic or forcibly relocated subclans are often spread throughout the length of Somalia. Nomadic clan families such as the Issaq, Hawiye, Dir, and Darood believe that they are pure Somali

61

compared to others, particularly those who come from southern parts of the country.

Somali history is a strange read. The Somalis are a people who have lived largely in a state of continuous intertribal conflict. Except for a few Arab trading posts on the coast (Mogadishu, Marka, Brava, Kismayu, and Berbera), the country existed unchanged for a millennium right up until the latter half of the nineteenth century. This had its good and bad points. Somalia produced no Thomas Edisons, but neither did it produce any Hitlers. Nobody paid much attention to Somalia, and Somalia, by and large, returned the compliment.

In the latter part of the nineteenth century, Somalia was divided for colonial administration between southern Somalia (Italian) and northern Somalia (British). British Somaliland was an arid, inhospitable place that was taken over mainly by the British for the port of Berbera, its proximity to Aden, and its strategic location at the southern entrance to the Red Sea. There was little colonial development in British Somaliland, and most of the inhabitants continued the pastoral, nomadic lives they enjoyed before the arrival of the British.

The period of British administration produced one of the few nationalist heroes in Somali history. Mohammed Abdullah Hassan was known by the Somalis as "the poor man of God" and by the British and Italians as the "Mad Mullah." Mohammed Hassan was a holy man of enormous charisma who detested all foreigners. He had a vague vision of a Somalia-for-the-Somalis kind of homeland. This vision did not include tribal equality, because he frequently engaged in raiding and livestock rustling against other Somali tribes and clans as well as the British. What Mohammed Hassan lacked in any clear objectives in his conflict against foreigners he more than made up for in sheer, stick-to-it persistence. From 1898 to 1920, he raided and fought with the British and their tribal allies, occasionally raiding Italian territory as well. The British mounted no less than seven major campaigns to eliminate him as a threat. They finally succeeded after World War I, when they were able to use airplanes to chase and bomb the Mad Mullah and his fellow tribesmen. Although they succeeded in finally overawing Mohammed Hassan's followers with a combination of displays of military power and dogged pursuit, the British never actually captured the Mad Mullah. He died of old age, in the bush, recalcitrant and unbending to the end. He is the one national hero of recent years (to a culture where each man can recite his lineage back seventeen generations, between eighty and a hundred years ago *is* recent) whom all Somalis agree on. It was a pity that we didn't pay more attention to the true lesson provided by this historic figure. Somalis fight, even when it's smarter not to, even when there's no chance of winning. There's a cussedness and an orneriness about them.

Only peripherally involved in the fight against Mohammed Hassan, Italian Somaliland prospered. The colony included the rich farming country of the Juba and Shabele valleys. In contrast to British Somaliland, the Italians developed significantly in their colony. The city of Mogadishu grew as the colonial capital, and the towns of Marka, Afgoi, and Kismayu became important transportation hubs. Many Italian colonists came to Somalia and established cordial if not close relationships with most of the tribes that lived there. Many of the Somali tribesmen enlisted in the Italian colonial army. In 1934, an Italian force had a small border incident with the Ethiopians at a place called Wal-Wal. This incident led to the Italian invasion and conquest of Ethiopia. One Italian army invaded Ethiopia through Somalia, using Mogadishu as its major logistics base.

Italy declared war on the British in June 1940 and invaded and occupied British Somaliland for one of the few Italian victories of the war. This minor success gained them little, however. British forces invading from Kenya took Italian Somaliland in February and March 1941 and soon eliminated all Italian forces in Ethiopia and the Horn of Africa. After the war, Somalia was placed under UN administration (ironically, southern Somalia was administered by the Italians) until 1960. On 1 July 1960, southern and northern Somalia were officially joined and Somalia became an independent nation.

Somalia staggered along until March 1969, when the last

free and fair (by Africa standards) elections were held. It must have been quite a free-for-all, with seventy political parties and more than a thousand candidates for the 123-seat national assembly. These elections have been characterized by some historians as "unusually violent," because clans tended to vote for candidates who would increase their clan's power. Opposing clans accused one another of ballot stuffing; the results were riots. These were not immediately put down by the military, because the military was made up predominantly of members of the Darood clan, and they were too busy making sure their candidates won. The result was a parliament with no majorities and fractional voting blocks. Although the elections were more violent than previous ones, the results were not dramatically different. There was little chance of anything serious coming out of such a national assembly. However, as long as the presidency remained intact, it was assumed that Somalia would stumble along as it always had. Unfortunately, President Abdirashid Ali Shermarke was assassinated on 18 October 1969. Three days later, Gen. Siad Barre, the head of the armed forces, seized power and declared himself president of the Somali Republic.

Siad Barre was a true piece of work, an eight on the scale of one to ten when it comes to nutty, emerging-nation dictators, topped only by the likes of Idi Amin. Siad Barre was a man who thought big. His idea was to take Somalia into "scientific socialism." He disbanded the old national assembly and set up a twenty-five-person Supreme Revolutionary Command Council. One of his first acts was to outlaw all references to clans or clan membership. In a single edict he attempted to do away with a social structure that had been in existence in Somalia for millennia. Marriages had to take place in community centers, and mandatory political education for everyone was decreed. The concept of trying to make the Somalis into African clones of the East Germans was bold but unrealistic. The very idea of these people, proud and independent as Lucifer, willingly becoming a lined-up, downcast crowd of lumpenproles is ludicrous. But that's what Barre tried to do.

Some analysts think that scientific socialism was Siad Barre's way of currying favor with the Russians, who were the close allies of the People's Democratic Republic of Yemen, across the water on the southern edge of the Arabian Peninsula. A socialist allied state on the Horn of Africa would give the Russians friendly territory on both sides of the southern entrance to the Red Sea. It would also give them air bases reaching out into the Red Sea and the Indian Ocean. Siad could expect significant support from the Soviets and the Communist bloc. It was a shrewd calculation and one that for a short time worked. Siad Barre signed a treaty of co-operation and friendship with Soviet president Podgorny in July 1974.

Declaring scientific socialism didn't mean Siad Barre meant to live by it. Of the twenty-five men in the Supreme Revolutionary Command Council, more than half were from Siad Barre's own clan. Siad Barre was actually no more a confirmed socialist than he was a Roman Catholic. He did, however, use scientific socialism brilliantly to justify the assumption to power of his Marehan clan. He also brought into government many of his relatives, the most infamous of whom was Brig. Gen. Mohammed Said Hersi (aka Morgan), his son-in-law. Morgan was trained by the East Germans, and his secret police organization was one of the most ruthless and feared in Africa.

Siad Barre tried to use some of the trappings of modern socialism to keep his political enemies weak. He forcibly relocated entire clans from their traditional homelands and put them into areas in which they had never lived. This mix-up of clans helped minimize the power of clan elders. He also stressed an equal role for women and had ten clan sheiks executed for opposing the government's sexual equality policy. Although Siad Barre was the champion of the modern socialist Somalia and women's rights, he was careful not to have women in any position of power. His stressing of sexual equality was yet another ploy to use a Western political model to break the power of clan elders and punish his enemies.

Still, if Somalia had gone on like this in its own internal

politics, it would have been no worse than any one of a dozen dictatorships in Africa during the 1970s. Unfortunately, in late 1972, some American oil prospectors in the Ogaden desert of Ethiopia near the border with Somalia found natural gas deposits and made the announcement that oil might be there as well. The Ogaden area has a high number of ethnic Somalis. Siad Barre immediately began his backing of the Western Somalia Liberation Front, whose purpose was to liberate the Ogaden and place it under Somali control. This situation smoldered for a number of years until it finally came to a head in 1977.

The first critical event in 1977 was that the Ethiopian government changed hands. The new leader, Mengistu Haile Mariam, seized power in a bloody coup and was immediately congratulated by the Soviet ambassador. Mengistu from the very beginning cultivated a relationship with the Soviets. This threw Siad Barre into a quandary. The Soviets were his patrons, but now they looked to be leaning toward the Ethiopians as well. This state of affairs made Barre's plan to invade and occupy the Ogaden awkward, to say the least. Nonetheless, on 23 July 1977, Somali forces launched a full-scale attack into the Ogaden to "liberate" their Somali brethren and return the Ogaden to "rightful" Somali control.

Timing, in this world, is everything, and Siad Barre's couldn't have been worse. Had he invaded a year earlier against the previous Ethiopian regime, there can be little doubt that the Soviets would have supported him. As it was, when forced to choose between lush, mineral-rich Ethiopia and impoverished Somalia, the Soviets didn't hesitate. After a few abortive attempts to get Siad Barre to see reason *(The Ethiopians are now your socialist brothers. No, really.)*, they broke relations with the Somalis. All Russian advisors left the country, and the Russians managed to sabotage a great deal as they left. They started one of the most massive airlifts in modern military history to Ethiopia, bringing in not only thousands of tons of equipment and war materiel but hundreds of Soviet advisors and several thousand Cuban troops. The rejuvenated and reinforced Ethiopian army soon had the Somalis in full retreat. The last elements of the Somali army finally staggered back across the border in March 1978. Siad Barre's attempted expansion of Somalia had been a total fiasco.

The reaction to this was not long in coming, because a coup attempt was launched against Siad Barre only one month after the last troops came home. The coup plotters were members of the armed forces and the Majertain clan. Although the coup failed, it could be seen as the first defiance to Barre. He reacted savagely to it. His secret police and army conducted a brutal campaign against the Majertain, killing and jailing many and collectively punishing the whole tribe by destroying their rainwater reservoirs. Many more Majertain, along with thousands of their animals, died on the waterless plains of northern Somalia. The surviving coup leaders fled the country. From exile they formed the Somali Salvation Front, or SSF. This became the first of a number of groups organized in the next decade to resist Siad Barre.

Siad held a couple of showcase Soviet-style elections in 1979 and 1984, but he never released his grasp on power until it was torn from him. He did make new overtures overseas and secured some modest support from the United States (who at the time looked upon Somalia as a counterbalance to the burgeoning Soviet presence in the Horn of Africa). In 1980 Somalia signed an agreement with the Carter administration for access to the Somali port of Berbera, on the northern shore of Somalia. The Somali economy, not healthy in the best of times, took a nosedive in 1984, when a cattle plague caused the Saudis to ban the export of Somali cattle (Somalia's largest export product). Inflation went from 25 percent to near 90 percent in less than a year. The International Monetary Fund provided a temporary panacea for the Somali economy, but with no mineral wealth to speak of, and a subsistence farming economy that was constantly being interrupted by low-level guerrilla warfare, the chances for significant economic recovery were not good.

Meantime, internal unrest continued to bubble in Somalia. In 1981 the Somali National Movement (SNM) was formed in London. Made up mainly of Issaq clan members, it was focused on the events in northern Somalia. In 1983 there was sporadic tribal warfare between the Issaq and the Dolbuhanta tribes. Dolbuhanta clansmen raided Issaq villages, killing men, women, and children and taking massive amounts of livestock. The Issaq and their SNM sponsors responded and were soon embroiled in a low-level guerrilla war with Dolbuhanta militia and the Somali regular army.

Siad Barre continued to become more and more paranoid. In April 1986, he ordered the arrest of more than two hundred officers for possible coup plotting. His rationale was that there had recently been coups against other dictators who had relationships with the United States. He became convinced that the United States had similar plans for him. Shortly after this, he was badly injured in a car accident and flown to Saudi Arabia for treatment. He was replaced in the interim by Brig. Mohammed Ali Samantar, who attempted to form a government of national reconciliation. Samantar was foiled in this by Siad Barre's immediate family members in government. Barre came back to Mogadishu from Saudi Arabia and publicly humiliated Samantar but, curiously, did not have him removed from government. In December 1986, Siad Barre was reelected to the presidency without opposition. He continued to place his relatives into positions of national importance, for which they were ill suited. This was particularly true of his appointment of Jama Barre, his nephew, to finance minister. Jama Barre's opposition to International Monetary Fund–mandated reforms had a negative effect on an already unhealthy economy.

All during this time, a low-level guerrilla war continued on the border with Ethiopia between the Ethiopian-backed Somali National Movement and the Somali-backed Western Somali Liberation Front. Realizing his weak position, Siad Barre tried to negotiate an end to hostilities with the Ethiopians. An accord was reached with Ethiopia on 4 April calling for normalized relations.

On 23 May, SNM guerrillas from Ethiopia attacked into northern Somalia, taking several towns and cutting off Berbera from the rest of the country. The Somali army could not defeat them but did manage to slaughter thousands of their fellow tribesmen for assisting the insurrection. This campaign of repression caused one of the first major refugee migrations since the Ogaden war. The campaign by the Somali army did not, however, break the power of the SNM. The SNM had significant support among the tribes of northern Somalia, and members of the Somali army found themselves fighting outside of their tribal territory in what was becoming a full-blown civil war.

The situation became so violent and precarious that the UN evacuated all refugee assistance personnel from northern Somalia in June. In November, the United Nations High Commissioner for Refugees (UNHCR) began to minimize its staff in Somalia as a whole due to the widespread corruption and interference by Siad Barre's government. All UN workers were scheduled to leave the country by early 1990. Assistance from the United States had already been cut off, and Siad Barre was informed by Secretary Baker that no more U.S. aid would be forthcoming until the Somali government's human rights record improved. Meanwhile, the fighting intensified in northern Somalia, and defections by Siad Barre's troops to the SNM grew.

Siad had dissent in Mogadishu to deal with as well. The Catholic archbishop of Mogadishu, Salvatore Colombo, a longtime Barre critic, was assassinated on 9 July 1989. Five days later, large-scale riots broke out following the arrest of several prominent sheiks for complicity in the archbishop's murder. Siad Barre put his son Mohammed Said Masalah in charge of the repression of these riots. The police killed a great many rioters.

Siad Barre tried to buy himself time by declaring that multiparty elections would be held by the end of 1990. Unfortunately at the time of this declaration, August 1989, things had spun out of his control. The SNM had tasted success in the north, and other Somalis were beginning to break from Barre's camp as well. In November 1989 the Somali army's

4th Division mutinied and Siad Barre sent his all-purpose thug Mohammed Said Masalah to put down the mutiny. This he did by savage repression of the mutineers and the surrounding countryside. The mutineers and townsmen who survived escaped to join the growing resistance to Barre's rule. By January 1990 it was estimated that Siad Barre's forces had killed more than fifty thousand people during the last eighteen months.

The war between Barre's forces and the growing alphabet soup of resistance movements continued to sputter for the first few months of 1990. In May 1990 a group of 114 political moderates, made up mainly of men from the pre–Siad Barre government, published a manifesto calling for ceasefire and national reconciliation. They were arrested. Siad Barre shortly afterward attended a soccer game to show his people that he was not afraid to appear in public. He was pelted with food and roundly booed by his subjects. His guards panicked and fired into the spectators, killing sixty-five. More people were killed at protests over the arrest of the signers of the manifesto. Barre's hold on power became more tenuous by the day. He continued to reshuffle his cabinet and make proclamations about constitutional referendums and multiparty elections, but by now no one was listening. On 2 October the main Somali resistance groups—the SNM, the United Somali Congress (USC), and the Somali Patriotic Movement (SPM)—signed an agreement that had the common objective of defeating the Barre government. Over the next few months, the combined forces of the resistance movements closed in on Mogadishu. Barre reacted to the protest within Mogadishu with mass arrests. There was a general decline in public order in Mogadishu. By early December the U.S. embassy began voluntary evacuation of U.S. and other Western nationals. By the end of December the rebels were at the outskirts of Mogadishu, and fierce fighting took place in the city. Amidst all this, the U.S. embassy was evacuated on 5 January 1991, with Marine helicopters doing a daring evacuation on the eve of the Gulf War. Almost immediately, the U.S. embassy was stripped to the point of telephone wires being torn out of the walls. Only relief workers and the Red Cross were left in Somalia.

Siad Barre offered to resign if the rebels would agree to a cease-fire; his offer was summarily rejected. On 27 January he fled Mogadishu for Kismayu, hoping to rally his forces there. However, the rebels understood that he was on the run and did not let up on their pressure. Forces of the USC took Kismayu in early April 1991. The remnants of the Barre forces, under his son-in-law Mohammed Hersi Morgan, remained in southern Somalia. In July 1991 northern Somalia, calling itself Somaliland, declared independence. The decision was referred to as "irreversible."

Although the different tribal and political factions had held together loosely in their opposition to Siad Barre, his ouster was the signal for the fracture of any consensus. It was difficult to tell all the players, even with a scorecard. Each group protected the interests of a particular clan or subclan. Many were affiliated with one another (like code-sharing airlines). For example, both the Somali National Alliance (SNA) and the Somali Democratic Movement (SDM) were loyal to Mohammed Farah Adieed. Adieed was also a member of the United Somali Congress, as was his archenemy Ali Mahdi, who also controlled the Somali Patriotic Movement and the Somali National Movement. There was also the Somali National Front (SNF), the remnant of forces from the subclan of Barre. In addition, there were smaller groups, such as the Somali Salvation Democratic Movement (SSDM), made up mainly of old resistance fighters against Siad Barre not affiliated with Adieed or Ali Mahdi. A relief worker running into any of these groups at a road checkpoint would be robbed and see his supplies confiscated.

On 18 August, Ali Madhi, the titular head of the USC, declared himself the president of Somalia. The SNA commander, Mohammed Farah Adieed, immediately rejected this. Within a few days there was open conflict between the forces of Adieed and Ali Mahdi, both in Mogadishu and throughout

the countryside. This lasted through September, then sub-
sided but never really stopped. Ali Mahdi tried to form a cabinet with all clans represented in October 1991, but this was
not recognized by Adieed or other warlord chiefs. Fighting
flared up again in November when Ali Mahdi forces attempted to capture Adieed. The general lawlessness in the
city increased as supplies of food and commercial goods became scarce. The Italian embassy was looted by Adieed
forces, but none of the remaining diplomats was injured. By
the end of December 1991, it was estimated that more than
five thousand people had been killed in Mogadishu alone during the fall fighting and more than twenty thousand were
wounded. In addition, there were thousands of uncounted
deaths in the countryside. Large populations of people were
displaced and starving. By January 1992, widespread deaths
from starvation were being reported for the first time. The
armies of Adieed and Ali Mahdi, as well as warlord groups
with no major affiliation, all interfered with food deliveries to
rival clan locations. Conflict continued through the spring,
with the bodies piling up and little real advantage being enjoyed by either side.

Then in April 1992, a truly bizarre note came to an already
strange civil war. The forces of Siad Barre launched a counterattack from their base camp around Baidoa in an effort to re-
assert their control over the country. (You have to hand it to
Siad Barre: for sheer persistence, he's a hard guy to beat.)
Unfortunately, he staged his comeback a tad prematurely. His
forces got as far as Afgoi before being soundly beaten by
Adieed's troops and driven all the way south to the Kenyan
border. Forces loyal to Adieed under Gen. Omar Jess occupied Kismayu, and Siad Barre finally called it a day, crossing
the border to Kenya and eventually ending up in Nigeria,
where he would be granted political asylum. His son-in-law,
with the remainder of his army, remained in southern Somalia, meanwhile, waiting for new developments.

By June 1992 Somalia had degenerated into a state of
"Mad Max" anarchy, with warlord groups controlling their
turf like groups of freebooters in the Thirty Years' War in Eu-

rope. The biggest antagonists, Adieed and Ali Mahdi, were involved in a death struggle in Mogadishu. Their countryside adherents tried to exert pressure on one another by delaying or confiscating relief supplies meant for starving refugees and populations in opposing clan or political faction territory. Relief supplies also became a kind of currency, and anyone with half a dozen men and some rifles could set up a few old tires and an iron bar over the road as a "checkpoint" and exact tolls from the relief convoys. The media started paying attention to Somalia. For the first time, the West began seeing pictures from the areas most affected by food deprivation.

With the civil war stalemated and social situation in chaos, General Adieed grandly gave permission for the UN to come in and escort food convoys. Adieed did this out of calculated thought that if the UN treated him as the dominant authority in Somalia, this would bring him closer to recognition as the legitimate government. In fact, Adieed and Ali Mahdi controlled only relatively small numbers of hard-core followers in Mogadishu. They had forces all over Somalia, but these and their local commanders were not under complete control. Many set up their own authority and fiefdoms and were at best loosely affiliated with the major warlords. They might provide troops and follow some orders, but they were also not above looting and raiding on their own. Humanitarian relief organizations found it increasingly difficult to get supplies to the most stricken areas. More and more of the food was denied to starve the other side into submission, or it was simply siphoned off by local gangs who used it as currency. Being more sensitive to international opinion, Adieed saw his acquiescence to UN presence as a propaganda and political coup. The first UN troops arrived in June, and by September there was a Pakistani battalion at Mogadishu International Airport.

August saw the first U.S. intervention in the Somalia civil war, although initial efforts were modest. President Bush authorized the delivery of relief supplies to Somalia starting on 14 August 1992. Using C-130 transports, which were secured during their short ground time in Somalia by Special

Forces soldiers, the air force began flying in food, medicines, and other relief supplies to airstrips in the places worst affected by starvation. This operation (named Provide Hope) was fraught with problems from the beginning. It brought food into the country, but the distribution of it was still a major problem. Although the warlord forces and bandits never tried to engage the aircraft or Special Forces soldiers while they were on the ground, C-130s flying into and out of the airstrips soon began taking fire from disgruntled or bored bandits. The United States finally shut down these flights on 19 September after several C-130s had been hit by ground fire. Provide Hope increased the amount of food coming in but did not address the problem of food distribution. It basically got more food on the ground to be stolen. The starvation problem seemed as bad as ever.

Although the Pakistani battalion was in place by September, Adieed reneged on his offer to let the battalion escort food. The battalion basically controlled part of the Mogadishu airport and was helpless to prevent the looting of relief supplies flown in. Unclear of their authority, with a vague mission from the UN, these troops stood by helplessly as Adieed's troops looted relief supplies with impunity. After a few weeks, the Pakistanis were bunkered in at the airport and were occupied mainly with protecting themselves. The fighting in Mogadishu continued, and disease and anarchy spread.

While all of this was going on, there was a fateful meeting of the U.S. National Security Council in Washington on 21 November. The council was trying to decide what, if anything, could be done about Somalia. Then chairman of the Joint Chiefs of Staff, Colin Powell, urged intervention. His rationale was twofold: (1) the scale of the suffering in Somalia demanded action and (2) the United States was the only country that could do something about it. Although recently defeated for a second term, President Bush saw Somalia as a clear test of the "new world order." If the United States and the industrialized nations of the West and Asia, along with their regional allies, could not intervene and end the suffering in this poor African country, there didn't seem much hope for the post–Cold War world. Bush believed that going to Somalia to end the suffering there was the moral thing to do. He gave the order to intervene in the Somali civil war. This new operation was to be called Restore Hope. It was a noble decision—motivated by thoroughly decent impulses—but the wrong one.

Five

Alert (November–December 1992)

I first learned of the deployment while watching television news during Thanksgiving weekend. The Somalia situation in and of itself was nothing new. Watching the wretched misery of the Somalis on TV, I'd felt sorry for them but had not thought of intervention. Imagine my surprise when I saw on the news that soldiers from Fort Drum, New York, and U.S. Marines were to be committed to a humanitarian mission in Somalia within the next few days. Fort Drum meant the 10th Mountain Division, and that meant our battalion. As DRF-1, we would be the first to go. As soon as the story was over, I called Lieutenant Colonel Sikes. He couldn't confirm it, but we met at the battalion to review procedures for when and if we got the word. It came the next day.

The next ten days were a blur of activity. Although as DRF-1 we were ready to move in eighteen hours, the actual time line was a bit friendlier. The Marines wouldn't land until 9 December, and the first unit from 10th Mountain wouldn't arrive in country until 13 December. This gave us a little more time to plan and go through last-minute checks and inspections. There was some confusion as to exactly what the plan was for entry into the country. Initially, the word was that the battalion would fly into Mogadishu. Then we got word that we'd fly into Baledogle instead. This was a major air base, built by the Russians, about fifty miles from Mogadishu. Then we were told that initially the airflow would contain only three C-141s, with the rest of the battalion fol-

76

lowing three days later. This was due to competing priorities for the U.S. Air Force airlift.

This put us in a dilemma. Three C-141s could not hold even a quarter of the battalion's assets. What would we take? I spent some hours in the battalion conference room with Lieutenant Colonel Sikes, Joe Occhuzzio, the company commanders, and the staff. Sikes finally decided upon the following configuration for an advanced party:

- battalion TAC-CP (TAC-2) and a command and control team from the S2 and S3 sections commanded by me
- support platoon slice (three vehicles under Lieutenant Van Hoesen)
- one AT platoon under Lieutenant Criswell
- Alpha Company under Capt. Gordy Flowers
- TACSAT team
- detachment from the division's long-range surveillance unit (LRSU)

Division directed the inclusion of this last element. I wasn't especially pleased with it. At this early stage of the game, why I needed a long-range patrol squad was beyond me. I told Lieutenant Colonel Sikes as much, but the bottom line was that the division planners were adamant. The previous commander of the LRSU had the reputation of being something of a loose cannon, and I had never worked with any of the LRSU squads. I just hoped they wouldn't be in the way.

The other issue was what to do about Charlie Company. Sikes's misgivings about sending the company away during DRF-1 were now seen as well founded. Division tried to get the company released from the JRTC tasking, but apparently a real-world deployment to a potential combat zone was not considered sufficient reason for Forces Command (FORSCOM) to relieve the 10th Mountain from the tasking. The 10th Mountain Division instead had to replace Charlie Company for the Somalia deployment with a company from the

1-87 in the 1st Brigade. The news of this was a crushing disappointment to Capt. Kelly Jordan and his men, who were already in the process of planning their return from the JRTC.

It was disappointing to me as well. Charlie was a solid company. The platoon leaders had been in their jobs for a while and had done well on the recent platoon live fires. Kelly Jordan was my old assistant S3, Frank Kirsop's predecessor. Osteen's scout platoon was a solid, well-trained outfit as well. I was considerably relieved to learn that the Alpha Company 1-87, under Capt. Geoff Hammil, would be our stand-in company. I had worked with Geoff before when he was in the 1st Brigade S3 shop and we were supporting 1st Brigade exercises. His professional knowledge and calm demeanor had impressed me. Alpha 1-87 turned out to be a fine outfit that never failed to carry its share of the load. In addition, we got the 1-87 Scouts under First Lieutenant Harvey. This platoon turned out to be an aggressive and well-led outfit and would figure prominently in most of the actions fought by battalion troops. At the end of the tour they would be second in the battalion for number of gunmen captured or killed.

In the meantime the division was getting all sorts of conflicting signals from the 18th Airborne Corps and the Joint Staff. At first, the entire 2d Brigade and most of the division support troops would go. Then we got the word that artillery was to be left back (the word came in after some units had actually loaded their equipment on ships). This confusion came from an arbitrary personnel cap announced by the secretary of defense. The total army forces in country were limited to no more than 10,200 soldiers. This included all the important nondivisional support elements (such as aviation, engineers, and corps support group units) that would make up the bulk of army forces. Because of this, planners from the division had to go back and try to cookie-cutter an organization to support the mission out of the arbitrary personnel ceiling. The upshot of all this was that over the next two weeks, 2d Brigade was cut one infantry battalion (the 2-14) and its direct support artillery battalion. Initially only the 2-87 Infantry and the 3-14 Infantry would go. The 2-14 had a date with history in Somalia, but it did not come until almost a year later, on 3 October 1993, when they led the attack to rescue the trapped Rangers. Now in early December 1992 they had been pulled back from Fort Pickett, Virginia (where they had just been deployed for training exercises), after less than one day. Lieutenant Colonel Bill David, the battalion commander, was not pleased about losing almost three weeks of training and then not being able to deploy to Somalia. The imposed shortsighted personnel ceiling policy had similar ripple effects up and down the division.

We spent the next few days reconfiguring the battalion for the deployment. We also held last-minute training and preparations, reconfirming weapons zeros, and conducting classes on rules of engagement, first aid, and what to expect in Somalia. Each day we received updates on the activities in Somalia and watched the news for images of the place that was to be our area of operations. It seemed pretty wild—gunmen and anarchy and a sea of miserable faces. We were to be the cavalry coming to set it all right. Nonetheless, the troops in general seemed enthused about the mission. I had a vague sense even then that it would be a can of worms, but it really didn't matter that much to me. I was a soldier and this is what I did. In truth everyone was looking forward to an active deployment. Most young soldiers join the army for the adventure of it, and most old ones stay in partly for the same reason. Somalia in December sure looked a lot more interesting than training to go to the Joint Readiness Training Center.

The battalion's families were making the sudden adjustment that had become so common for soldiers in the nineties. "Whoops, Daddy won't be here for Christmas after all. Sorry, kids." Soldiers were making arrangements to send their families home, have relatives come up, or just have Christmas early. Everyone put a brave face on it, but you could tell that a lot of the wives were frightened and a little dazed by the suddenness of it all. My own situation was better than most, with Donna's family being close by in Toronto. We had planned on visiting there over Christmas anyway. Now she and John would just go without me. Donna was taking it in stride, although after two years of marriage she had weathered the Gulf War, then Hurricane Andrew, and now this. I'm sure she was wondering what she'd gotten herself into marrying a soldier.

Lieutenant Colonel Sikes held a briefing for the battalion families and explained our mission (as best he knew it) and what kind of conditions we would be facing. He had put a lot of effort into the briefing and provided every scrap of information, both about the mission and what agencies were available to assist the families in their soldiers' absence. It was typical of him to work hard on such a thing. Afterward he wondered aloud to me whether he'd done enough. Every family was briefed by support agency representatives, and the complete phone lists of family support groups and service representatives were published. I honestly couldn't see what else could be done by either him or the battalion staff, and I told him so. He shook his head and said there had to be something else. I told him to stop worrying or he'd spoil the deployment.

That night on TV, we watched the Marines come ashore. We were, to a man, sickened and outraged by the TV floodlights on the beach. I wondered how much of a pain the reporters were going to be. I vowed privately that if anyone did that to me, I'd break every light set out there and maybe a few cameramen too.

The next day was even more hectic as we continued to prepare for movement. I put together a couple of training memoranda on convoy security and checkpoint operations. Lieutenant Colonel Sikes liked them and had me give several classes on the subjects. One of the classes was interrupted by the Chief of Staff of the Army, General Sullivan, who came by to give us some words of encouragement. Later that day we were tasked to provide an officer to accompany Brigadier General Magruder, the assistant division commander, for maneuver. He would be bringing an advance team from division to establish liaison with the Marines and coordinate our reception of the division's elements into Somalia. Sikes detailed Kirk Haschak to go, reasoning that HHC would be broken up among other elements, and Kirk was a seasoned enough officer to help prepare for our entry into the country.

Later that afternoon we issued the battalion operations order. This was the first of many, and it detailed the scheme of deployment that I have already mentioned. The battalion TAC-2 and attachments would deploy first, along with Alpha Company as the battalion advanced detachment (ADVON), and Lieutenant Colonel Sikes and the main body would deploy five days later. Sikes personally read the mission statement and gave his commander's intent:

"TF Condor conducts strategic deployment, establishes lodgment, assists in the transition of division ready brigade elements into the tactical area of responsibility (TAOR), and establishes a security zone in assigned TAOR to ensure delivery of food, water, and medical supplies by UN-sponsored NGOs; on order, transition responsibility for the conduct of relief operations to follow on UN forces and conduct redeployment.

Commander's Intent for All Operations

Force protection is paramount (trust no one). Use the buddy system. Keep your head down. Resist the pull of compassion that can lead to complacency. Doing what is right for the soldier may not always be the easy way. Remember and follow your training. Winning is maintaining the moral high ground.

- Establish a security zone for the safe conduct of humanitarian assistance operations.
- Secure movement of humanitarian supplies in TAOR.
- Secure critical humanitarian relief sites in TAOR.
- Maintain task force discipline and show of force operations through constant aggressive activity.
- Reinforce the hope of life in all Somalians. Be light infantry ambassadors for the American way of life."

This was vintage Jim Sikes: he was succinct and to the point but at the same time optimistic and upbeat. He could say something such as "Reinforce the hope of life" and "Be light infantry ambassadors for the American way of life" and not get a single soft snicker or subtly rolled eyeball. He had that knack for bringing out the best in people.

Our mission was fairly simple initially: secure Baledogle airfield for use by the JTF as an additional airhead into the country in order to take some of the pressure off of Mogadishu International; assist NGOs in the area with food distribution; and be prepared to execute further missions.

Initially, we would have our hands full just securing the large Baledogle airfield complex. Because we really didn't have any idea what NGOs and food distribution sites existed in the area of Baledogle airfield and the nearest adjacent town, Wanwaylen, we would have to make that a primary task for reconnaissance once we got there. This translated as showing up and announcing to the locals, "Okay, here we are. What's going on?" We didn't have any specific intelligence on hostiles in the area either (although we did have some good intelligence summaries on some of the major warlord forces and the nature of Somali factions in general, thanks to the efforts of Mike Klein). In short, we really didn't know a lot, but we generally knew what we had to do—secure the airfield.

So, on December 11 we were off. Donna and John dropped me at the battalion, and with a lump in my throat I watched them drive away. I sighed, then got down to the business at hand. I met for the first time with the division LRSU detachment, and many of my fears were allayed. Staff Sergeant Hillard, the squad leader, seemed like a pro, and the prospect of any cowboy action on his part now seemed a lot less likely. My TACSAT operators from 18th Airborne Corps also showed up, and we redistributed the load to take some of the burden off these two guys. Gordy and First Sergeant Choinard had their people well in hand, and all of Alpha Company seemed really pumped. We had a final roll call of the ADVON, did a last equipment check, then boarded buses for the trip to Griffiths Air Force Base. We were brought to a big hangar next to where B-52 bombers were kept. There we palletized our cargo and got our vehicles inspected. Then we sat down to wait. There was some initial confusion as to whether we would be flying out that day or the next.

After a few hours, three C-141B transports showed up and we were informed that we would be flying out that day after all. We loaded the planes in short order and were soon ready to go. I would be in the lead plane with the command and control vehicles and a platoon of Alpha Company. Gordy would take the next plane with the rest of Alpha Company, and Bob Van Hoesen would follow in the third plane with the support platoon and Echo Company elements. I put out some last-minute instructions to the plane commanders, avoided the members of the press who were there to see us off (thankfully, a division public affairs officer representative was there to help), and boarded the aircraft. After a short safety briefing, the big plane taxied out to the runway and with a sudden surge of thrust we were airborne. The faces of the people around me were composed but excited at the same time. This wasn't another training exercise. We were the first army troops flying to Somalia. I confess to feeling a little elated myself. Part of me missed Donna and John already, but that part was locked away in its little compartment. Mostly I was thinking of the mission and wondering what we'd find.

Six

Getting There (11–13 December 1992)

The flight was long and boring. The troops didn't say much. The unknown nature of what we would be facing must have weighed on them. First Sergeant Choinard and I spent time walking along the aircraft's cavernous length and talking to the troops. I'm not sure how much it helped them, but it helped me. The hours dragged on. The flight crew was a pleasant and congenial group who allowed anyone to visit the cockpit, a few at a time. About halfway across the Atlantic we conducted an in-flight refueling, with all sorts of strange and disconcerting noises coming down into the cargo bay. From the cockpit the tanker looked impossibly close, and my stomach dropped when I saw it. The flight crew was nonplussed, however, and the whole operation was carried out with detached and businesslike serenity. Refueled, we flew on into the night. A few people tried to sleep but most were too keyed up. Eventually, I pulled out the book I had brought with me, *Bataan, Our Last Ditch*. The travails of the defenders of Bataan helped put things back into perspective. I mean, compared to that, how bad could Somalia be? Soon, I drifted off.

It was daylight when we reached Egypt and Cairo West Air Base. I awoke and went up to the cockpit to see a tan world bathed in the sunlit glare of the desert. After more than a dozen hours in the dull lighting of the cargo compartment, the world seemed unnaturally bright. In the distance we could see the Egyptian air base where we would land and refuel before continuing. The pilot put the aircraft into a slow, lazy descent, which allowed me to get a good look at the air base. A big, sprawling complex in the desert to the west of Cairo, through the good offices of the Egyptian government, it was to become a major staging base for operations in Somalia. Ours were the first Somalia-bound planes landing there. We circled and landed, with the flight crew showing the same matter-of-fact ease with which they did everything else.

On the ground we were met by an air force colonel, the leader of the advanced liaison team sent to work with the Egyptian air force. We were informed that we would have to hold overnight because the airfield we were supposed to be flying into (Baledogle) had not been secured yet by the Marines. Hold one day and fly into Somalia to either Bale-dogle or Mogadishu tomorrow.

Unfortunately, there were no support facilities on the airfield to feed and billet 150 men. In a few weeks the advanced base at Cairo West would, with the assistance of the Egyptian air force, accommodate such an element, but in these first days there wasn't anything there. The lack of facilities presented us with a problem. We could have stayed in a hangar, but there was no food and water available. As a result we would have had to break into the supplies we were carrying for the mission. Because I didn't know how long we would have to subsist on them in Somalia before we could be resupplied, I didn't want to touch them.

Instead, the air force colonel in charge of the airfield liaison and control group made arrangements at a local hotel for us to stay overnight. I was not entirely pleased with this, nor was Gordy Flowers, who cautioned me about the troops losing their combat mind-set. But there was nothing else. Besides, I thought, it might be the last decent night's sleep or good meal they would have for some time. We piled our men onto buses and rode to the hotel. In the distance we could see the pyramids.

The hotel kitchen was amazed at the amount of food 150 American soldiers can eat on a buffet line. Other than a minor misunderstanding about room service (some of our troops had decided that the buffet wasn't enough), the night passed without incident. The next morning we returned to the airfield, and after a short delay we were off. Even at this point we didn't know if we were flying in to Baledogle or Mogadishu. At any rate, we were Somalia bound.

We were about halfway through the flight when I was told that we were going to Baledogle. The last few hours were spent doing weapons and equipment checks and munching on food saved from the hotel. About an hour out we broke open the ammunition and issued everyone his basic load. The aircrew was not pleased with this and mentioned that it was a violation of Military Airlift Command (MAC) regulations. I told them their concern was noted and to report me to the MAC chain of command if they felt that strongly about it. I was goddamned if my people would get off the plane without ready ammunition. This little tiff over, they couldn't have been more helpful. The crew chief took last letters from us to mail when they got back to the States.

I was in the cargo compartment when we landed, so I had no impression of Baledogle. The plane taxied to the northern end of the runway and let the ramp down. Instantly a blast of humid heat hit us. The next thing I could see was a mob of about fifty cameramen and reporters running for the back of the plane. I'd meant to record the name of the first man off the plane so he could have the honor of being the first U.S. Army soldier in Somalia, but unfortunately I didn't get to see who jumped out first, so his name is lost to history. We pretty much all piled out together anyway.

I told First Sergeant Choinard and Lieutenant Criswell to get the plane unloaded, then I went out to make a short statement and keep the press at bay. I spoke some inanity about being glad to be here to help (and thinking, but not saying, that we were especially glad to be out of Fort Drum in winter) and about our admiration for the relief agencies who had been here during the crisis—real Christian charity stuff. I then told them to leave us alone while we were unloading and to stay off the airstrip because there were two more planes coming in. Among the reporters were two Marines sent by the commander of the task force that had secured the airfield a few hours before. I went with them to meet their commander.

Baledogle (13–31 December 1992)

The Marines from the battalion task force commanded by Lieutenant Colonel O'Leary had set up a temporary command post in the old airfield headquarters building, which doubled as the control tower. I had Specialist Henry park TAC-2 and I walked up the three flights of stairs to the Marine CP. The heat was already oppressive and I was sweating profusely under my full combat load, flak jacket, and helmet. The Marine task force commander, a friendly, tobacco-chewing major, couldn't have been nicer. He was pleased to have us there to take over the airfield from him, because they were already being tasked to move farther inland to Baidoa and Bardera. We agreed that he would maintain the perimeter guard on the airfield for that night, and my troops would take over in the morning. This would give my men a chance to do recons of the area and the troops a brief opportunity to acclimatize before we assumed the responsibility for airfield security. We had just completed agreeing on where my troops would assemble for the night when I felt a tap on my shoulder.

Turning around I was astonished to see David Hackworth, a reporter for *Newsweek* and an old acquaintance. Dave is a character I'd bumped into several times the previous four years at Fort Irwin and in the Gulf War. Now he's the first guy I meet in Somalia. It was spooky. Dave was (and is) a controversial figure—a highly decorated retired colonel and "military reform" guru not loved by a great many in the military's hierarchy. I was sure that his presence would raise the pucker factor for the joint task force public affairs officers. I didn't always agree with him, but I liked him. At least he knew enough about the army to keep out of the way while he was watching stuff. In any event, it was nice to see a friendly face so soon after landing, and we caught up on old times for a few minutes while the second plane came in and landed. The troops' vehicles and equipment were then quickly guided to their assembly areas. Staff Sergeant Brown, Henry, and the TACSAT team began setting up a command post for me below the control tower.

Right after the third C-141 landed, a smaller twin-engine prop plane came in and Brigadier General Magruder and Kirk Haschak came out to the headquarters building. I briefed Magruder on the plan for security and he nodded his assent. He then told me that the plans for occupation of Somalia had changed greatly. Task Force 3-14 infantry would no longer be coming to Baledogle but would be going directly to Kismayu, along with various supporting elements and Division Artillery (DIVARTY) headquarters. Magruder would be the designated commander of JTF Kismayu. The 2d Brigade would base its operations out of Baledogle, and the division headquarters would establish itself in Mogadishu. For the short term I was to be the officer in charge at Baledogle until Lieutenant Colonel Sikes and Colonel Ward showed up. I was instructed to support the Marines in any manner in which they asked and to rely upon them for supplies. I had already made arrangements with them for a resupply of water and rations. Brigadier General Magruder also told me that Ambassador Oakley would arrive at the airfield either tomorrow or the next day and I was to arrange a meeting between the ambassador and the local leaders. It was getting dark by the time the general finished briefing me. After wishing me luck and leaving me Kirk Haschak, he left for Mogadishu.

After Brigader General Magruder left we did a quick check to ensure that everyone was bedded down and secure for the night. There were no real worries in that regard; Gordy and his people knew they were competent. Lieutenant Van Hoesen and the support platoon guys were on one side of the headquarters building and Lieutenant Criswell's antitank platoon was on the other. I positioned the ADVON headquarters next to the Marines on top of the old operations and control tower building.

The building itself was a U-shaped, three-story structure

that was in surprisingly good condition considering that all the windows were missing. The control tower was on the top of the building and offered a commanding view of the whole complex. We immediately chose the building for our headquarters. Besides nests of scorpions and bats, there was a lot of debris in many of the rooms, but with some work it would make a good brigade headquarters. The air force control team that came in with the Marines was detached to us and set up shop in the control tower. I had Kirk put our little headquarters in the room beneath it and set up our communications antennas and TACSAT on the roof. We put up our big aerial photo of Baledogle on a piece of cardboard and covered it with plastic acetate. It was as good as a large-scale map of the area, so we used it to apportion parts of the airstrip complex to different units in the next two weeks as more units moved in.

Our sleeping area was on the roof beside the control tower. Dave Hackworth and I sat under the stars and talked for a few minutes about the mission and what we expected to see. Then I peeled off my sweat-drenched shirt and spread it out beside me to dry, feeling the warm breeze blow over me. It was a moment of rare beauty and luxury. The dark expanse of Somalia was spread out below us, with every star in the sky vivid and seeming almost close enough to touch. I lay back and ate my MRE dried fruit, chasing it down with a little water. I soon fell asleep.

In the morning Kirk Haschak and I reconnoitered the airfield and its environs. Baledogle airfield was a surprisingly large complex, about three kilometers long and half as wide. There was a single main airstrip and a large taxiway running parallel to it, which could serve as a second airstrip in a pinch. The facilities had been built by the Russians in the early seventies and for the time were close to state of the art. The airfield, however, had been wrecked. Some damage was done by the Russians when they withdrew in 1977, the rest during the civil war. What hadn't been destroyed or shot up was looted by the villagers from nearby Wanwaylen. There wasn't a window or an electrical socket left in any building.

At one end of the strip were the shells of large, modern hangars with their roofs mostly gone. In and around the hangars were a half-dozen Chinese MiG-19s stripped of their cannons and other equipment with stagnant pools of rainwater in their cockpits. The power plants had been destroyed by the Russians, and huge rusting generators sat half off their mountings as if moved by an earthquake. All the streetlights were missing bulbs (an indicator of the true dedication of the looters). Garbage and debris were strewn all over the place.

The other part of the air base complex that demanded my immediate attention was the munitions bunkers, about a half mile from the control tower. I had thought that most of the ammunition on the base would have been looted. However, we found that most of the bunkers were still full of aerial munitions, mainly Russian bombs and French rockets. Many of the rockets were broken open, and propellent was spilled on the ground. All the munitions looked highly unstable. Upon seeing them I gave a low whistle and backed out as quickly as I could. I gave instructions that no one should go into that area until it was made safe by explosive ordnance disposal (EOD) personnel. Later, when they came, the EOD men were impressed with the find. It took them a long time to dispose of it all, often in fairly innovative ways.

There were no people actually living at the airfield complex, which was a help, but there was a small village outside the gate. The village sustained itself by running a "checkpoint" on the main road from Wanwaylen to Baidoa and taking a percentage of relief supplies from relief trucks (or from out-and-out highway robbery). One of the first things we did was tear down their checkpoint and inform them that they were out of business. This caused consternation at first, but our armed presence combined with more and more planes flying in every day made our point, and we had no actual trouble with them.

Baledogle was to be our home for some time. On first glance it looked unrepairable, but on closer inspection it would serve. It was definitely the country's biggest airfield outside of Mogadishu. I felt confident that it would soon be taking a large percentage of the airlift currently stacking up to get into Mogadishu, but that was the air force's concern. We were just securing the place.

During my meeting with Brigadier General Magruder, he'd instructed me to make contact with the local tribal authorities in Wanwaylen and tell them that Ambassador Oakley would like to meet with them. The next day I made my first trip into Wanwaylen, accompanied by the Marine major and a security detachment made up of the LRSU team and a squad from Alpha Company. Wanwaylen was about seventy kilometers to the northwest of Mogadishu and about ten kilometers from Baledogle air base. I noticed that the highway leading to Wanwaylen and Mogadishu was still in pretty good shape. There were no large potholes, which seemed encouraging. When we arrived at Wanwaylen, I got to see the face of Somalia that would become familiar to me over time: a small town crowded with people who weren't doing anything in particular but who all seemed to be moving. The streets were strewn with debris (nonedible), and the whole place had sort of a tumbledown, dog-patch air.

The majority of the battalion, with its promised attachment of a civil affairs section, had not yet closed on Baledogle, so I was without any interpreters or civil affairs types. Beyond that, I had no idea what to expect when I went to Wanwaylen. I didn't know what to look for in terms of leadership, and, given that I had no Somali speaker assigned, I felt like a Martian about to land there and say "Take me to your leader." So we drove into town, stopped in the marketplace, smiled at everyone, and said, "Does anyone speak English?" Of course someone did, a man named Mohammed, who said he'd be delighted to translate for us. Soon we met another man named Idris, who also spoke English and told us that Mohammed could not be trusted. An argument ensued between them, which I broke up with some difficulty. I told them they could both be my interpreters and one could tell me if the other was lying. After some minor alrums and excursions, we met with a group of young men who claimed they were elders but who

I found out later were officials of the Somali National Alliance. We subsequently met an older group of gentlemen who were the real elders. This led to confusion as to who was in charge, which I settled by telling them that they could both make representations to the United Nations Intervention Task Force (UNITAF) forces in the area. I then met with the leaders of the militia unit that seemed to have the real power in Wanwaylen. I told them they were to take down all checkpoints and not interfere with traffic on the road from Afgoi. The next day I met with the elders of the town to set up a meeting with Ambassador Oakley the following morning.

While this was going on, the remainder of the Marines of Lieutenant Colonel O'Leary's Marine battalion landing team arrived to join the rest of their men at the Baledogle airstrip. They would stage there for the push to Baidoa and Bardera the next day. Also with them was a detachment from the French Foreign Legion. They pulled in to our perimeter and conducted maintenance and resupply while they prepared to move on. O'Leary issued his unit operations order later that afternoon. I attended their meeting as the senior army officer present. After the back brief, an officer pulled me aside and made a request. The Marines had a trail of reporters almost as big as their column itself following them from Mogadishu. They wanted to slip out of the Baledogle airstrip as quietly as possible early in the morning in order to lose some of their hangers-on.

This was easier said than done. The reporters clung to the Marines like a remora on a shark. Although I had not personally seen the entrance of the Marine and Legion column into Baledogle airstrip, I was told that the number of reporter vehicles made it look like a Gypsy caravan. I could sympathize with the Marines. The last thing I'd want as a tactical commander heading into the unknown is a forty-car caravansary of four-wheel-drive vehicles complete with hired Somali gunmen following me around. I wasn't sure of the legalities of holding up the reporters, but I figured I'd give it a shot just the same. I instructed Gordy Flowers not to let anyone else out of the gate once the last Marine vehicle had gone through. He grinned happily at me when I told him. I had to admit that the whole thing did take on the aspect of a Halloween prank.

The troops were interested in the Foreign Legion detachment accompanying the Marines. Here were the fabled mercenaries working on their vehicles and preparing to move out, creatures from history inadvertently thrown among us. The actual sight of them was disappointing. It was not that there was anything wrong with them; they were conducting their precombat checks like any professional outfit. Rather, I half expected them to be wearing their kepi blanc (they keep it for ceremonial use only, I was told). But I guess the letdown was the realization that they looked like us. There were a few conversations between our troops and the Legionnaires, but they were busy in their preparations for the next day and we really didn't have anything to trade. (No Legionnaire in his right mind would have traded French rations for MREs.)

Going back to the headquarters, I was approached by an attractive young reporter who asked if it was safe to go to Mogadishu to file her story. Curious, I asked her what she meant. Stepping closer to me, she looked up and, batting her eyes, said in a breathless kind of way, "Are they going to move out tonight or can I go to Mogadishu and be back tomorrow morning?"—all the while making sure I got a good look down her semiopened shirt.

I was momentarily taken aback by the brazenness and stupidity of her act. Here was this late twenties Mata Hari wanna-be, trying to get me to tell her about the plans for an imminent operation, all because of a smile and a peek down her blouse (which I will admit was quite nice). I hadn't been away from home for even a week and had Ward Cleaver written all over me. So I managed a slight smile and told her in a low, conspiratorial whisper that yes, I thought it was safe for her to go to Mogadishu and file her story. Giggling her thanks, she scampered off. It was the only time I actually lied to a reporter during the whole deployment. Sorry, Edward R. Murrow, the devil made me do it.

In spite of my concern over their ability to get out in the

morning without the locust horde of reporters finding out about it, the Marines and the Legion managed to do exactly that. They rolled out of the Baledogle perimeter around 0230, quiet as armored church mice. The reporters didn't learn this for about three hours, and by then the Marines were well on their way to Baidoa. We managed to stall the reporters for an additional hour or so at the gate before finally letting them go to further plague our Semper Fi friends and the Legionnaires. Most were less than gracious as they left. Oh, well, you can't please everyone.

About this time we had our first Elvis sighting. Lieutenant Van Hoesen informed me that he'd seen Elvis on one of the Marine trucks as it was pulling out of the airfield. I asked him how he could be sure, and he told me that it definitely looked like the "king." Soon the battalion was awash with Elvis sightings. (By the time we reached Marka, the TACSAT guys were actually keeping a chart tracking the various sightings.) It was Van Hoesen's way of keeping the tension down, and we all appreciated it.

The Canadians showed up later that day. We'd been told to expect the 1st Canadian Parachute Regiment to fly in to Baledogle in the planning phase and now, sure enough, here they were. They had flown all the way from Canada in slow C-130 transports and had been almost thirty-six hours in transit. They came off the plane as we did, fully kitted out with flak jackets and full fighting loads, carrying enormous rucksacks. Not knowing what to expect, they immediately formed a perimeter around the aircraft with weapons facing out. It looked a little foolish, but then I reflected that we too hadn't known for sure whether the Marines would be there when we took off from Cairo West, so these guys were just being safe. As soon as they realized that we were there and had already secured the airstrip, they collapsed their perimeter and began unloading their aircraft in a businesslike and professional manner. The base element of the Canadian force (the airborne regiment) was about the same size as the 2-87 (three rifle companies and a headquarters company), but they had been augmented with a company of light armor (six-wheeled versions of the MOWAG Piranha known as Grizzlys or Cougars). They also had a robust logistics support element. All in all, they were almost twice the size of the 2-87.

I met Lieutenant Colonel Matthieu of the Canadian air-borne regiment and reported the status of the airfield and its perimeter to him. He graciously left me in charge until the rest of his battalion flowed in the next day. After that, we tem-porarily came under his command (he was then the senior coalition officer on site) until Lieutenant Colonel Sikes and Colonel Ward showed up. After showing Matthieu the loca-tion for his battalion HQ, I left him to supervise the arrival of his battalion and prepared for my next big event of the day, the arrival of Ambassador Robert Oakley. Around 1400 his plane landed and I greeted him and his small entourage. To be truthful, I hadn't known what to expect.

Ambassador Oakley was a revelation to me. My previous exposure to State Department personnel had not always been uplifting. Most of them seemed to be young, immaculately suited, yuppie-preppie types named Kent or Chip or Buffy who had majored in condescension at some Ivy League school. Ambassador Oakley was the genuine article. A career diplo-mat of extraordinary intelligence and personal magnetism, he had been at posts in Africa and southern Asia for more than thirty years. He had been the ambassador to Somalia previously and knew all the players, the local language and customs, and what line to take. His sheer physical presence commanded respect. He was a tall, rangy figure whose craggy, weather-beaten face projected purpose, self-control, and tre-mendous dignity. He was a diplomat who personified the power and rectitude of America. He summarily dismissed any Somali young man with sunglasses who claimed to be an "official" and instead concentrated on working with the el-ders, who were the backbone of Somali society. It was quite a sight to see the tall, dignified Oakley, who towered over most of the elders, speaking to the old Somali men who sat uncom-fortably on their chairs, with their carved, inlaid walking sticks beside them. He impressed upon them that the salvation of their community lay with them, and they had to cooperate. They seemed receptive. (I later observed that most people had a hard time saying "no" to Ambassador Oakley—not just Somalis either.)

We were on the ground in Baledogle for five days before Lieutenant Colonel Sikes and the rest of the battalion started to flow in. During this time, other units had traveled through Baledogle and Wanwaylen, and a Marine helicopter unit arrived to set up operations within our perimeter on the Baledogle airstrip. Its commander, Lt. Col. Mike Boyce, was a friendly, commonsense sort who deferred the defense of the perimeter to us and provided us with a list of his assets on hand in case of tactical emergencies. He also offered us support in terms of rations, and potable water, which was gladly accepted. We exchanged call signs and radio frequencies and confirmed that we all had the same password. It was amazing how relaxed everything was: no contest over who owned the airfield, no interservice rivalry, no problems. We were just a couple of midgrade officers figuring things out in the middle of nowhere like the government pays us to do.

As units such as the Marine helicopters set up shop on the airfield complex, I realized that I'd better start some space management. Although the Baledogle complex was large, most of it was in an unserviceable condition. Usable building space and hardstand was at a premium. I put Kirk Haschak in charge of space management, giving him the charter of placing people according to their operational requirements as opposed to their druthers. This ruffled a few feathers (especially when people who had become comfortable in an aircraft maintenance space were told to move to accommodate the Marine aviation, who could actually use it), but all in all it was accepted without a whole lot of fuss. Kirk did a super job on this; months later, Baledogle was still fundamentally configured the way we originally laid it out.

As the battalion and the 2d Brigade headquarters began flowing in, we learned that the brigade's 3d Battalion, 2-14 Infantry, would definitely not be coming. On top of that, neither would the 2-7 Field Artillery, as we had expected. As bad as this was, it was not as immediately calamitous as the news brought to me by the U.S. Air Force Tactical Airlift Control Element (TALCE) running the airfield. The airfield would have to be closed to C-141s because of the damage they were causing to the poorly maintained runway. Fortunately, by the time this decision was made, most of the battalion and a good portion of the brigade HQ had already landed at Baledogle. As Alpha 1-87 and Bravo Company came off the plane, they were given places on the perimeter, thus giving Gordy Flowers's people and the Canadians smaller pieces of the overall defense of the airstrip. One of the last aircraft to land before the air force shut down the runway to C-141s brought Lieutenant Colonel Sikes. My little independent command was over.

The boss was not in the best of moods, and after hearing his story I could understand why. He would have arrived days earlier except that his aircraft had to divert to Spain due to an inflight emergency, causing a delay of more than twenty-four hours. He also was concerned that soon after we arrived I had allowed soldiers off of the defensive perimeter to divest themselves of their flak jackets; however, after seeing the situation on the airfield and experiencing firsthand the almost crushing heat of the place, he conceded that I'd been right.

Looking around, he could see that quite a bit had been done, and his normal good humor soon came back. He then met with Lieutenant Colonel Matthieu and took command of the airfield from him (anticipating the arrival of Colonel Ward). The remainder of the battalion (with Joe Occhuzzio in the last plane) and elements of the 2d Brigade HQ flew in to Mogadishu the next day. I traveled to the city to link up with them and show them the way to Baledogle, really a recon for me as my first trip past Wanwaylen.

There wasn't much in the fifty miles between Wanwaylen and Afgoi, just scrub and a few hut villages. At Afgoi we crossed the bridge over the Shabele River to Mogadishu. The nearer we got to the city, the more refugee camps we saw, and the crowds alongside the road became larger. As we got close to Mogadishu, we saw that all the houses and buildings we passed were missing roofs, as in Wanwaylen and Afgoi. I wondered if there were any buildings in the country with roofs. There weren't many, and so a roofless building would always be the symbol of the Somalia deployment for me.

Because the U.S. embassy compound was on the way to the airfield, I decided to stop to learn how to locate exactly where to link up with the newly landed units. The compound was in what could best be described as an organized state of pandemonium. The JTF, under Marine lieutenant general Johnston, was establishing its headquarters there, and the 10th Mountain Division HQ was setting up alongside as the army forces component (ARFOR) headquarters. The embassy buildings had to be seen to be believed. They had been completely gutted of everything, including electrical wires stripped from the walls. The whole place was a beehive of satellite antennas, humvees, and tents, with helicopters landing every few minutes. When I learned at 10th Mountain HQ that the 2d Brigade staff had indeed landed, I resolved to go down to the airfield and find them.

I went farther into the town toward the K-4 circle (the scene of heavy fighting during the October 1993 battle). It was peaceful, and the streets were filled with people, dilapidated vehicles, and vendors. Business was definitely back, and everyone—in the short run anyway—seemed to be prepared to let it stay that way. No one was threatening, and although many people begged for food, none looked starved. I was trying to reach the 2d Brigade on the radio and wondering just how I could find them when I ran into their lead element heading out for Baledogle. They were as happy to see me as I was to see them (and as surprised). Turning around on a street that looked like a crowd scene from *Raiders of the Lost Ark* was not easy, but Terry Henry managed to do it quickly without running anyone over.

Major Dave Wood (the brigade S3) and I compared quick notes, then he called the remainder of his march elements, telling them the way. After that, it was smooth sailing out of Mogadishu toward Wanwaylen and Baledogle. The sheer size and crush of Mogadishu had been sobering; I did not envy the Marines their task of keeping order in the city.

After the brigade arrived, the efforts to clean up Baledogle airfield began to pick up steam. We now had good relations with most of the people and tribal groups around Wanwaylen because of the initial meetings with Ambassador Oakley and the subsequent meetings, which I chaired. We soon were traveling to town daily to arrange for labor to help clean up the facilities at Baledogle airfield.

During one of these meetings, we had some excitement when a few shots were fired outside the room where the elders and I were gathered. My stomach leapt at the sound, but silence soon returned. No word from my escort meant that no Americans had been hit. I didn't want to lose face by leaping up and running outside. The elders all started talking at once and I had to command them to silence in a loud voice. They assured me that the firing was not from one of their men and had to be some individual just shooting on his own (at what, I wondered). After admonishing all of them to discipline their men against random fire, I continued the meeting. We never did figure out who fired those shots or at what they were aimed.

The mortar platoon, which was providing my escort, had taken cover and was tactically deployed around the meeting site. The men were still pretty pumped and the platoon leader (Lieutenant Genega) was convinced he'd taken fire. I wasn't so sure and in the absence of any evidence I let the incident drop. It had been a good reaction drill. The funny thing was that Lieutenant Van Hoesen was returning on a convoy from Mogadishu and heard Lieutenant Genega's call reporting the firing. Turning his vehicles around, Van Hoesen came barreling back toward town, intent on adding the rifles of his escort to Lieutenant Genega's platoon. Fortunately they were not needed. This little incident told me a lot about the discipline of our soldiers and the common sense of most of our junior leaders. Observing the mortar platoon as I came out of the meetinghouse, I wouldn't have wanted to be a Somali who walked up to them carrying a weapon just then. On the other hand, they had maintained discipline and hadn't fired a shot for lack of a clear target. The troops were showing that they could handle scary situations without resorting to needless firing. The presence of mind shown by Genega in securing the site and by Van Hoesen in not waiting for orders but immediately moving to the place of contact was encouraging. The incident also showed me that all the major players in Wanwaylen wanted peace with us, at least for the time being.

Meanwhile, the battalion's command sergeant major, Hubert Key, also met with the elders to arrange for people to work at the airfield. After about a week, more than a hundred Somalis came daily to clean up debris and assist in making the place operational. Key was responsible for organizing and assigning the details, and he was the obvious choice for this. His commanding presence, deep bass voice, and unwavering gaze were perfect for dealing with the representatives of each faction. From the start, keeping order among prospective workers was an issue. We could not designate a single local headman to bring us labor, because he would choose only men from his faction, thus fomenting discontent among the have-nots. Command Sergeant Major Key ensured that each group got equal representation in the job availability. It was impressive how he managed this without violence. Faced with challenges to his authority, he would stop work for a couple of days, then call in all the leaders and read them the riot act. Then work would start again, but only on his terms. Baledogle soon began to take on a much neater aspect. It wasn't beautiful, but at least it wasn't the pesthole it had been when we'd first landed.

The workers were paid in Somali currency, which was carried by the field ordering officer. This was one of the first lessons I learned. One of the most useful men in the task force is the field ordering officer, who comes with a suitcase full of money and buys locally whatever the task force needs. This was also one of the oddest aspects of the Somali deployment. With no central government, no banking system, and no national treasury, the Somalis still insisted on doing commerce in their own national currency. Most would not take any other currency, including U.S. dollars. This aspect of U.S.–Somali relations went well. We had brought employment and stability. People seemed genuinely glad to see us.

During the first week at Baledogle, we also made contact with the nongovernmental organizations in Wanwaylen, represented by a woman from Irish Concern named Mary. She ran a feeding center and relief supplies distribution center there. She looked to be having a good degree of success, and most of the children in the town wore the kelly green T-shirts donated by Irish Concern. The Somalis appeared to respect her operation, and she said that she was in little need of assistance. She was grateful for our presence, because thieves were always a problem, but basically her organization was self-sufficient.

I soon learned that although there was privation in Wanwaylen, there were no people in the pitiful state of starvation that we had seen on television prior to deployment. In dealing with the locals, I got the impression that we (the UN forces in general and the Americans in particular) were looked upon as cash cows to be milked for all we were worth. Early on, Somali National Alliance officials tried to charge us rent for the (abandoned) Baledogle air base. Then, each group or tribal representative tried to ensure that only his people got to work in helping to clean up the base. We were, moreover, repeatedly asked for building materials to help rebuild schools and other buildings. These same buildings had been dismantled, and their roofs sold, by the same people now asking for more materials. The Somalis were sharp traders who recognized our unfamiliarity with them. As a result the early meetings between the Wanwaylen elders and SNA officials and the Americans took on a "Green Acres" aspect, with my being besieged by a dozen African versions of Mr. Haney, all of whom had "great deals" for us. I promised only things that it was within my power to give and said I would relay the other requests to "my general." I was glad when the brigade headquarters arrived and took the civil affairs responsibility for Wanwaylen from me.

As we became established, the 1st Canadian Parachute

Regiment and our units conducted a number of operations together around Wanwaylen. The early ones involved helping Irish Concern keep order during food distribution and, in general, acting like the new law in town. Our relations with the SNA gunmen in Wanwaylen were curt but cordial. We told them to remove their armored cars and 85mm guns from their position along the road to Mogadishu, and they did so without protest. One of them (a Panhard armored car with a 90mm gun) needed a tow, so we tied a cargo strap to a five-ton truck and pulled it to the place we had designated for them to park. This done, the gunmen kept a low profile and did not again attempt to regulate traffic on the main road through Wanwaylen.

The local patrols around the Baledogle airstrip were mostly boring, and the troops made no hostile contact. David Hackworth spent the next week tagging around with the troops floating from platoon to platoon. His presence was by now accepted by everyone, mainly because he was the only reporter we'd seen to that point who stuck around for more than a day and who wasn't a geek. Around that time, another reporter also appeared named Sean Naylor, of *Army Times*. Sean was another interesting character. He was a young man who had no previous military experience but had been a reporter for *Army Times* for several years. He had a boyish face and slight build that made him look younger than he was (in his late twenties). He was also diabetic, but this did not prevent him from tagging along on our operations. Sean was to stay with us for more than a month, living as we did and never complaining. He shared our contempt for day-tripper reporters. He was almost enough to restore one's faith in journalists. Almost.

Headquarters for both battalion and brigade were co-located in the large control tower building on the airstrip. The troops along with Command Sergeant Major Key and his work crew of Somalis did a superb job of cleaning these buildings. Sergeant First Class Hardcastle and Frank Kirsop soon had the TOC erected, complete with a briefing area and a chalkboard they had scrounged. Radios were remoted to antennas on the roof and generators were emplaced and sandbagged. The S3 section knew what was happening in the perimeter and where everyone was located. Along with the S2, they also kept track of all patrols. Mike Klein's S2 section updated information about the locals from the patrols we sent out and through intelligence updates from JTF. Command Sergeant Major Key's workers were also a good source of intelligence, but we realized that you had to take what they said with a grain of salt. Nonetheless, we were building up a good picture of what was around us.

The rest of the staff was clicking too. The S1 had already set up the unit mailroom and had processed the battalion's first emergency leave. Their busiest task was keeping accurate figures of how many people were actually on Baledogle airfield. Due to the constant in- and outflow of units, this was not easy. Captain Michael's S4 section occupied more room than the rest of the staff combined and was busier than anyone else with the effort of keeping the task force and its attached units supplied. The change in the place over the first two weeks was remarkable. The bat-infested, gutted ruin had been transformed into a functioning headquarters building. All these efforts were orchestrated by Joe Occhuzzio, the executive officer and chief of staff. The expertise that was in evidence in our soldiers in these first two weeks was one of the side benefits of our previous experience in Hurricane Andrew. The battalion staff sections were all old hands at setting up in devastated areas; we hit the ground running.

Having brigade headquarters right across the courtyard turned out to be an advantage too (although no one really wants to be positioned in his boss's lap during operations). We could leave them to monitor the overall situation and coordinate actions with the JTF while we concentrated on our own little patch of Somalia. I could wander over and talk to Dave Wood several times a day, getting updates and discussing possible future operations. This was invaluable in the fast-paced and constantly changing operational environment we experienced in the first month of the deployment.

We spent the rest of December patrolling around Baledogle and Wanwaylen and gearing up for relief missions, the
first of which was kind of a bust. We were supposed to accompany the Italians to Gialassi as they established operations. The only trouble was that, although the Italians showed
up at the appointed time, no food convoy appeared. Forming
the convoy was taking too long for the taste of our coalition
partners, so they left while the NGOs were still marshaling
the trucks. Here were the Italians at Baledogle, armed to the
teeth (they had some really neat kit, too—robust, little Fiat
four-wheel-drive trucks mounting .50-caliber machine guns
on pedestals, with lots of places to hang their gear over the
sides), with nothing to escort. Lieutenant Colonel Sikes (ever
tactful) inquired politely if it wasn't a good idea that when
this joint American-Italian convoy showed up at Gialassi, we
could bring some food. It took another day or so to sort this
out. Eventually, an MP platoon from division helped the Italians move the food to Gialassi. We had already been tasked
for other missions.

Christmas Day came and we had a service with a tree decorated in tinfoil, old candy wrappers, and any other shiny
refuse we could find. We didn't have any way of getting a special Christmas dinner to the troops, so it was MREs for most
of the guys. The Canadians had flown in some extra chow and
could accommodate about fifty of our men for Christmas dinner. Lieutenant Colonel Sikes sent a group of junior enlisted
men to this unexpected feast. We also managed to trade for
some Canadian field rations, which were much superior to
MREs. This was a reflection of one of the greatest ironies of
the whole Somalia intervention: for the first month, the Canadians (who scarcely have a military worthy of the name in
terms of numbers and capabilities) were ridiculously better
supplied than the Americans. The single battalion-sized element they sent (the 1st Parachute Regiment with a few attachments) had an entire Canadian navy supply vessel with a
helicopter detachment allocated to it. This meant that while
the Americans were rationing drinking water, the Canadians
were flying in fresh food and cold beer. It was an interesting

experience to be the poor relation for a change in a coalition operation. Fortunately for us, members of the 1st Canadian Parachute Regiment were gracious enough to share their largesse with their threadbare neighbors to the south. Theirs was the only Christmas gift the battalion received.

After the service we went right back to work, and the rest of Christmas passed like any other day. Dave Hackworth left that day and Gordy Flowers's company gave him a small farewell party. In truth, I was sorry to see him go. He was always quick with a friendly word or a joke and had been a congenial presence. He got along well with the troops. No doubt many of the public affairs officers in the JTF breathed a sigh of relief though.

Christmas night fell and I lay on the roof of the control tower building and thought back to the many Christmases I'd spent away from home—the DMZ in Korea, at Fort Lewis, in Saudi Arabia, and now here. I thought back to the previous Christmas when we'd brought John home for my parents to see for the first time. I thought about Donna and John and wondered how they were doing. I didn't do this in any maudlin sense. It was more like a year-in-review type of thing, like a TV program. The airfield complex was dark and shadowy in the moonlight and the whole world was quiet and still except for the faint, distant hum of some generators. So I lay on the roof and hit "playback" on past Christmas days while waiting for the next morning to come. It wasn't a bad pastime, and I fell asleep feeling content and rather lucky.

Right after Christmas we got orders that changed the whole complexion of the operation for us. Previously we had known that we would continue operations around Baledogle and that Task Force 2-14 infantry would come in to reinforce us. In time we would expand out to occupy Marka. This changed shortly after we arrived, with 2-14 and 2-7 Field Artillery being officially dropped from the deployment. The plan was then for 2d Brigade to do Marka and Baledogle with just us and the Canadians, but this changed again. The Canadians would not work for 2d Brigade but would instead be attached to JTF for command and control purposes and would be given their own humanitarian relief sector (HRS). The sector was to be determined within the next few days. Not only had the 2d Brigade lost two of its three infantry battalions and its direct support artillery battalion, but now it had to do without the attached Canadian battalion as well. The brigade still had to conduct security operations around Baledogle, protect food sites in Wanwaylen, and ensure the free flow of traffic from Afgoi to Bur Acaba. In addition we were to expand out to conduct security operations in Marka. It became apparent to me that this mission was being grossly under resourced. I listened to Colonel Ward and Lieutenant Colonel Sikes talk about the taskings we had to accomplish from JTF, and I wondered how we'd get all of this done.

Around December 26 we got the order to execute an air assault to secure the airstrip at Belet Uyene in order for the 1st Canadian Parachute Regiment (Para) to establish a base camp for HRS in the area. Although we had known this was coming, it was looked upon as a most unfortunate turn of events. Task Force 2-87 and the 1st Canadian Para had become close in our two weeks since they began operations at Baledogle. The Canadians had been a dependable adjacent unit whose professionalism could always be counted on. More than that, they had been good friends. Their congenial presence would be missed. A last-minute flurry of rations trading took place, then we all got down to the business at hand in preparing for the operation.

The planning for the mission to Belet Uyene was fairly involved. As an air assault problem, it was a real bear. We (the 2-87, with 2d Brigade HQ in overall tactical command) would conduct the actual air assault into Belet Uyene to seize the airstrip. We would then be followed by the balance of the Canadian airborne, landing on the newly secured airstrip in C-130 transports. In the meantime, a ground logistics column of the Canadian forces would drive up from Baledogle to Belet Uyene, leaving the day before the air assault and arriving after it occurred. This was going to be a hard mission to execute. The part about securing the airfield was simple enough; the problem with the Belet Uyene mission was the sheer distance of the air movement. At 250 kilometers one way, it was by far the longest air assault any of us had ever planned. The aircraft available for the mission were UH-60 Black Hawks from the newly arrived 5-158th Aviation Battalion (a unit from Germany), UH-60s from the 10th Mountain's aviation brigade, and U.S. Marine Corps CH-53s. Helicopter gunship support would be flown by AH-1S Cobras from the 10th Mountain's 3-17 cavalry squadron, but their loiter time over the objective area would be limited. There were also fast movers (jets) from the naval task force offshore. Belet Uyene would be a stretch even for the Marine CH-53s, which had "longer legs" than the Black Hawks. Because of the distance, we would have a full two hours between lifts and would refuel after every lift. This would not only increase the time between lifts arriving into the objective area, but the amount of fuel would limit the load of people and equipment that could be carried by many of the aircraft. It was therefore important to carefully plan each aircraft load to get as much combat power onto the aircraft as possible.

Beyond those challenges, Belet Uyene was also a relative unknown. Although the CIA and State Department types would make their usual prelanding coordination visit to the area, we didn't know for sure if they could smooth out our insertion with all of the armed local groups. Hence we planned for a combat air assault. We weren't looking to go in shooting, but we were damned sure going to bring in enough combat power to win any fight we might get into.

Task Force 2-87 infantry's part of this plan was pretty simple. We would insert two companies and the dismounted battalion tactical command post (TAC-CP) onto the airstrip itself and secure the strip and the perimeter surrounding it. Once we had done this, a second lift would bring the brigade TAC-CP and some of the Canadians to expand the perimeter. Lastly, C-130s would begin landing more Canadian troops and supplies. As soon as the Canadians took the perimeter from us, the battalion would move back to Baledogle the next day.

Serious anticipation prevailed throughout the day prior

to the air assault on Belet Uyene. Securing Baledogle had been necessary but boring work. The situation in Wanwaylen didn't need much presence and security. Bringing stability into the lawless hinterlands of Somalia, however, was what this whole mission was supposed to be about. We at last felt as if we were going to do what we came here for.

The next morning we lined up on the airfield next to our helicopters. Because ours was the first lift, we had the unique experience of lining up on the pickup zone with the helicopters already there. Normally we waited in a field someplace and the helos arrived and we uploaded and moved out in a matter of seconds. Here they looked like large, sleepy insects in the morning sun.

I checked with my RTOs, Higgenbotham and Labonte, and both were ready and knew all the call signs and frequencies. I did a last-minute inspection of my own kit and conferred with Lieutenant Colonel Sikes. Joe Occhuzzio would stay behind in charge of the remainder of the battalion and continue preparations for our next mission (which was supposed to take us to the town of Marka, on the coast south of Mogadishu, though the mission execution time was still to be determined). At the appointed time, the helicopters cranked and all the troops uploaded. We lifted off, and the buildings of Baledogle quickly became small in the distance.

I had the good fortune to be next to a door gunner's window, and the breeze that hit me was wonderfully cool. I looked around at the troopers in my aircraft, Hig and Labonte, and soldiers from Alpha Company 2-87. All were alert but at ease. A few were eating, one was reading a paperback book, and others were checking their weapons one last time. This was clearly a good group to be with in adversity, so I felt pretty confident as we sped north. We were seeing some of the most desolate country I had ever flown over. There was literally nothing for what seemed like hundreds of miles. The only sign of man at all were a few stick huts next to some empty kraals. The rest of the time, it was nothing more than scrub bush and bleakness. Eventually the scrub bush thinned

out and stopped altogether and we were flying over desert
(which, for a change, our desert uniforms would actually
blend in with). The bleakness of the ground below us increased, and I wondered how people could live in a place like
this. Eventually the pilots said that we were five minutes out.
Looking out the front windshield over their shoulders, I could
see a large, dirty town looming in the distance. Everyone was
gathering up his equipment and getting ready for the mad
dash out of the aircraft once it landed. The door gunners read-
ied their weapons. I took a last look at the people with me;
their faces were composed but intent, like runners at the starting gate. The ground came up fast, and now the town was to
the east of our landing site. The helicopter flared out and
landed in a cloud of dust. The wheels touched and in a matter
of seconds we hurled equipment off the aircraft and jumped
after it, running about ten meters and throwing ourselves flat,
the normal drill. The helicopters lifted off in a cloud of dust,
which enveloped and choked us. Then they were gone, and
their fading noise was quickly replaced by the sounds of
squad and platoon leaders yelling directions to their troops.
Hig and Labonte had their radio antennas up quickly, and I
was in communication with Lieutenant Colonel Sikes less
than a minute after I landed. From my place on the airfield, I
could see the whole objective area, so I stopped quickly to
take stock of the situation.

Almost immediately I could see that the plan needed modi-
fying, and fast. The all-around defense we had planned for
was not useful. There was no threat coming from the unin-
habited side of the airstrip. As it turned out, there wasn't
any "threat" at all, in the armed and dangerous sense of the
word. There was, however, a big crowd-control problem on
the town side of the airstrip. I contacted Sikes in the command and control (C2) ship and received permission to move
Alpha Company to assist Bravo Company in keeping the large
crowd of curious Somalis away from the airstrip. This was
probably the biggest show to hit Belet Uyene since the Ogaden war of the 1970s or maybe even the Italian invasion of

Ethiopia in 1935. Several thousand people thronged to see the helicopters and the C-130s land. They were all dressed in brightly colored clothes, which looked shocking and slightly incongruous given the scorched brownness of the place.

Within minutes, Colonel Ward and Colonel Matthieu landed and went to talk to the local elders and SNA representatives along with the State Department and CIA types. The intent was to have sort of a Welcome Wagon/get acquainted meeting. The landing and off-loading of the Canadian C-130s proceeded apace throughout the afternoon and early evening. We maintained the perimeter guard in the stupefying heat while the Canadians flowed in. Digging in to the hard-baked earth required no small effort, and we consumed prodigious amounts of water. Fortunately we were able to prevail upon Colonel Matthieu's men for extra bottled water; otherwise, we probably would have had heat casualties. Just as the last helo was lifting off, I was told to return with it and begin planning our next operation, the occupation of Marka, which had been moved up to 31 December. I protested to Lieutenant Colonel Sikes that this would leave him without any second in command on site, but he was adamant. The Marka mission was a go for execution, so we needed to get a jump on planning. He could run the battalion without me for a night. Feeling a bit unsure, I went to collect my equipment. The pace of this deployment was beginning to frighten me a little as I flew back to Baledogle, studying my map of Marka as I did so.

I missed a wild time. The Somalis, celebrating the arrival of the relief forces, had an all-night drunken party and spent a lot of time firing randomly into the air. Sikes had to order the troops into their foxholes around the airfield as "happy bullets" pinged through the perimeter. Fortunately no one was hit, and Task Force 2-87 elements flew back to Baledogle the next day, leaving our comrades in the Canadian airborne at Belet Uyene. We were sorry to lose the 1st Canadian Parachute Regiment. They had been good friends and fine professionals to work beside. No one suspected the tragedy that would befall them at Belet Uyene. Later in the deployment a few soldiers were found to have beaten and tortured a teenage

Somali thief who had broken into their camp; he subsequently died from his beatings. This isolated incident of soldier indiscipline and junior leader failure was blown out of all
proportion in the Canadian media and eventually caused the
disbandment of this fine regiment.

Seven

The Big Picture: Part 2 (December 1992)

After we had secured Baledogle and begun building up the base there, the Marines under Lieutenant Colonel O'Leary went on to the towns of Baidoa and Bardera, where some of the worst starvation in the famine had occurred. On 17 December the French were sent to Oddur to establish their base of operations. The Italians meanwhile had set up their base north of Mogadishu at Gialassi, and on the twenty-ninth the Canadians assumed responsibility for the area around Belet Uyene.

Joint task force headquarters (which went by the title of UNITAF, short for United Nations Intervention Task Force) had placed troops in most of the major population areas to the north and west of Mogadishu. On 18 December the Marines secured Kismayu airport and were soon relieved by the Belgian 1st Parachute Regiment and a task force from the 10th Mountain Division consisting of the Division Artillery headquarters and the 3-14 Infantry, along with various support elements. The combined joint task force was designated JTF Kismayu and was placed under the command of Brigadier General Magruder.

To date, there had been only a few isolated incidents of violence, the most serious of which was on 11 December when a group of technicals (the Somali term for four-wheel-drive trucks mounting heavy machine guns or recoilless rifles) opened fire on U.S. Marine Corps (USMC) helicopters and were destroyed for their pains. For the most part the political factions were willing to stand by and let UNITAF work with the NGOs and orchestrate the distribution of food.

This was the period of the most optimism in Restore Hope. Troops from many countries were protecting food convoys and feeding centers. The NGOs were able to go about their business without any interruption or disturbance from the political factions. This was when news reports showed smiling children waving, along with debilitated and starving people tearfully greeting the Marines and soldiers who escorted the food convoys.

It was hard to credit it then, but several momentous decisions were being made that would have a direct effect on the outcome of the operation. The two most serious were the decision to hand over control of the operation to the UN as soon as possible and the decision not to disarm the warlord groups and political factions, instead allowing them to retain their arms under certain conditions.

The decision to transition to UN control did not have consequences until the actual handoff to UNISOM II (the UN mission after U.S. intervention) in May 1993. However, it flavored the whole operation as temporary and something that was being done on the cheap. It kept forces from being deployed that were needed to secure the environment properly and did not allow the civil affairs units, the NGOs, and the UN sufficient time to build a stable civil structure. Basically, the U.S. government made the decision that once everyone got fed and no one was actually starving, we would hand over the whole deal to the UN. This was like a doctor going home once the cancer patient was sedated but before the tumor was removed.

In this case, the tumor was the presence of more than a dozen armed political factions, and the decision not to disarm them was, to me, the critical mistake of the intervention. In the beginning, the forces of the United States and other nations overwhelmed and intimidated the Somalis. An ultimatum for disarmament of all sides backed up with force would have been a concrete first step toward reestablishing civil order. It is true that some factions would have fought an effort to disarm, and others would have sought to avoid it. A clear and abrupt military defeat of one of the major clans at an early stage in the campaign would have had a tremendous effect on the remainder of the Somali factions. Disarmament would have taken months or perhaps even a year, but in the end it would have firmly established the international intervention forces (U.S.–led transitioning to UN–led) as the ultimate (albeit temporary) authority in Somalia.

As it was, we didn't confiscate their weapons but set out a series of confusing restrictions on the major groups. For example, you may not have a "technical" unless it's parked here in this collection yard, or you cannot be showing any visible weapons. This conveyed to the Somalis that we were afraid of (or at least concerned about) their power. This, combined with our rules of engagement, soon caused a change in attitude of the Somali political factions. Instead of being fearful of the UNITAF forces, they looked for ways to circumvent and work around them.

Meanwhile, the actual establishment of the UNITAF presence in the country continued to go smoothly. The 10th Mountain Division headquarters established itself in the embassy compound beside the 1st Marine Expeditionary Force (1 MEF) headquarters, and the port of Mogadishu began off-loading military equipment and supplies in earnest. Mogadishu airport was going constantly, with dozens of air force transports landing every day and bringing in more Marines and soldiers as well as more equipment.

The only area in the country that had yet to see any UNITAF troops was the lower Shabele valley, south of Afgoi and north of Kismayu. The last large town that had yet to be occupied by UNITAF was Marka, and Task Force 2-87 was given the warning order to conduct an air assault into Marka to occupy the town and establish operations in the lower Shabele valley. The order came in the middle of the Belet Uyene mission, so by 30 December we were back at Baledogle and busy preparing for this new mission. Before we could embark upon it, though, we had to break up a little riot in Wanwaylen.

Eight

The Wanwaylen Riot (31 December 1992)

After returning from Belet Uyene around 1700 on 30 December, the battalion staff and I spent the rest of the day coordinating the operations order for the Marka mission. The next day (New Year's Eve) was extremely hectic, with the battalion simultaneously ferrying troops back from Belet Uyene and preparing for the upcoming operation. The operations order (OPORD) for the Marka mission was given at 1100. Almost immediately, changes were necessitated by newly obtained intelligence. An updated OPORD was given at 1300. Soon after this, while attending the brigade daily meeting, we were interrupted by a member of the SNA from Wanwaylen—one "Colonel Mohammed"—who brought news that the Red Cross food warehouse in Wanwaylen was being looted. The SNA official requested assistance. Because I'd had the most contact with the Wanwaylen villagers, I was told by Lieutenant Colonel Sikes to take the reaction force platoon and elements of Echo Company to investigate the situation and secure the warehouse.

Looking back on it, the Wanwaylen riot, in contrast to events that occurred later, was a modest affair. We didn't have to kill anyone and none of us was hurt badly, so compared to some of the later actions, it was small change. It was, however, our first true taste of the anarchy that surrounded us. That and its sheer duration (almost seven hours) caused it to stay in my mind clearly. I was the senior man on the scene initially and was responsible for the major decisions for the first few hours.

Not all these decisions were correct ones. They were made in good faith, but many were made from an ignorance of the true situation and the nature of the people around me. The warning signs were there, but I had too little experience in country to appreciate them. At the time I felt pleased with myself. I had reacted well under trying circumstances and kept my cool. As I became more experienced in country, though, I came to realize that there were other courses of action that I could have taken.

The force I took with me, one rifle platoon under Lieutenant Christiansen and one antitank platoon under Lieutenant Criswell, was all there was available at the time. All other units were either involved in local security operations or preparing for the next day's mission. In addition to the two platoons, I brought Captain Wilk, the Echo Company commander, to act as my assistant and assume tactical command while I talked with the locals. Also accompanying me was Major Beal, the brigade FSO, who had been given the temporary mission of brigade S5 (civil affairs officer). He was newly arrived in country, and this was to be his first trip to Wanwaylen. I talked to the platoon leaders and Captain Wilk, then gave them a few minutes to brief their subordinate leaders. Because I was completely ignorant of the situation, my briefing was nothing more than a quick review of the rules of engagement (ROE) and an admonition for minimum use of force. We left the airfield at about 1340 and reached Wanwaylen in about fifteen minutes. The column threaded its way through the streets of Wanwaylen without difficulty and turned at the intersection in the main market area that led to the warehouse.

When we turned the corner, we came upon a scene of considerable mayhem. There were several hundred people gathered in a milling mass around the food warehouse. Food bags were being dragged from the door and ripped open by looters. People were fighting one another for the rice, whacking one another with sticks, pots and pans, and whatever else they had

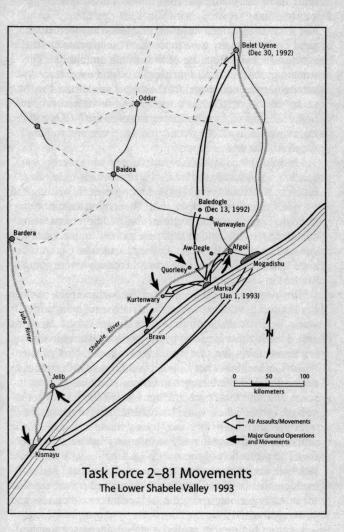

Task Force 2–81 Movements
The Lower Shabele Valley 1993

brought to carry rice in. Mohammed started gibbering urgently, "You must stop them. You must stop them. Please!" I told Lieutenant Christiansen to dismount his people, then I went forward to get a better look. At that moment several shots were heard from the crowd, which undulated wildly. I went to ground, as did all the people behind me, but soon got up again. I was concerned that someone might start shooting at movements or suspicious windows or in the general direction of the firing. I needn't have worried; the NCOs had the troops well in hand. All were deployed, prone and waiting for the word. The word was with me.

I looked at the looters. My instructions were pretty clear: I was to go and secure the food site. I personally didn't have a problem with this. I would have done so even if the thing had been left entirely at my discretion. The looting looked wrong; it did not conform to the norms of civilized behavior I was accustomed to. This kind of situation was new to me, but I was confident we could handle it. I called Lieutenant Christiansen and Captain Wilk to meet me and told them we were going to secure the warehouse.

This was the crucial decision of the day, and for a number of reasons I have come to view it in retrospect as incorrect. It was a decision made in good faith (as most bad decisions are). I could excuse myself by saying that I was only following instructions, but that would be a cop-out. Neither Lieutenant Colonel Sikes nor Colonel Ward was so inflexible as to demand mindless adherence to orders. Had I called from the scene and said that it was my opinion we should not get involved, I'm sure they would have trusted my judgment. Faced with the anarchy before me, trying to stop it seemed the proper thing to do. After all, wasn't that what we'd been sent for? The protection of these sorts of supplies was the whole rationale for the deployment. I was confident that I had sufficient combat power to handle any armed resistance and that the infantry platoon with me could secure the warehouse and eject any looters.

Ejecting the looters proved a straightforward enough affair. I instructed Christiansen to have his platoon fix bayonets and move on line to the warehouse to push the rioters out of the area. I instructed Captain Wilk to overwatch us with his M60 machine guns mounted on humvees and to react to any fire we might receive. Both elements were deployed quickly, and I gave the word to Christiansen to advance and clear out the warehouse. With bayonets fixed, the troops advanced at a fast walk, which broke into a jog. As they approached the warehouse they began to shout at the top of their lungs. The sight of this line of shouting soldiers closing with fixed bayonets was enough to cause most of the looters to bolt. Only a few stayed to try to get more food. These were ejected in short order. We managed to clear the warehouse with only one soldier slightly cut (on a piece of corrugated iron) and no major wounds to any Somalis, although a few required blows with rifle butts before they would stop resisting. The infantry platoon formed a tight perimeter around the warehouse, and the TOW humvees with their machine guns were brought up. The crowd did not disperse but hung on the periphery watching us. They made no threatening gestures. At any rate, we'd secured the warehouse.

Unfortunately, I did not fully appreciate the real problem of securing the warehouse—namely, now that I've got it, what will I do with it? We couldn't hold onto it for long. The battalion was conducting a major air assault operation into the town of Marka, on the coast, in a little more than twelve hours. Nor did the elements being left behind under brigade control have sufficient forces to secure the warehouse. When we left for Marka, there would be only one rifle company remaining to guard the whole Baledogle perimeter, of several miles. Our presence held the crowd at bay for the moment, but as soon as we left, anarchy would break out again.

I looked at the crowd. For the first time since I'd come to Somalia, I saw people who looked hungry—not on death's door, but definitely the worse for wear. I asked the SNA official where the people had come from and why I hadn't seen them before. His answers were vague and noncommittal. Another Somali man came up and said that the International

Committee of the Red Cross (ICRC) official (a Somali national) who was running the feeding center was keeping the food and giving it only to his own people and selling the rest. The riot apparently had started when villagers saw a truck belonging to the ICRC official come up and begin to upload food. The shots were fired by the ICRC guard, who was overwhelmed. The crowd continued to grow but kept a respectful distance.

Basically here is the situation I faced. My considerations for any decision were based upon the following factors:

- The battalion was conducting an air assault to secure the port of Marka the next morning. This operation could not be postponed or canceled.
- The forces left at Baledogle were insufficient to maintain a permanent guard on the warehouse and effectively secure the airfield too.
- No reinforcement was in the offing. The Marines were stretched too thin. The 3-14 Infantry had been sent to Kismayu. There were no other forces available in the short term.
- Apparently an inequitable distribution of relief supplies had caused the riot.
- If I pulled out with the food still in the warehouse, the rioting would resume.

The crowd, although still growing, was not challenging us in any way at this time. It appeared as if the presence of armed troops had cowed them for the moment. I reasoned that we couldn't just leave and let the riot recommence. This would have been an admission of impotence. And because the food was the cause of the riot, I had to remove the food from the warehouse.

I made the decision to hand out the food to the people in the crowd in a controlled manner, using my troops to keep order. I reasoned that if we gave out the food, the people would disperse and go back to their homes, and any disturbances that occurred would at least be of a minor, interpersonal nature. There were only a few hundred bags of rice. I didn't think distributing it would take more than a few hours. Afterward, with the people fed and the riot dispersed, we could return to the Baledogle airstrip and complete the preparations for tomorrow's mission.

Unfortunately, I did not understand one of the basic economic realities of Somalia at the time: relief supplies were *money*. When I began handing out supplies, it was like handing out free money. Although there were hungry people present, what caused the riot was not the desperation of the hungry but the avarice of the greedy. Most of them had not been stealing the rice to eat but to sell. In announcing that we were going to hand out the rice, I had in effect unwittingly provided the catalyst for violence in what I thought to be a situation-defusing good deed.

Of course things got worse. The realization that we were going to hand out the food made the crowd extremely agitated. We were soon being pressed back to the point that I was becoming concerned for the troops' safety. I radioed to battalion for a company of reinforcements. With order restored, hopefully we could finish handing out the food and leave. The reinforcements took time to get to Wanwaylen. Fortunately, the battalion scout platoon, which was returning from a convoy escort mission to Mogadishu, heard my request for reinforcements and diverted to Wanwaylen. I gladly fed the scouts into the perimeter. The crowd continued to grow and become more unruly. At this time it had enlarged to about a thousand people. I requested that further assistance be expedited.

The handout of food proceeded slowly. Many people were pushing and trampling one another to be first. The troops had to use their rifle butts to keep them back. We fired shots in the air to momentarily cow the crowd, but this worked only for a short time. We also tried to use our vehicles as barriers to keep the Somalis from trampling us. The noise of the crowd grew in volume, and it became difficult to communicate orders verbally. Several Somalis tried to break into the warehouse and had to be removed. The crowd continued to press in, egged on by more aggressive individuals. Even with the reinforcement of the scout platoon, the soldiers were being pushed back and threatened by the crowd, which was becoming increasingly more violent. At one point I was convinced that unless something was done to force back the crowd, our soldiers were in imminent danger of being trampled. Withdrawal was not an option; the warehouse was completely surrounded by the mob. The threat to the troops was such that I resolved to shoot one of the agitators in the hopes of dispersing the crowd. It was my estimation then, and is still my judgment today, that the troops were in danger of being overrun, and only reinforcements or an extreme measure such as lethal violence would prevent us from having our people killed or injured. I picked out a man in a green knit cap who was constantly haranguing the crowd. I would shoot the man personally, the act being mine alone. I passed the word to the officers and NCOs as to what I was about to do.

Fortunately, before I had to carry this out, the reinforcements under Lieutenant Colonel Sikes arrived in a fury of pushing, butt stroking, and firing into the air. With these extra men we managed to reestablish the perimeter. Also with Lieutenant Colonel Sikes was the PSYOPS team with a loudspeaker truck. The reinforcements and the loudspeaker again temporarily restored the situation. Then Colonel Ward flew by in a helicopter, dusting off everyone with rotor wash, but couldn't find anywhere to land. The helicopter temporarily cowed the Somalis and gave us a few minutes' more respite. However, the handout of food was still going too slowly. In addition, groups of thugs were robbing the people of their rice sacks almost as soon as they left the perimeter. We would not be out before dark, so Lieutenant Colonel Sikes directed me to get the battalion mortar platoon into position to fire illumination if necessary. Lieutenant Genega soon had his people in position and had illumination registered. It was getting harder to keep control of the situation, and Sikes said to prepare to pull out. Sergeant Anderson (Sikes's driver) accidently ran over my foot with his humvee as we were organizing to move out. My upbraiding him for this, combined with his air of injured innocence, provided the soldiers with the only moment of comic relief they'd had all day.

Finally at 2045 we piled the remaining sacks of rice in the road outside of the warehouse and withdrew under mortar illumination. Units confirmed accountability of personnel and equipment and mounted the trucks. I brought up the rear in my humvee. The last thing I saw as I turned the corner was a large crowd of Somalis fighting over the remaining bags of rice in the light of the mortar illumination.

As we rode back to Baledogle airfield, I breathed a big sigh of relief that we were out of there with no fatalities. I was also thinking about what I had just experienced and what the lessons were. Some of the main ones were as follows:

• The most basic mistake I made was to become involved in the first place. Knowing what I know now about crowds of rioting Somalis, I can say that the forces at hand were completely inadequate for the task. Even had they been adequate (one or two companies), the next day's mission to Marka precluded their use. I completely underestimated the time it would take to resolve this situation.
• My inexperience in crowd control led me to believe that the Somalis would remain nonviolent. I was at the time unfamiliar with the incredible speed at which a relatively peaceful crowd can become a rock-throwing mob.
• Handing out the food as a crisis-defusing mechanism failed disastrously. In retrospect, I could have informed representatives of each tribal group that I would hand out a portion of the food to them for distribution. This would have put the onus of protecting their "share" of the food back on the Somalis. This might not have worked for several reasons. First, many of the people involved in the riot were refugees with no local tribal affiliation. Second, the crowd was looting the food store because of a basic lack of faith in the distribution supervised by

their authority figures. Third, I didn't know if all the players were on hand; I could have alienated a large group of the population by unwittingly not including them. Having said all this, such an action could not possibly have resulted in any bigger mess than the one we ended up with.

As I look back on what I was thinking when I first saw the riot, I realize that my basic error was in looking at it from a normal American frame of reference. Taken at face value, what I saw was an appalling thing: people stealing food meant for the starving. It looked chaotic and lawless and, yes, wrong. We had been sent there to stop this sort of thing. I thought we could, and I didn't think more deeply about it than that. In retrospect, what I should have asked myself was, is this worth getting any of my soldiers hurt? Is it worth killing any Somalis to accomplish it? What are the consequences of doing nothing?

In this case, the consequences of doing nothing would have been minimal. The warehouse would have been looted, and any violence would have been done by Somalis against Somalis. The majesty of the UN forces and the U.S. Army could have withstood this inactivity, and we could have used this riot as a warning that future shipments of food to this warehouse must have a substantial guard on them. As time went by during our deployment, we realized that despite our best efforts, a certain amount of relief supplies would be looted, and it was better to send more relief supplies than guard each food warehouse.

The "don't just stand there, do something" impulse is a formidable one. Soldiers are trained to act, to exercise initiative. The danger is acting out of ignorance. Had I been forced to shoot the Somali in the green hat in order to disperse the crowd, the resulting ill will could have soured relations in the area for months to come.

The incident also provided us some tactical lessons in riot control that stood the battalion in good stead for the remainder of the deployment: •

• Size of the force employed. For use of nonlethal force, the Wanwaylen riot made me leery of employing anything less than a company-sized element of at least a hundred men. A good rule of thumb is that the more troops you can devote to a riot early, the better your chances of peacefully dispersing it before it can spread.

• Units must be properly equipped for riot control. We were woefully short of critical riot control equipment, particularly concertina wire and CS gas. These two items would have made a tremendous difference in the Wanwaylen riot. The wire was not available due to shortages at the time. The CS gas was not available because CS release authority was held at UNITAF level by Lieutenant General Johnston, the 1 MEF commander. This effectively precluded its timely issue and use. I still do not fully understand why this nonlethal munition was so tightly controlled. The CS gas and pepper spray release authority was eventually delegated down to battalion task force level (where it should have been all along) when rioting developed in Mogadishu. Riots develop quickly, and there is no time for a local commander to communicate through three levels of headquarters more than two hundred miles apart to ask, "Mother, may I?" to use CS. Deprived of these tools, we did riot control the "old-fashioned way," with rifle butts and bayonets, at greater risk to our troops.

• Firing in the air can scare a crowd, but it works only for a short time. The Wanwaylen riot showed us that the nonlethal discharge of firearms can become counterproductive quickly, because it can make the crowd think we are only bluffing and will not shoot them.

• Troop leaders need bullhorns to shout orders to their subordinates. Shouted commands could not be heard over the screaming of the crowd, and the noise was such that half the time you couldn't even hear a radio speaker or handset. If riot control is anticipated in a deployment, each platoon leader and company commander should be equipped with a bullhorn to communicate orders.

• Vehicles can be effective as barriers, but troops must ensure that all pilferable materials have been removed from them.

• PSYOPS personnel can be effective in controlling and manipulating a crowd with their loudspeakers. This is especially true if they have a person fluent in the native language as opposed to canned tapes. However, the Wanwaylen riot also showed us that once a crowd has reached a certain level of hysteria, loudspeakers can have an agitating effect.

• Trained civil affairs personnel are indispensable in this type of operation. In Somalia, the 2d Brigade fire support elements (FSE) were initially used for civil affairs due to the lack of indirect fire assets available and the restrictions on the employment of what limited assets we had. (In four months, all we fired from our mortars was illumination.) However, in a more robust low-intensity conflict (LIC) environment, the fire support officer will have to do his own job of planning, coordinating, and directing indirect fires. Furthermore, no one in the infantry battalions or in the 2d Brigade FSE was trained in civil affairs operations. We worked hard and learned quickly, but our early efforts were clumsy. Units that are involved in humanitarian or LIC operations should have trained civil affairs teams assigned to them. The lack of civil affairs personnel in Somalia led us to more than one "by guess or by God" solution.

The riot was a sobering and eye-opening experience for us all. The lessons we learned, particularly the one about the importance of developing a maximum force presence early in a crisis, stood us in good stead in future situations that were decidedly more dangerous than the one in Wanwaylen. The riot also showed us again that little was as it seemed in this unhappy country. In a way, the riot inadvertently provided a confidence-building exercise for many of the battalion's soldiers in that it showed them that they could be involved in an ugly situation and not have to resort to lethal violence (al-

though we came close). The troops came out of the riot with
more confidence in the ROE than they'd previously had.

I barely spoke a word on the way back to the airfield. I
looked at my watch; it was about 2200. The first lift of the air
assault on Marka was due to take off around 0630 and I was
utterly drained. I limped into the TOC (my foot still hurt) and
found my night shift on duty monitoring the situation and
taking status reports. The off shift was finishing packing up
for the next day's move. Sergeant First Class Hardcastle
looked up at me and grinned. "Sir, you look like shit," he said
cheerfully (Hardcastle's way of expressing affection). Frank
Kirsop briefed me on the air assault operation and preparations for it, assuring me that he and Major Occhuzzio had it
covered and not to worry. He then handed me some mail and
said, "Sir, you look like hell," or words to that effect, and suggested that I get some sleep. I went over to brigade to see if I
could learn anything more from Dave Wood about Marka,
but there wasn't anything new he could tell me. I saw Lieutenant Colonel Sikes talking to Colonel Ward. I went over and
asked Sikes if he had anything else. (Why I did this is beyond
me; force of habit I suppose. I'd have shit if he'd said "yes.")
Fortunately for me, he smiled and said, "No, Marty. Go to
sleep, big day tomorrow." I went back to the TOC, sat down,
and looked at my mail—a letter and a package from my
friend Jim Good. The package held a *Playboy* magazine,
which I looked at for a few minutes, the winsome, large-
chested centerfold adding a final surreal touch to a strange
day. Then I went upstairs to my place on the roof and stripped
off my uniform. I didn't realize until then that it had been
completely soaked with sweat and was just starting to dry off.
I was so tired I shook for a few minutes. I looked at my watch;
almost midnight. Five hours of sleep until I had to get up for
the air assault.

Part Three
The Shabele Valley

Marka is a wonderful old Arab town on the coast about 100 KM south of Mogadishu. Five KM from Marka (an easy hitch) you can stay right on the beach in huts at Sinubusi beach where it's clean, quiet and there are few people. A hut for two costs SSh 400 with a basic bathroom. The sea is calm, clear and warm with no sharks due to a sand bank further out. There is a restaurant that has good grilled fish.

—*The Lonely Planet Guide to Africa*

Nine

Marka (1 January–20 February 1993)

The occupation of Marka went off according to plan. Once again, UNITAF had sent State Department and CIA emissaries to the town prior to the military forces showing up, so surprise was not a factor. Our original plan had been to cordon off the whole town and disarm everyone. However, negotiations with the SNA officials and the Ali Tihad Islamic fundamentalists resulted in their pledging to withdraw to their compounds and not interfere with our occupation of the town. Because of this, the plan was changed to a simple air movement of the infantry companies and the battalion TAC-CP, with the battalion support trains element driving to Marka in convoy under the command of Joe Occhuzzio. We could take only two companies with us, because one (Bravo 2-87) was to remain behind and provide security for Baledogle airfield.

Lieutenant Colonel Sikes went in on the first lift with Gordy Flowers's company, and they landed in the city's port. There were some tense moments as Ali Tihad gunmen, who had been controlling the port, were startled by the abruptness of our force's arrival. There was a short, tense confrontation, with both sides handling their weapons as if they expected to use them. However, after a quick meeting between local leaders and Lieutenant Colonel Sikes, the gunmen agreed to withdraw to their compound (as had been previously negotiated by the CIA and State Department advanced team) and leave us in possession of the port. While this was going on, I waited with the last lift at Baledogle, getting reports from brigade headquarters.

After rehearsing our organization for getting onto the aircraft and checking with Geoff Hammil to ensure that everyone was ready, there was nothing to do but wait. It was a pleasant morning—sunny, cool, and breezy and most refreshing after the previous day's exertion. I sat in the sun and let the breeze wash over me. Five hours of sleep, a quick wash with a canteen of water, and a clean uniform did wonders for me. I sat on the grass by the airfield with the rest of my aircraft load and thought about the previous day's riot, which seemed unreal somehow. First Lieutenant Van Hoesen came by just before the ground convoy pulled out and asked if I'd seen Elvis just then. "Where?" I inquired. "He was in one of the UH-60s as a door gunner, sir. You couldn't miss him." Elvis apparently got around.

After an hour or so, the UH-60s showed up and we uploaded without difficulty. Elvis wasn't the door gunner on my bird, so I missed him again. The flight to Marka was different from the one to Belet Uyene. The terrain below that flight had been parched scrub and desert. Going toward Marka, the farther we traveled into the lower Shabele valley, the more lush and verdant the ground became. There were villages thronging with people and numerous cultivated fields. The Shabele River itself was wide and brown and meandered the length of the valley as far as the eye could see. There were plenty of irrigation canals. It was hard to reconcile this part of the country with the starvation I had seen on TV.

Unlike the mud and brick huts of Wanwaylen, Marka's buildings were mostly tan and white masonry. The town had a strong Italian flavor; it had been something of a resort during the days of Italian colonization. It was nestled at the base of a steep hill on the water. Although a few tracks came directly over the hill, to most vehicles the slope was not trafficable, and the only road into the town ran along the coast from Shalamboot, to the south. There was a road to the north that ran toward Mogadishu, but it petered out after twenty kilometers. The road over the coastal ridgeline from the small town of

Shalamboot was the only way commercial traffic could get into town.

Outside Marka where the Shalamboot road came over the hill was a small clump of buildings centered around a derelict police barracks. There was a large, flat field by this unused compound that the second helicopter lift used for a landing zone. Once we landed, I linked up with Lieutenant Colonel Sikes and we began to establish the battalion command post in the only building that still had a roof. We wanted to establish our base camp outside the actual environs of Marka and separate from all other habitation so we could set up a defensive perimeter with good fields of fire. The location chosen was adjacent to the abandoned barracks, about five kilometers outside of town. From here the battalion command post established communications with 2d Brigade and the convoys en route to Marka. While we set up the CP, Sikes and the companies conducted a sweep of Marka proper.

The troops moved slowly through the town, taking their time, two companies abreast with two platoons each on line and a third in reserve. There was no resistance. Everywhere were painted signs welcoming the "saviors of Somalia." It looked as if the local warlord leaders had once again figured that if you can't beat 'em, join 'em, at least temporarily. There were certainly a lot of people in Marka, and the troops' sweep of the town was carried out under the curious but not unfriendly gaze of thousands of Somalis. The operation was a pain for the TOC to track, however, because only a few members of the battalion had satellite photograph maps of the town. As a result we spent a lot of time in the TOC, translating latitude and longitude coordinates of the units into actual map locations. (For example, "Alpha Company, you're two hundred meters short of Phase Line Cougar. You should see a large runoff ditch paralleling the road by the mosque near the top of the hill.") It wasn't the best way to command and control, but we had to make do. The sweep ended with most of the troops outside the town. They were then pulled back to our base camp, leaving one platoon in the port of Marka to establish security and guard the relief supplies on the beach.

The port was a small affair, barely worthy of being called one. There were a few office buildings and a small, broken-down warehouse, all of which were missing the roof. The port had no serviceable pier that ships could tie up to; instead, they had to off-load offshore and lighter their goods onto the beach, where they would be stacked by manual labor, as in the nineteenth century. When we took over the port, there were thousands of bags of rice and lentils along with hundreds of five-gallon drums of cooking oil waiting for transportation to feeding centers. Although you couldn't tell it from our peaceful reception, Marka was notorious for robbers and pirates. The hulk of a large relief ship, which had recently been boarded, grounded, and looted, still sat forlornly off the beach.

The Ali Tihad had actually done a good job of protecting the relief supplies from wholesale looting. Nobody in Somalia while I was there could stop pilferage completely. They had neatly stacked all the sacks of rice and lentils and drums of cooking oil on the beach and even covered a few with tarpaulins. In fact, supplies were stacked up all over the place, because no relief convoys had left the port for some months. One of our highest priorities was to get these convoys moving again.

We spent the next few days running patrols in Marka to establish our presence there. The sight of our disciplined soldiers moving through the town had a calming effect on everyone. Shops opened up again, and Marka returned to, if not quite normalcy, a sense of equilibrium. Lieutenant Colonel Sikes went about meeting some of the key players in the town. He conspicuously avoided the local SNA officials, instead meeting with only the elders of the town. This was a deliberate move based upon what he had been told by the civil affairs personnel and Ambassador Oakley. The elders of each town and tribe were the traditional authorities and arbiters of disputes in the country. Their authority had been subtly undermined during the twenty-one-year rule of Siad Barre and subsequently eclipsed by the political factions with the advent of civil war. In meeting with the elders and helping to establish a town council, he pointedly wanted to show the people of Marka that the young men with sunglasses and guns no longer ruled. He stressed to everyone that we would be the only people in town who would carry weapons. Sikes made it clear that all technicals and crew-served weapons must be turned in, that no small arms would be permitted to be carried on the streets of Marka, and that anyone seen carrying a gun would have it confiscated by U.S. soldiers. The SNA members balked at this of course, but after a few searches of their houses and the confiscation of their technicals and crew-served weapons, they got the message. The Ali Tihad agreed to consolidate their arms in their compound, centered around a large house on the outskirts of town. As was to be typical of our entire stay in Marka, the dreaded Ali Tihad Islamic fundamentalists turned out to be the most organized and cooperative of all the different political groups and factions.

We also met with members of the NGOs, finding that the two people of the Red Cross in the town were an odd pair. At first they did not want anything to do with us, feeling that such contact would compromise the integrity of the International Red Cross. On the other hand, they could not get any of their food convoys out because of bandits in the valley and the extortionate prices charged by truck drivers. They wanted us to get rid of the bandits and protect the convoys but not actually be seen with them. We explained the impracticality of this, telling them that their convoys would be escorted whether they liked it or not. On hearing this, they swung 180 degrees and asked if we could also secure their funds, because they were afraid of thieves coming to steal from them. I got the feeling that they were not impressed with the whole disaster relief scene in Somalia and wished that the ICRC had given them something more palatable and romantic. Although they had lived in Marka for some months, they had few friends among the Somalis that I could see. Their mannerisms were diffident and effeminate, and truck drivers and workers made great fun of them.

Better off (at least more organized) was the Médecins Sans

Frontières group that ran a small hospital in Marka. Its staff didn't require much direct help from us but welcomed the stability that we brought. Their doctors and nurses were volunteers and were by and large admirable people who treated the tragedy around them one person at a time. They were easy to work with, not at all prone to hysteria, and reasonable in their demands.

The other aid worker in Marka was a middle-aged Italian woman named Anna Togalise but known to one and all as Sister Anna, although I don't believe she was ever a nun. Anna had lived in Marka for decades and was one of the forces who held the community together during the worst of the civil war. She established the hospital where the Médecins Sans Frontières worked and had tremendous influence with all of the elders in the town of Marka. She was soft-spoken and gracious. I had expected to meet someone like Anna Magnani in *The Rose Tattoo*—all hand gestures and talking a mile a minute. Instead I met a quiet, pleasant woman of middle height who had an air of purpose and intelligence and who clearly did not frighten easily. Fortunately for us, she was both welcoming and supportive of our efforts.

After a few days we moved into the barracks proper and made them our permanent base camp. Like 90 percent of the buildings we saw in Somalia, the barracks had no roof or electrical fixtures. By placing our encampment there, we controlled the road into Marka but were not actually in the immediate vicinity (small-arms range) of Marka itself.

In the middle of these hectic first few weeks in Somalia, President Bush decided to visit the troops. I liked Bush as a president, but it seemed to me that his visit was inopportune. UNITAF was trying to get set up in this lawless, devastated place right at the outset of the mission and, boom, here he was. Thankfully, he went to Mogadishu first. This gave us just enough time to complete the Marka occupation before he went to Baledogle. As Maxwell Smart would have said, "He missed us by *that* much." The men who stayed behind at Baledogle said it was something to behold. The Secret Service placed requirements on them, such as no troops with weapons within five hundred meters of the president and no armed Somalis within one kilometer. When told that the perimeter did not go out that far, they were visibly shaken. Furthermore, they were told that there was no way the soldiers and Marines would ground their weapons. The farthest we'd go was no magazines in the rifles. Of course President Bush didn't dictate any of this. It was just some overzealous jerk from the Secret Service protection detail. The guy must have thought he was in downtown Atlanta. The president and Mrs. Bush were wonderful and were well received. In spite of the heat, they stood in the crowd for hours, and anyone who wanted his picture taken with the "Pres" got an opportunity. Then Bush was off to see the Marines at Baidoa. Despite the visit going well, I still have mixed feelings about it. In a way it was good that he came; he was, after all, the one who ordered us to Somalia. On the other hand, the president does bring a lot of support staff and equipment wherever he goes. There's no such thing as his just popping in, so his visit was a distraction we could have done without. Beyond that, I still think Somalia was the worst mistake of his presidency. I'd vote for him again, though.

To control Marka, Lieutenant Colonel Sikes decided that we needed to keep a permanent presence in the port and patrol around the clock elsewhere in town. We also needed to control access to the town and check all traffic entering and exiting. To this last end we occupied a house about halfway to Marka from the police barracks and established a platoon-sized strongpoint there. This was to be our checkpoint and vehicle inspection station for traffic coming to Marka. The port of Marka had a platoon. Our attached sapper platoon strung concertina wire fences around the supplies on the beach. With this approach, the overall mission for security operations in Marka could be performed by a single rifle company securing the port, establishing the checkpoint outside town, and providing a third platoon as an immediate reaction force. One rifle company was already detached to brigade control at Baledogle, along with Echo Company to conduct convoy security operations. Thus, when the Marka security missions were factored in, the 2-87 had one remaining rifle company along with the scout and heavy mortar platoons with which to patrol the town of Marka, conduct counterbandit operations in the Shabele valley, and ensure relief supply convoy security. It was a tall order any way I looked at it.

While we were setting up shop in an abandoned house, we were accosted by several individuals. Each claimed to be the owner of the house and all wanted monthly rent, one guy to the tune of $20,000 a month. Obviously they had word that the Americans would believe anything and pay exorbitant prices. These gentlemen were told politely by Mike Klein that the army appreciated their public-spirited gesture of offering us the building to work from, and we would see that their names would be mentioned in dispatches. This didn't work nearly as well as cash, but once they realized it was all they were going to get, each cleared out quickly.

We were assisted in this by our new interpreter, Ahmed Omer. He was an American citizen of Somali extraction who was born in Somalia and still spoke the language fluently. He had been hired by the Department of Defense (DOD) at the outset of the operation because of the absolute dearth of Somali speakers in the army. He'd left his job in New York and come to the land of his birth to help out. He was saddened by what had happened to Somalia and was at a loss to explain it. He was an idealist and an incredibly brave man, always at Lieutenant Colonel Sikes's side even in the thick of the fighting. He was initially unarmed; indeed, we were not supposed to arm him. However, after a while it became clear that for his own personal protection he needed a sidearm. We gave him a captured pistol and allowed him to practice with it. He stayed with the battalion for the whole period, then volunteered to stay with our replacements. He was an invaluable addition to the battalion, because his advice was invariably correct.

After a few days in Marka, we received orders from division that we would be getting a large food convoy escorted by Italians. As soon as we took over security from the Italians, we would escort the convoy to feeding centers in our humanitarian relief sector. We expected the Italians around noon.

The next day Sikes and I were a little skeptical about the time line (our previous experience with the Italians not exactly boosting our confidence), but the division operations officer swore up and down they'd be there on time. The only problem was one of protocol. The convoy escort would be commanded by an Italian colonel. We had to have a field grade officer there to meet him. This sensibly fell to me, being the junior major. Joe Occhuzzio was busy supervising the camp setup. I mentioned to Sikes that because the Italians were sending a full colonel, it might be politic for at least a lieutenant colonel to greet them, but he cut me off by saying, "You don't expect *me* to wait for the bastards, do you, Marty?" The TOC was already set up and operations for the next day were already sorted out. Mike Klein and Hardcastle could handle emergencies until I got back from over the hill. I called division and coordinated the linkup point to be the turnoff to Marka in the village of Shalamboot.

We did another sweep of the town the next day using the remaining rifle company, making a point to have patrols walk down every street. No shots were fired, but we did have to disarm several gunmen to prove that we were serious about the no visible weapons rule. I monitored the operation from the TOC, keeping track of movements and doing command and control work, as on the previous day. I wasn't really needed, but I didn't have much to do until going to meet the Italians. Supposedly they had left Mogadishu on time and were on schedule. At 1130 I went over the hill in TAC-2 with Terry Henry and a security team. There was no sign of the Italians, but I reasoned that we were early, so we set up security and waited. And waited. And waited.

The Italians finally showed up about six hours late. Just as it was turning dusk, the convoy drove into view and one of those nice Italian trucks that we'd admired previously in Baledogle came up to us. A short exchange with the officer in charge (OIC) convinced me that he had no useful information to impart (such as how many trucks were in the convoy and where they were). I did manage to gather that there had been numerous "breakdowns" en route and many trucks had been left along the road. Most of them promptly came back to life and drove off to sell the relief supplies as soon as the Italians were out of sight. The Italians were clearly eager to leave because it was getting dark. They did not want to be near Marka, where threats had been made against Italians, who were not popular with most of the people because of their colonial past. When I told their commander that we assumed responsibility for the convoy, he disappeared like a scalded dog, taking his people with him. Sighing, I told my people to police up every relief truck they could find and get them to the assembly area we'd established on the other side of town. We would have to wait there until morning to get the convoy to Quorleey.

Getting some of the trucks over the hill was another adventure, because most of them were overloaded and asthmatic. Several broke down and had to be towed or pushed over the crest. Added to this was the challenge of making sure that none got "lost" because the drivers could sense a new administration in their security and wanted to take off while they thought they still could. Several had to be pointedly told to get back in the line of trucks waiting to climb the hill. We finally had them all turned around and lined up on the road facing back up the hill, waiting for morning. We placed roving guards around the trucks, and only a few bags of supplies were lost to pilferage.

I found Sikes eating an MRE by his little one-man tent and explained the whole fouled-up day to him, adding a few choice words about our coalition partners, Somali drivers, and life in general. Being Jim Sikes, he just let me vent and grinned. Thoroughly pissed off about the whole thing, I walked back to my quarters and went to sleep.

The next day we set out for Quorleey. The escort was a heavy one, with the mortar platoon and a rifle platoon and command vehicles. I was the commander of the whole mess, with Kirk Haschak tagging along to get familiar with the area. Sean Naylor, the *Army Times* correspondent, came along as well.

The drive to Quorleey turned out to be something of a

yawn. There were no bandit ambushes, nor were there many people to be seen on the way. We quickly came to learn that no bandit in his right mind would attack an escorted convoy, because it was much easier to steal from an unguarded distribution site. The route for the most part was an improved dirt road and well maintained. What was striking was the countryside—cornfields and banana plantations abounded as far as the eye could see. About an hour into the trip, we had passed so many crops that I began to feel vaguely silly about bringing a load of relief rice and lentils to this land of plenty. Sean Naylor wondered aloud about this too. Kirk Haschak (who was quicker on the draw than I was) quipped, "Hell, I don't know, Sean, maybe they don't eat corn." This was subsequently published in the *Army Times*, and we both ended up getting a talking-to.

Upon reaching Quorleey, we encountered a huge crowd of people jumping around and cheering our arrival. It was quite a spectacle, something straight out of a *Rama of the Jungle* movie. The townspeople swarmed about our vehicles, and we had to dismount to guide the trucks through the crowd. I was worried that these were starving people come to steal the food. But this wasn't the case. We were the first UNITAF soldiers these people had seen, and they were coming out to see their "benefactors." The food was unloaded in the warehouse at Quorleey (using local labor paid for with MREs), and the convoy returned to Marka without incident. It had been a strange but happy mission, and one of the few times in the whole deployment when I thought that we actually might have helped a few people.

The Marka Town Council

Lieutenant Colonel Sikes spent the next few days meeting with the key players in Marka. He was following the previous guidance he'd had from Ambassador Oakley and the JTF about restoring the authority of clan elders. As with everywhere else in Somalia, this would be easier said than done, because there were the inevitable SNA "officials" around. However, things at Marka were slightly better than in many other places. The Ali Tihad had prevented the SNA or any other warlord group from making significant inroads into the community. On these trips Sikes took with him a newcomer to the battalion who was to have an extremely positive impact on our operations. Major Walt Wojtas was a civil affairs officer who came with a large amount of experience under his belt from participation in Operation Desert Storm and Provide Comfort, as well as from training exercises in Africa. Although civil affairs had been around since World War II, until the aftermath of the Cold War it hadn't received the limelight in military operations. Now in the post–Cold War "new world order," civil affairs people were in great demand. They were finding themselves employed as never before in what was called military operations other than war (MOOTW) and what would be called stability and support operations (SASO), which sounds like an underwire bra. Anyway, Walt was one of a few men in the army trained to work with local civil authorities in establishing, or reestablishing, a civil government. He had been home fewer than six months in the previous two years and seemed at first to be burned out, but he soon fell into the groove of operations and was a tremendous help to us. His insights from his tour in northern Iraq were most helpful, and his advice was always well thought out. Moreover, both he and Sikes had the gift of gab and putting people at ease. They were also quite pointed about the fact that the only authority that the battalion (and UNITAF) was prepared to recognize in Marka was that of the clan elders. As a result, these leaders came forward more quickly than in other towns in the lower Shabele valley.

Clans dominated every part of Somali life. What family and clan a person belonged to was of vital importance to every Somali. In a country with less than 50 percent literacy, virtually every man could recite his lineage back several dozen generations. None of us really understood the clan structure. The idea of tribal extended families encompassing hundreds of thousands of people was alien to us.

Lieutenant Colonel Sikes tried. He and Ahmed Omer would sit down in front of a butcher paper easel and Ahmed would attempt to explain the clan structure. The butcher paper eventually filled up with a wiring diagram of tribes and subtribes and a sort of pecking order among them. Ahmed Omer tried his best to explain that certain tribes and clans were part of certain political alliances (for example, the Somali National Alliance, or SNA, was made up mainly of Hawiye and Habr Gedir clan members, of whom Mohammed Farah Adieed was the head man). The dominant clan around Marka was the Dir, but there were so many subclans and sub-subclans that the fact that most of them were ultimately re-lated under the Dir didn't mean anything. I confess we had a hard time figuring out who belonged to what clan. I'd ask Ahmed if there were any signs, such as facial markings or distinctive dress, that a person could see in order to tell clans apart. No such luck. Then I asked him how he could tell peo-ple apart and what clan they were in. He told me you could tell by the way they talked and carried themselves. I went to sleep that night with the sobering realization that there was exactly one man in the task force who could tell these people apart and he wasn't even a soldier. What motivated many of the clans was no mystery. The obvious things (at least to me) were loot, money, and the desire to dominate the other clans around them. The ultimate goal was more obscure. No one group had the power to dominate and, as a result, Somalia was in chaos. In any event, we worked hard to develop an ac-curate clan picture of the lower Shabele valley.

Ahmed Omer's description of clan structure gave us some insight into the Somalis, but we never really got to know them. Because their affiliations were loose, for every hard-core, disciplined clan fighter there were dozens of armed men whose sole function seemed to revolve around robbery and looting. Although ostensibly part of a major political faction and responsible to it, these men were only nominally under the control of anyone. The group of Somalis whom we feared the most in those initial days was the Ali Tihad (the Islamic fundamentalists). Ironically we ended up having peaceful relations with them. Their overall impact on Marka was actually beneficial. They had taken over the port of Marka and driven out the SNA. They ran port operations and continued to bring in supplies. It was another example of how you couldn't take any intelligence at face value. We'd gone into Marka expecting to have to fight the Ali Tihad.

The man who had his work cut out for him in all of this was Mike Klein. As the intelligence officer for the battalion, he had to identify the threat and come up with their likely courses of action to give us a basis to plan operations against them. In normal conventional warfare (such as training at the NTC or the Gulf War), he would have at his disposal a formidable array of information provided by higher headquarters. This information could come from national reconnaissance assets such as satellite imagery, or higher headquarters military intelligence assets such as radio intercept, aerial photography, or thermal imagery. Normally, Mike would get an update from higher echelons that would give him a fairly detailed overall picture, from which he could begin his work. He would fill in the gaps of the initial intelligence provided by reconnaissance patrols from the scout platoon and the line companies and his own intuitive analysis through a process known as intelligence preparation of the battlefield (IPB). Mike was good at IPB analysis, and he used the whole staff in his war gaming of enemy courses of action.

Like all of us, Mike had to come to grips with a new and vastly different situation. He started out in Marka with literally nothing. It took time just figuring out where all the main clan families lived. There were no "green lines" separating the clans the way the buffer zone separated the factions in Beirut. In many places, the clans lived superimposed on one another and with little enclaves in territory populated by majorities from other clans. Mike had to identify where the major political factions were based—for example, distinguishing a Somali National Alliance (SNA) area from that of a United Somali Congress (USC). Also, he had to identify the villages and outlying areas that had an affiliation with the Ali Tihad.

On top of this, the S2 section had to track bandit activity in the town of Marka and the surrounding countryside. At first, this came in after the fact from reports of bandit robbery. Later, as people opened up to us, we started getting reports of groups of bandits located near villages or by isolated stretches in the road. There was a certain calculation to this. In many cases, a rival bandit group would turn in another, with the hope that we would disarm them. The rival bandit group would then victimize the disarmed bandits or at least muscle in on their territory. We would tell newly disarmed bandits that their only hope for safety lay in telling us where the other bandit groups were. This sometimes led to our disarming other groups.

The S2 section had to be somewhat critical when evaluating voluntary information, because the Somalis had a fine gift for drama and exaggeration. A report that fifty armed bandits were going to raid a food warehouse in Aw-Degle normally meant that four Somalis were getting together to steal some goats. Ahmed Omer was of tremendous help in these interrogations, not only for his knowledge of the language but of the culture as well. When his antenna went up, chances were that we were onto something. Otherwise, we had to be skeptical. Occasionally this skepticism led us to make the wrong decision and not protect something we should have, but we were right a lot more with our jaundiced eye than we were wrong.

Mike doggedly kept incident overlays on the maps of our areas of operation showing every robbery or instance of clan violence. He started a new overlay each week and compared his current overlay with those of the previous weeks. As patterns began to develop, we would shift our patrols to those areas to capture or suppress the bandits. We never had enough assets to do the thorough job needed, but we could keep the main roads policed and shift our patrols to keep the bandits off balance. Mike and the S2 section were tireless in their efforts, updating their database on the town and the valley, talking to Somalis, sending out recon patrols, debriefing convoy escorts, interrogating captured bandits, and working with the town council. Mike was forever looking for any scrap of information. His work was never ending and unglamorous, but we couldn't have succeeded without it.

Logistics at this early stage was a jury-rigged affair as well, but we couldn't have sustained ourselves without the superb efforts of Captain Michaels and his S4 section. All our support came out of Baledogle. Daily logistics runs by Black Hawk helicopters brought us critical supplies. We had an attached reverse osmosis water purification unit (ROWPU, pronounced "row-pew") that made enough drinking water, but we were entirely dependent on MREs for food. It was all the S4 and the XO could do to keep us in operating supplies such as fuel, batteries, and ammunition. Vehicle maintenance was also a challenge. Although we had a maintenance contact team forward, we had no spare parts, because they are consolidated at brigade level in a light division. Any major vehicle repairs necessitated either parts being flown down or the vehicle being sling loaded back to Baledogle to be repaired in the maintenance shop. On one occasion we lost a vehicle when the sling load became unstable and the helicopter pilot had to cut the load or risk crashing. A humvee dropped from about three hundred feet compresses down into a mass about the size of a large riding lawn mower. Lieutenant Colonel Sikes was not pleased. In spite of these travails, Joe Occhuzzio and Steve Michaels continued to coordinate supplies from the Marines in Mogadishu and make the system work with our forward support battalion in Baledogle. As more assets arrived in country, the supply situation improved, but the logistical support of Task Force 2-87 in Marka in the early days was indeed a challenge. Fortunately for us, our logisticians were up to it.

One of the best things about Marka was the beach. About a half mile from the battalion's encampment was a large cove inside the reef line where the water was never more than five feet deep and always crystal clear. The ever-present danger of sharks was much less there, so Sikes authorized bathing parties as long as there were armed lookouts. After three weeks of constant operations under water rationing, even a saltwater bath was wonderful. My small bottle of saltwater soap was a big hit with the staff and soon disappeared. Nonetheless, it was a grand sensation to strip off the same uniform you'd been wearing for weeks and wade into the warm ocean in the bright sunshine, feeling the little waves lap over you as you sat with your bare ass on the clean sand of the bottom and scrubbed. Life's little pleasures.

Washing clothes was difficult in the saltwater. The soap wouldn't lather, but at least a person could manage to get off the first layer of grime. Troops would use some of their precious fresh water ration to rinse the clothes. We had to watch this initially because the ROWPU was not operating to full capacity. Later on when we had more water, it became easier. Still later we were able to wash our clothes (and ourselves) in fresh water.

The first bathing party became quite a show for the Somalis, most of whom had never before seen a naked Caucasian. By the time we started to leave the water, there was a good crowd of Somalis watching us, pointing and laughing. I was a little embarrassed, standing up to my waist in the water looking at a hundred giggling Somalis. Mike Klein, however, was in grand form. "It's a curse," he said, "even here in Africa." I asked him what he meant. "Well, sir, wherever I go, people come from miles around just to get a look at my hog." He shouted, "Behold!" and emerged from the sea like Neptune, with arms held high over his head in triumph. The Somalis clapped and cheered. They appeared highly pleased (although shriveled as we were, I doubt they were very impressed).

There was a small, strange footnote to our bathing in the sea. About a month later, Sikes was notified that a reporter for a Canadian newspaper had complained that we had offended the "Islamic sensibilities" of the Somalis by washing naked in the sea in front of them. The article ignored the fact that hundreds of Somalis did the same thing daily on the beach outside Marka and that our bathing beach was about five miles outside of town. If they wanted to see us, they had to walk out there. This was of course just another reporter determined to do his best to show the U.S. military in a bad light. The division public affairs guys voiced some concerns about it, but Sikes just ignored them. His position was that when sufficient water and shower units were on hand, we'd wash in fresh water; until then we'd continue to wash at the beach.

Soon after the first meetings in which we managed to identify most of the players in Marka, Lieutenant Colonel Sikes and Major Wojtas met with the elders to set up the Marka town council. Made up of people originally from Marka, the council would work toward reestablishing the authority of the elders, which had been compromised by the political factions. The council met daily at first, then weekly or whenever a meeting was necessary. It would regulate the distribution of relief supplies within Marka (initially under our close watch to ensure that no one was left out) and coordinate rebuilding sections of the town wrecked earlier. Most important, the reestablishment of the tribal elders as the local authority would allow them to adjudicate interpersonal and interfamilial disputes, without bloodshed. Most Somalis still set great store in the opinions of the tribal elders (something one would expect in people who could recite the names of their seventeen previous ancestors). Having the elders there to arbitrate disputes and negotiate compensation (for example, so many goats and/or camels for a murder) cut down considerably on the amount of feuding.

The town council initially consisted of twenty-five persons, to include Sid Abukar and Princess Manna, a Somali woman who was the last daughter of Sultan Sid Abukar Hagi Abdalla, an important elder. Lieutenant Colonel Sikes went to these meetings and chaired them initially, gradually passing the chairmanship to Sid Abukar. The town council was one of the major success stories of our stay in HRS Marka. It remained in operation long after the U.S. military had left the sector.

A subsequent step after the creation of the Marka town council, one that initially raised a few eyebrows at JTF, was the formation of the Marka police force. This was the first local authority of its type set up anywhere in Somalia and probably the most successful. It was made up of former members of the Somali national police and volunteers approved by the Marka town council. Many former national policemen still retained the old national police force green uniform and blue beret. The force started out with twenty members and grew to more than forty by the time we left. The members of the police force had tremendous pride in their prior affiliation and were eager to return to duty. Earlier in the deployment, after the Marines landed, former members of the defunct police had gone out on their own to direct traffic in the newly peaceful Mogadishu. This kind of willingness was also evident among the Marka police. Initially, their duties were limited to accompanying the patrols of Task Force 2-87 soldiers through Marka and conducting patrols around the port of Marka. At first they were constrained by being armed only with billy clubs. Later, we armed them and their duties expanded significantly. They never let us down.

Our operations in Marka revolved around manning the checkpoint outside of town, dealing with the port security detail, and patrolling the town itself. The three operations each took a rifle platoon; the detail for Marka security was rotated between companies. The checkpoint was located on the only trafficable road to the town. We were able to stop and search all vehicular traffic going into and out of Marka. Each vehicle and person entering Marka would be searched for weapons. This occasionally ruffled feathers with the proud Somalis, but usually they took it in stride. Individual weapons would be checked in a weapons holding area and receipts would be provided. All crew-served weapons would be confiscated. Period.

A typical vehicle to be searched could be anything from a single man in a Datsun pickup loaded with produce to a dilapidated Bluebird school bus with about a hundred people and their belongings. Vehicle searches began with the passengers exiting the vehicle and standing in a waiting area. We had learned the Somali words for these instructions, but

half the time the passengers looked at the soldiers uncompre-
hendingly and the troops had to resort to pantomime and
hand gestures. Occasionally someone objected and had to be
manhandled. Two soldiers would then cover the occupants—
nicely, mind you, no weapons pointing right at them, just at
the ready in case someone made a false move or produced a
hidden weapon—while the others inspected the vehicle. They
used mirrors to check the undercarriage and would check
all the vehicle's compartments, including the engine. Sometimes this would be a challenge, because the compartments
would not come open; such occasions are why we had crow-
bars. What we were looking for was weapons, ammunition,
and explosives.

After the vehicle search, the cargo would be inspected,
bundles opened, boxes opened, fluids poked with sticks to
ensure they really were as deep as the container. The three
men searching would carry out their task briskly but thoroughly. If a weapon was found, the soldiers would check to
see if the carrier had proper authorization to carry it, such as a
UNITAF card identifying him as an NGO security guard. If
so, the weapon would be checked and returned when the vehicle left Marka. If not, the weapon would be confiscated.
Most of the trouble and hard feelings at the checkpoint came
from the confusion over weapons policy, which persisted
throughout our time in the Somalia deployment. However,
people soon learned not to try to bring weapons into Marka.
We were the only law west of the Pecos and we had things
our way.

Each vehicle search took about five minutes, except for
large ones. Once the search was completed, the vehicles' occupants would be invited to repack their property and allowed
to proceed. Vehicle searches at the main Marka checkpoint
were probably carried out twenty to fifty times a day.

We had one tragic incident when a Somali man was killed
by an accidental weapons discharge by a soldier clearing
his weapon. Fortunately, it was witnessed by numerous Somalis and Americans, all of whom agreed that it was an accident. The only other major incident involved a truckload of

Somalis that appeared to try to run the barrier, then crashed directly into it. All weapons covering the checkpoint were instantly up and ready as the Somalis in the wrecked truck frantically held up their hands and signaled their nonhostile intent. It turned out that the vehicle's brakes failed, and the driver was powerless to stop it in time. This once again made me proud of the discipline of the soldiers and junior leaders. All weapons were instantly covering the truck but no one got trigger-happy. What could have been a tragic incident turned out semicomic.

Patrols were run in the town twenty-four hours a day. There was never a period in which a squad-sized patrol was not walking through the streets of the town, maintaining a presence. The battalion maintained a reaction platoon ready at all times, in case a patrol got into trouble, but we never had to deploy it. The troops generally enjoyed the patrols, because they offered a chance to get away from the boredom of checkpoint and guard duty.

A typical patrol consisted of a squad of six to eight men armed with one or two M203 grenade launchers and one or two squad automatic weapons, the rest rifles. The troops would also have AN/PAS-4 night sights and AN/PAS-7 night vision goggles. Additional equipment would be a PRC-77 radio and a first-aid bag. Each soldier wore his Kevlar flak vest, helmet, and load-bearing equipment (LBE) and carried a two-quart canteen on a strap. The patrol leader was normally a three-stripe sergeant (E-5) or a staff sergeant (E-6). Occasionally the platoon leader or platoon sergeant would take a patrol. Normally, however, it was a squad leader's mission.

The patrol leader was given his patrol route in the TOC and a list of checkpoints to call in. He would be given an intelligence update by the S2 NCO on duty or maybe by Captain Klein himself. He would then go brief his people and conduct precombat checks. These included things such as weapons cleanliness, equipment serviceability, ammunition readiness, troop knowledge of the ROE, and patrol standard operating procedures (SOPs). All of it was old stuff to the troops but necessary before going out. The troops would move by truck to the port, then wait for the appointed time to begin the patrol.

At the designated hour, the troops would depart from the port and walk into the town. They would pass the USC headquarters on their right, where a few toughs would be hanging around in the front wearing the surly looks of juvenile delinquents who don't like being ignored. The troops would glance at them for signs of anything other than the normal animosity, but they were punks, nothing like the hard cases in Kismayu or Brava.

The troops would then ascend the paved road into the plaza of the town, where there were several Italian-style cafes and what used to be a theater. In the daytime, there were always a lot of stalls with people selling everything from khat (a stimulant) to cigarettes as well as produce and stolen relief supplies. Here they would meet with only cursory looks from the people, who had gotten used to their presence quickly. The patrol would fan out and take security positions while the patrol leader and the attached Marka policeman talked to a few people to see if anything was going on.

The image of soldiers taking cover with weapons at the ready in a normal, busy, day-to-day market reminded me of news clips I had seen of the Brits patrolling Northern Ireland. If the Somalis generally ignored the patrols, the soldiers didn't ignore the Somalis. They were constantly watching the surrounding people for signs of hostility or suspicious acts.

After a few minutes in the market, the patrol would move on. Although lightly laden, the troops would be sweating under their flak jackets and helmets. The canyons of three- and four-story buildings effectively prevented any sea breezes from penetrating the town and also helped trap the humidity. Occasionally, a wheezing car or truck would ease its way down the street and the troops would watch it go past, its black smoke adding to the claustrophobic atmosphere. Also contributing to the general malaise were the dozens of charcoal cooking fires coming from the houses. It was hard to see how the Somalis managed to cook on open flames every night and not burn down half the town.

The soldiers would stop warily whenever they were passed by large groups of young men. Soldiers moving on the opposite side of the street would instinctively stop and subtly cover their squad mates until the youths had passed. The patrol would move at a slow pace. There was no point in hurrying. A person could walk from one end of the town to another in twenty minutes, but the patrol's mission was to be out for three hours, "maintaining a presence." They would scan the windows of the buildings around them for any hostile intent. A soldier on patrol must pay attention and be alert. Marka was by and large a laid-back place, but there were incidents, such as the patrol in Bravo Company that got into a fight with bandits and had a Marka policeman wounded. A bandit was also wounded and captured in this encounter, but for about a minute there were bullets flying all over the place. There were a few incidents of sniping that just missed soldiers as they walked the streets. The soldiers didn't live in a constant state of fear, but neither was this a mundane, pleasant walk in the sun. Soldiers would study the faces of the people and look for any telltale signs of trouble, such as no children around, people not on the street, or an excess of young men hanging around in one area. Our men got to learn the signs after a while.

After patrolling for a while, the men got to know some people by name. Some of these would greet them in their broken English or give friendly waves. Children would follow, but they didn't come as before because they'd learned that it was no good asking for anything. The soldiers on patrol were all business. It was a nice thing to smile at the kids; any show of friendliness was helpful. The kids played ball in the street or chased one another around and made a lot of noise. They normally had shirts and shorts on; only a few were naked. All were skinny, but they seemed energetic.

The patrol leader would call in his checkpoints to the TOC as the patrol passed them. This kept the TOC appraised of where the patrol was in case there was trouble and the reaction force had to be sent in. It also allowed the TOC to vector the patrol to a potential trouble spot in town more quickly. It was a milestone for the patrol's movement, a way of marking time. The patrol wound its way through the twisting streets of the town, mingling with the townspeople but at the same time apart from them, as if on a different plane of existence.

Occasionally a patrol would happen upon violent scenes of Somalis beating up Somalis. These could be arguments over ownership—what we would call "domestic abuse"—or just plain old feuding. If it looked as though someone might get killed, the troops would intervene and disperse the people; otherwise, the smartest thing to do was to let them fight it out. The raucous screams of the spectators would echo in the soldiers' ears as they continued on their patrol. Some soldiers would look back and shake their heads, thinking that these people are all crazy.

The patrol would reach the northern outskirts of town and swing back south on another street. The leader would look at his watch—halftime. It took discipline not to walk too fast and to halt for security checks every ten minutes or so. The patrol leader knew that half the reason for a patrol such as this was presence. The patrol could have done the entire designated patrol route at a brisk walk in forty-five minutes, but most patrols were scheduled to take three to four hours. So there was no point in being in a hurry.

The soldiers would continue to walk south back toward the town center and the port of Marka. They had to negotiate a series of ravines that went through the town. Normally used for refuse disposal, they could be smelled when the houses still blocked them from view. The stench of garbage and dead animals on some days was almost overpowering. This was one place where almost no patrol did a security halt. The best time to walk by the ravines was after a hard rain.

The patrol would continue south on the hillside and be sure to swing by the Ali Tihad compound. Not because the Islamic fundamentalists were giving us a hard time, but just to remind them that we knew where they lived. Men in the outposts outside the compound (with no visible weapons) would watch the patrol impassively, but on the whole the reception was less nasty than outside the USC building. A few

Ali Tihad guards would even wave now and then. The patrol would continue south toward Princess Manna's villa. Maybe there would be a whispered question, "Is she a real princess, Sarge?" to which there would be a gruff retort, "How the fuck do I know? Maintain your sector and be quiet." The villa was nice but small, no bigger than a suburban ranch home. It still had a roof, however, and looked undamaged.

The patrol would finally, gratefully, turn back toward the port of Marka. The troops would be getting thirsty, and the two quarts of water they had started with would be greatly depleted. They would walk down the sandy road past Sister Anna's TB hospital and trade uneasy glances with the Somali patients, who looked dully back at them. Traffic from the checkpoint to the port of Marka would pass them. The beach would look particularly inviting after the long walk, the sea breeze a refreshing change from the stifling atmosphere of the town.

Finally the patrol would reach the port and be admitted through the gate. The leader would ensure that all soldiers cleared their weapons, then he reported completion of the patrol to the TOC. If anything significant had happened, he'd tell the port security commander and make arrangements to go and debrief Captain Klein immediately. If not, all the troops would refill their canteens and board the truck to return to base camp. Facing out, they'd watch the port recede into the distance and look forward to standing down for a few hours, another patrol completed.

The port security detail consisted of a platoon stationed inside the wire at the port of Marka. The concertina fence put in by our engineers created a decent barrier, but it required constant patrolling to be effective. Duty in the port was perhaps the most miserable of all the Marka security missions, both because of the stationary nature of the security detail and the fact that mosquitoes swarmed thicker in the port than anywhere else in Marka.

The first few weeks guarding the port were interesting, however, because there were numerous attempts by local toughs and entrepreneurs to steal food from the stockpiles kept there. This was not an easy undertaking for them. We had put up a good triple concertina fence all around the food site, and the port was at all times guarded by a platoon of alert soldiers with night vision devices. In addition, none of the food kept there was in what could be considered "pilferable" quantities. The rice and lentils were in hundred-pound sacks and the cooking oil came in clumsy five-gallon cans. It was not the sort of stuff a person could easily run away with. As with our previous experience with warehouse pilferage in Wanwaylen, it wasn't the starving or the wasted people who were pilfering food. The thieves in Marka were, as everywhere else, well-nourished young men who were stealing the food to sell it. This gave the prevention of theft a different perspective in the soldiers' eyes, making them take their security duties seriously.

There soon developed a predictable pattern that became a bizarre nightly ritual for a few weeks. The thieves would gather after dark and skirt the barbed wire fence. They would test it and wait for a reaction from the soldiers. If there was no reaction, one or more of them would begin to practice running up to the fence in preparation for jumping it. The thieves would measure and gauge and experiment, and when they thought they had it down, they would then remove all of their clothing and try to leap over the triple concertina fence. Most of them would make it, to be promptly seized by soldiers who had been watching the whole thing in their night vision sights. A few would misjudge and have to be cut out of the barbed wire while they screamed and thrashed. All captured thieves would have their cuts treated by the platoon medic, then would be flex cuffed and placed in a storeroom with good ventilation—known to the soldiers as "Motel 6"—to await the morning. In the morning they would be released, naked, out of the main gate, to the general merriment and amusement of crowds who would come to watch. On a good night there were usually between five and ten naked, bemused men sitting in detention waiting for the morning release. Our record was, I believe, a dozen. It was fortunate that no one was seriously hurt during these attempts. Later on, when the Marka police force was established and the Somali police patrolled the outer perimeter of the port, theft attempts dropped precipitously.

After a week in our initial position, we moved into the abandoned police compound, about a kilometer from the house we had initially occupied. The buildings had no roofs and the compound had trash all over the place, but we soon set that right. It was a more defensible position, and we increased its value by surrounding it with several layers of barbed wire. The headquarters was installed in the old station building. The aid station was in a roofless building we called Club Marka. Because our battalion's divisional call sign was Condor, we referred to our new home as Condor Base.

Because it now appeared that Marka would be our operations area for some time into the future, and because life was starting to develop a semblance of a routine, we began to establish a training regime. A small-arms range would be nothing ambitious, largely to re-zero our weapons and zero night sights. It would give the troops a place to practice shooting whenever we got the chance. I picked out a spot near our bathing beach and gave Gordy Flowers the task of turning it into a range. It was crude, but it served our purpose. We rotated companies and platoons through it as we could. No one got much shooting done because of our mission operations tempo, but everyone got to re-zero night sights before patrols. It was a rare week that didn't have somebody using the range to shoot. A major challenge was keeping curious Somalis away from the downrange impact area; this was a chore, but doable. It was actually good to have spectators. The sight of the Americans constantly practicing combined with the professionalism with which our troops carried out their sweeps and searches probably deterred a few potential criminals.

Except for the thieves, Marka was quiet. It was certainly not a hotbed of incidents as was Mogadishu. The people of Marka could have their wild moments, however. The one ugly riot we had there was when the Italian navy showed up and tried to land supplies over the shore. It turned out that this had supposedly been coordinated with Princess Manna, but she had forgotten to tell the rest of the Marka town council. It didn't matter, because the Italians hadn't coordinated with us either. I received an exasperated radio call from Joe Occhuzzio while we were on an operation around Kurtenwary asking if I had given permission for the Italians to land in the port. I replied with an indignant negative. In the meantime, hundreds of Somalis gathered on the shore and near the port and began to hurl stones at the Italians. Our men tried to hold back the crowds. The Italians were dissuaded from continuing operations. They returned to their ship and sailed away. Marka certainly lived up to its reputation as an Italian hostile area. I was glad no one had been shot.

Meanwhile, back in Baledogle, the battalion had its first lethal firefight with bandits. Echo Company was conducting a routine mounted patrol of the roads. As twilight was starting to set in, the lead vehicle encountered a stopped pickup truck with a large crowd of Somalis around it. Suddenly the patrol started taking fire from the crowd, with bullets hitting two of the humvees. The lead vehicle immediately responded with M60 machine-gun fire, and other members of the patrol dismounted and returned fire. The firefight lasted almost five minutes. Six Somalis were killed and five wounded. The gunmen broke contact and one rifle was recovered. Sadly, an investigation revealed that most of the casualties were innocent Somalis who were being robbed by bandits when the patrol came upon the scene. Only one of the bodies on the scene was positively identified as a bandit. Several other of the bandits had been hit by the patrol's fire and managed to escape with the aid of their companions. One of the wounded bandits was confirmed to have later died; we lost track of the others.

The tragedy was unavoidable. The bandits had opened fire on the soldiers, and they reacted in the only way they could. They returned fire in accordance with the ROE. In the twilight, it was impossible to tell who had a gun and who didn't. All they knew was that they'd come upon a large group of men who had started shooting at them. The soldiers in the patrol did not know that they had happened upon a highway robbery. This was one of the more unpleasant aspects of fire-fights in Somalia, one that the battalion was to encounter re-peatedly. There were always innocent bystanders around the contacts between hostiles and soldiers. Only rarely did we engage bandits without having to be cautious about hurting bystanders.

A friend from my advisor days in Saudi Arabia, Jim Good, sent me a box of novelties and magic tricks with which to im-press the natives. Most were simple parlor tricks, which I gave away to soldiers in the battalion, but a few were gems. One trick was fake cigarettes that emitted puffs of authentic-looking smoke. I had tremendous fun putting out a cigarette in the palm of my hand in front of the local tough guys, one of whom tried to emulate me, much to his discomfiture. The capper, though, was the old bag of laughs: the battery-powered laugh recording inside a little orange bag. The So-malis were convinced it was some sort of demon that we kept in the bag. Mike Klein, that master of psychology, put it to brilliant use on a thief we'd caught inside our compound. Af-ter having the man escorted to the front gate, Mike took out his strobe light (an aircraft signaling device) and flashed it on the man twice. He told Ahmed Omer that he now had the man's soul in the little orange bag and if he tried to steal from us again he'd throw the bag in a fire. When Ahmed finished translating, Klein squeezed the bag, which set off the laugh recording. The poor wretch screamed and took off like a bolt of lightning toward Marka, never to bother us again.

Troops would spend what little off time they had doing various things. Letter writing was always popular, as was reading. Magazines and paperback books were passed around until they fell apart. Portable video games were beginning to make an appearance then; and you could always see some kid lying flat on his cot with his fingers working frantically on a game as it made little bleep-boink-burp sounds. Seeing it was enough to make a major feel a hundred years old. Games of all types were hits: card games, chess, checkers, occasionally

Risk. Once I saw people playing the old "paper-scissors-stone" game with their hands. After the video games, I found that oddly comforting. The weight sets brought by Alpha Company were popular; the big iron was never left idle for long.

Despite all the exertions of their duties, some troops were determined to leave Somalia "huge." Men would run extra laps around Condor Base. A few hardy souls entered an MRE eating contest in which the winner claimed the prize by eating eight MREs. Never was the motivational factor in winning so apparent. As the winner said, "Sir, you just gotta want it bad enough." We weren't exactly overrun with spare time, so these diversions were about as far as we ever got. Later, a few lucky souls went to Mombassa on a four-day R and R and came back telling wild tales of hotel rooms on the ocean, booze, food, and babes. Only a fraction of the troops were able to go.

Kirk Haschak and I developed an after-dinner ritual. Once the last meeting and instructions for the night were done, we'd meet in his tent and play "Pigs." This is a German game in which two small plastic pigs are thrown, and how they land determines the score. We'd normally play for about half an hour and talk about what went on that day and what was coming up. Kirk's wife, Monica, and Donna were good friends, so we'd catch each other up on the home front whenever either of us got mail. He'd tell me about the travails of horse ownership. Monica, a veterinary assistant, had a horse. I'd fill him in on John's progress. It was a small link to the other world of Fort Drum, and it helped pass the time.

It was during this period that we conducted one of the most pleasant, productive, and hilarious missions of the battalion's stay in Somalia, Operation Condor Tow Truck. There were so many derelict cars and trucks in Marka's streets that many streets were literally only one vehicle wide. There were places where you couldn't even get a humvee through because of the clutter. This had a negative impact on our ability to transit through the town and on commerce. The Marka town council asked Lieutenant Colonel Sikes for his assistance in clearing the streets. Sikes agreed to improve the trafficability in the town, both to assist us in our tactical operations and to improve the quality of life for the Somalis in Marka.

We decided to clear only the main thoroughfares and public areas initially, because there was so much derelict stuff in Marka that a thorough cleaning would take a week. We used five-ton trucks from the support platoon, under the indefatigable Lieutenant Van Hoesen. The trucks had dedicated security provided by a platoon from Alpha 2-87. The whole operation itself was commanded by Gordy Flowers; Sikes and I just went along as sightseers.

The operation started on the morning of 4 February and was instantly a big hit. Huge numbers of children would gather around as a five-ton truck would back up to the derelict and secure a tow cable around it, and off they would go. People were clapping and cheering, and kids would follow the burnt-out hulk and leap on it for a ride. The five ton would then drop its tow outside town and return for another trip, followed by hundreds of cheering, screaming, and gesticulating kids. It got to the point that the security detail with each vehicle had to devote some men to simple crowd control to allow the truck drivers to attach the tow cables. Even so, we were always careful to keep at least some soldiers in a position to engage any sudden fire we might take. Fortunately, nothing of the sort developed. The closest thing we came to in terms of resistance was a pair of opportunists who claimed that we had "illegally" taken their car, a burnt-out hulk blocking the street, and demanded payment of $20,000 U.S. They were politely told to go away. Looking at our guns, they did so.

In the meantime, Van Hoesen, Staff Sergeant Cronin, and the men from the support platoon were in their glory. Each time a truck pulled out another derelict, a great throng of people lined the streets cheering and waving. Van Hoesen was standing in a five ton, waving back and clearly delighted. The giant officer was a popular man with the Somalis anyway. This day he might actually have been Elvis.

We kept it up until more than twenty derelict vehicles had

been pulled off the streets, making trafficability much improved. Lieutenant Colonel Sikes was happy with the whole operation. Because it was getting dark, we called off the operation for the day. Sikes told me to plan for a Condor Tow Truck II, in which we'd start going after the side streets. Unfortunately, we never got to that because of other operational requirements.

Ten

The Big Picture: Operation RESTORE HOPE,
January–February 1993

By mid-January, UNITAF had designated its HRS sectors
into a more or less stabilized apportionment that would stand
for the duration of the Somalia deployment. The HRS would
change hands between the different nations of UNITAF and
later UNISOM, but the boundaries would remain the same.
The humanitarian relief sectors were HRS Mogadishu (USMC),
HRS Baledogle (Army Forces Central Command, or AR-
CENT), HRS Belet Uyene (Canadian), HRS Oddur (French),
HRS Baidoa (USMC, later to ARCENT control under the
Australians), HRS Gialassi (Italian), and HRS Kismayu
(ARCENT, later Belgian). Each HRS had in common the fact
that they were huge—either geographically, demographically,
or both. HRS Marka was as big as Connecticut and Rhode Island combined and was by no means the biggest HRS. Because of the vastness of areas to control and the paucity of
forces, UNITAF decided to designate a UNITAF reaction
force. Ideally, this should have been a force not dedicated to a
specific HRS. A Marine battalion afloat or an army battalion
staged by an airfield would have been logical choices. However, because one Marine task force was leaving and the other
was hip deep in Mogadishu, JTF decided to designate Task
Force 2-87 as the UNITAF reaction force.

On the face of it, this didn't make much sense. Our little
battalion task force was tasked with controlling a huge HRS
with only about half its combat power. A rifle company and

Echo Company remained in Baledogle under brigade control. We wouldn't get these forces back until the Moroccans showed up around the end of January to work under 2d Brigade control in Baledogle. Looking around, however, we could see that everyone else in all the other HRS sectors was in the same boat. JTF didn't have a lot of choice, because there weren't enough forces in Somalia available. So Task Force 2-87 maintained a company on two-hour recall from operations to assemble and conduct airmobile movement to whatever trouble spot the JTF directed. A battalion TAC-CP element would accompany it, and the rest of the battalion would follow as soon as possible. A complicating factor was that we would still have to leave a skeleton crew on hand in Marka during our absence.

This dual HRS and UNITAF reaction force arrangement was supposed to be temporary. Other multinational units continued to come into Somalia and swell the ranks of the UNITAF forces. The plan was for Task Force 2-87 to be replaced in HRS Marka by a battalion from a coalition nation and for us to move to Mogadishu and act solely as the UNITAF reaction force. This concept turned out to be a lot easier to formulate than implement. Getting another nation's forces to accept responsibility for HRS Marka proved to be difficult. UNITAF could not direct a nation's forces to do something without their government's agreement.

Many nations sent units with fairly stiff restrictions on them (for example, only to be used in Mogadishu). Others gave their commanders broad leeway to refuse UNITAF orders or restricted them to checking back with their government before they did anything not initially agreed to prior to their deployment. This put UNITAF in the position of a Century 21 Realtor trying to sell a property as opposed to a military headquarters giving directions to subordinate units. Representatives from various UNITAF forces came to Marka to "kick the tires" and see if they wanted the mission. The Saudi airborne battalion was a candidate for a short time, and I got to practice my Arabic on their visiting liaison officer. However, they dropped out because their government limited

them to Mogadishu. The Nigerians were candidates for a
time, as were the Botswanans, who had garnered a reputation
for kick-ass riot control. However, neither worked out. The
problem with Marka was its distance from the logistics hub
of Mogadishu. Many of the smaller national forces were not
robust enough to support themselves over a distance without
substantial help from UNITAF. UNITAF tried to find a taker
for Marka throughout our stay, finally getting the Pakistani
contingent to take it shortly after we were replaced by Task
Force 1-22. For the duration of our stay, however, we did the
double duty of UNITAF reaction force and HRS Marka unit.
It made life interesting.

For the most part, things in late January and early February
stayed quiet. There were occasional incidents in Mogadishu,
but the uneasy and ill-defined peace between the warlords
and UNITAF pretty much held. Of course, by not attempting
to confiscate weapons and disarm factions, UNITAF removed
one of the principal opportunities for conflict to arise. It also
destroyed any chance of the country getting back to normality. Somali weapons and their status caused a good deal of
confusion. There were no-visible-weapons rules (as if a hidden one was somehow better), no-crew-served-weapons rules
(easier to enforce), and several different versions of UNITAF
weapons permits, none of which were ever effective. There
was never a centrally recognized weapons registration card.
Nor was there any reliable way of tracking legitimately registered weapons. Somalis learned that the rules changed from
place to place and the best thing for them to do, even if they
were honest and not bandits or warlord gunmen, was to hide
their weapons.

UNITAF continued to direct the empowerment of the local
tribal elders and the return to traditional Somali tribal government structure. I wasn't informed enough on Somali culture then, or now, to know if this would work. However, it
seemed to me even then that the political armies had sup-
planted the power of the elders, especially after Siad Barre
had spent two decades marginalizing them. In the face of
armed thugs, who did not respect the moral authority they

represented, the elders were powerless. Without disarming the warlords, the elder councils we formed would have power only as long as they were backed by UNITAF troops.

This was the period of the famous mission creep (a term that, as far as I know, was first coined by Lieutenant Colonel Sikes). We (UNITAF) had come to Somalia to secure food convoys and feeding centers and to stop mass starvation. Well, the mass starvation was on the decline when we got to Somalia, and we had secured the feeding centers and food convoys in short order. The big question was, now what? Somalia was such an utter shambles that it was hard not to have mission creep. Feed the people and secure the convoys wasn't a strategy; it was merely a task. Faced with the chaos before us, it was instinctive to try to impose order, to reestablish services and some kind of authority. Better had there been a comprehensive plan outlining a long-term strategy for the reestablishment of government in Somalia. This would have made mission creep unnecessary. As it was, UNITAF proceeded further and further into nation building. We had gotten on this bus and now we didn't have a clue as to where it was going. We just knew we couldn't get off.

Eleven

The lower Shabele River valley is three hundred kilometers long and about a hundred kilometers wide. In peacetime about 2 million people lived there, according to the last known census. It had the reputation of being the breadbasket of Somalia; it was easy to see why. The land in many parts of the valley was green and cultivated. The sluggish Shabele River fed numerous creeks and irrigation ditches, and the land looked as though it could sustain several crops a year. In some places cornfields were dense and seemed to go for miles along the road. As Kirk Haschak said once, "This place looks like Ohio." Not quite (most farmhouses in Ohio have roofs), but I could see his point. The devastation and misery of Somalia that we had seen on TV wasn't in evidence. True, the place looked the worse for wear, and there was the occasional burnt-out piece of military hardware to remind you that there had been a civil war, but the thousands of starving people were nowhere to be seen.

The valley started at Afgoi, a midsized town at the hub of two major roads—the road from Baidoa to Mogadishu and the road from Kismayu to Mogadishu. Because of this, a lot of commerce went through Afgoi. As a result, there was also a large bandit presence in the vicinity of the town. UNITAF had to station a company of MPs there before the roads around Afgoi became reasonably safe for unescorted traffic. Afgoi was situated beside the Shabele River, and the town itself was a strange combination of cinder-block buildings and mud huts. It was also a big market town where farmers brought their produce to sell to businessmen who would take it back to Mogadishu. This was true before the war and to a lesser extent during our deployment. Fewer farmers worked the fields now; they had either been chased off or figured "what the hell" and joined a bandit gang or warlord group themselves. The relief supplies flooding the country made it unprofitable to farm anyway. All of this made Afgoi a town that bore watching.

The main road running south from Afgoi to Marka, Brava, Jelib, and ultimately Kismayu was a wide and mostly un-paved affair that had wildly varying conditions. Sometimes it was smooth and well maintained. In other places it was a washboarded mess, and driving along it would rattle your teeth and make every loose piece of equipment in the vehicle shake. There were a lot of little, one-horse towns along the road. The first one south of Afgoi was Lantabur, a nondescript village of mud shacks and a rumored den of thieves. Going south from Lantabur was K-50 airfield, a three-thousand-foot dirt strip with a dirt off-load ramp and a pole for a wind sock, long since stolen.

Off the eastern side of the road was a coastal ridgeline about three to five hundred feet tall with gradually sloping sides. The ridge was trafficable in most places by a humvee. There were also forests that started about a kilometer from the road and ran out past the Shabele River in the west and all the way to the Indian Ocean in the east. Toward the south, the forests gradually got farther away from the road until fi-nally in places they stopped altogether and the coastal ridge-line was bare except for scrub bush, as it was around Marka. Then the trees and forests started to pick up again until, by Brava, the coastal forests were almost as thick as they were by Lantabur.

On the western side of the road were farmlands, stands of trees, villages, and the river itself. The biggest villages not actually on the road were Aw-Degle, Jannelle, Quorleey, and Kurtenwary. All of them had improved dirt roads, which turned into quagmires when it rained.

Moving south from K-50 airfield, a traveler would first encounter the turnoff to Jannelle, which was marked with a derelict U.S. M101 105mm howitzer. In the distance a person could also see the red and white radio tower that marked Jannelle's location. Many (but not all) larger towns in the valley had radio towers similar to the one in Jannelle. They made it easier to navigate, especially by air, because they provided ready reference points along with the position of the river and the coastal ridgeline.

After Jannelle, the presence of cultivated farmland increased dramatically. There were banana plantations, cornfields, and fields of a plant I didn't recognize but later found out was sorghum. The houses were battered and roofless, but farming was still active here, although it did look as though the farmers could have done a lot more than they were doing.

The Marka turnoff was at Shalamboot, another side-of-the-road town whose houses were brick and stucco as opposed to the normal sticks and wattle that so many other Somali dewllings were made of. Shalamboot was in a little better condition than most places, and many houses still had their roofs. The road to Marka was easy to see off to the east as we traveled through town. The main road continued to the Quorleey turnoff and on southward, through more farmlands and small forests, toward Brava. The Kurtenwary turnoff road was to the west, just after crossing a bridge on one of the few stretches of road that had remained paved. The bridge was still, miraculously, in good shape. It could take two-way traffic with ease. The water that passed underneath it was sluggish, stinking, filthy, and not fit for putting out fires. Past the Kurtenwary turnoff, the road went through country more sparsely populated, nothing but thin forests and the occasional bus passing through to break up the green monotony of the grass. South of the Kurtenwary turnoff was Brava, the next major town. It was on the seaward side of the coastal ridgeline and had the smaller village of Mundun, with its defunct department of transportation compound, sitting on the land side of the ridgeline, similar to Shalamboot, outside Marka. Brava was literally the last civilization, if you could call it that, before Jelib, more than a hundred miles away. Task Force 2-87's tactical area of responsibility ended just south of the equator, which was about thirty miles north of Jelib. We used as our southern limit a tiny village without a name on the main road, which had yet another massive red and white radio tower erected next to it.

Most of the valley's population was north of Brava, with large refugee concentrations around Kurtenwary, Quorleey, Jannelle, Marka, Aw-Degle, and Afgoi. These refugee camps consisted of people living in wicker huts and plastic shelters. They seemed to spend their lives hanging around waiting for someone to give them something. The villages were listless, wretched places; I was always glad when I left one after a visit. There was little love lost among refugees being cared for by aid agencies and the local inhabitants. Each side accused the other of being bandits and robbing and killing people in the valley. Both sides were right, of course. Everyone spent a lot of time trying to win us over to "their side," but we were implacable.

Because this was Africa, all the troops were on the lookout for animals. Unfortunately, the lower Shabele valley wasn't something out of *Mutual of Omaha's Wild Kingdom*. There weren't a lot of animals evident in the northern part of the valley. What was there were mainly domestic ones, particularly goats, camels, and cattle. It was an irony of the famine that, even at its height in 1992, cattle were being exported out of Marka for sale in Yemen. Of the wild animals we did see, the most prevalent were warthogs. These were more common near the southern part of the valley, especially around Kurtenwary. They were large, violent animals; the Somalis were scared of them. One charged a group of soldiers, and it took a surprisingly large number of bullets before it finally keeled over dead. I was surprised the Somalis didn't eat the animals, but I was told that pork was *halal*. This seemed odd; I mean, the Somalis were not exactly fiercely Islamic in most other aspects of their lifestyle. It was strange that in the middle of a supposed famine they still drew the line at pork. There were a few antelopes that we saw only at extremely long range and which took off as soon as they spotted us. Clearly the locals eat those, I'd thought. There was also a small dog like an antelope that one of the soldiers gleefully identified as a dik-dik. All those nights watching the Discovery Channel weren't wasted after all, but there were no elephants or zebras.

There was a greater variety of birds: blackbirds that flew in great, cloudlike flocks and white birds with long bills that followed the cows around. In the forest there were some persistent birdcalls at night but nothing like the soundtrack of a Tarzan movie. The most noticeable bird in the valley was a cranelike white bird with a black head and a long beak that was bent slightly downward. It stood about three to four feet tall and traveled in flocks of twenty to thirty. It must have been the mating season or something, because every time we saw these birds they seemed to be humping one another or trying to. The troops christened them "black-headed fucker birds," or BHFBs, and the name stuck. They could be guaranteed to spook up if anyone got too close to them, making a squawk-shriek noise while doing so. This made them a serious impediment to sneaking up on anyone. Of course, it worked both ways: if a bunch of them took off in the distance, you knew that something had spooked them. The BHFBs were just another little weird thing we had to deal with. In the beginning of January, a few days after we were established in Marka, Lieutenant Colonel Sikes called the staff together and informed us that we would be responsible for the entire lower Shabele valley area from Afgoi to south of Brava. To keep control over this area—referred to as HRS Marka—and keep the relief supplies going, we had one understrength infantry battalion. My first impression when Lieutenant Colonel Sikes told me this was that he had to be kidding. UNITAF really didn't expect us to cover this whole area. It was silly to think we could. The whole 10th Mountain Division would have trouble securing it. Then I saw that he wasn't smiling.

Sikes gave us the gist of it in a few minutes. As bad as our area of responsibility was, we were by no means in a unique situation. He pointed out that the whole country was in the same boat. The Canadians with one battalion in Belet Uyene, the Marines in Bardera and Baidoa, 2d Brigade with just a rifle company and Echo Company in Baledogle. This last was really screwy. Here was our next higher headquarters being task organized to perform the same function of a rifle battalion (that is, control of an HRS) but having to borrow troops from us to do it because brigade headquarters is just that, *headquarters*. There are no line companies at brigade level; they're all down in battalions. This ad hoc solution was forced on Major General Arnold by the artificial troop ceiling placed on the 10th Mountain Division. More than ever, the shortsightedness of the troop ceiling that didn't allow us to bring the whole brigade of three infantry battalions and one field artillery battalion was having a negative impact on operations. Battalions were being asked to do much more than they were designed or trained to do. The 2d Brigade HQ was completely misutilized. There wasn't any choice.

Sikes, along with Joe Occhuzzio, me, and the rest of the staff, sat down to review our options. If the boss was good at one thing, it was defining a problem and coming up with a mission statement. On a piece of butcher paper he outlined the tasks facing us. The sheer magnitude of the thing stunned the members of the staff for a few minutes, but contributing to Lieutenant Colonel Sikes's analysis became productive. The boss had gotten us used to eating elephants a bite at a time. Besides, we were the 2-87 staff: pick up after hurricanes, deploy at Christmas, disarm gunmen, run an airfield, quell riots, escort convoys, and feed people—no problem. Now we were going to be the only law west of the Pecos, so to speak. As Mike Klein would say, "cool."

So we sat in a derelict house by the Marka seashore and came up with tasks to be accomplished. We were just a normal infantry battalion staff handed the reins of government: Jim Sikes, forty-one, from the Citadel; Joe Occhuzzio, thirty-seven, from Florida State; Martin Stanton, thirty-six, from Florida Tech. We were a normal group of men for what you'd find in a U.S. Army infantry battalion. Like improv actors performing without a script, we came up with thoughts and suggestions as to how we would go about business in HRS Marka. Sikes led the discussion and kept us on track with the guidance that was coming out of 10th Mountain HQ and the JTF. Our overall mission and the key tasks to accomplish it were pretty diverse. Broken down, the key tasks looked like this:

- Establish a secure environment for the NGOs to work in, for relief supplies to be distributed, and for commerce to flow freely.
- Restore clan elders as the authority in their communities.
- Establish governing bodies (town councils) in each town, based on the traditional tribal elder system, which were recognized and accepted by all clan members.
- Establish a HRS Marka regional council of elders from all the major population centers.
- Establish local police forces under the authority of these councils.
- Promote and assist in weapons turn-in from various armed factions, and promote the return of refugees to their native villages or, if those villages did not exist, to their nearest clan members.
- Assist UNITAF engineers in restoring the road network and other key public works.

Our first problem was establishing a secure environment, not only in escorting and protecting NGOs and UNITAF aid agencies but in providing security for the population of the lower Shabele valley against bandits. To do this we had to take on both the armed factions in the valley and the bandits. We started by putting the armed factions in HRS Marka into their place. One of the battalion's tasks was to enforce General Arnold's "four nos" (no crew-served weapons, no technicals, no checkpoints, and no bandits). The first two we accomplished relatively swiftly, those being the two easiest. What crew-served weapons we did not find and confiscate were hidden carefully against the day we would be gone. Technicals were either hidden or disarmed and turned back into pickup trucks. In a short time, the most visible signs of the anarchy in Somalia were no longer anywhere in sight. The armed factions, such as the SNA, the USC, and the Ali Tihad, agreed to keep their weapons on their compounds and not to put armed fighters on the street. Getting the armed political groups to toe the line was initially much easier than I had anticipated. However, it is useful to remember that this was during the early days of the deployment and the Somalis were still a little overawed by us. They had not yet learned of our limitations or our confusion in end-state objectives. For the short term, at least, we had a cosmetic victory.

Removing the bandit threat from HRS Marka would be a lot more complicated. If the first two "nos" were fairly straightforward, the next two—no visible weapons and no checkpoints—would be a lot more complicated. Removing these threats was central to what we felt "success" looked like for HRS Marka. One major reason that UNITAF forces deployed to Somalia was that bandit groups were preventing food supplies from reaching feeding centers and starving people. This threat was quickly removed by the convoy escort system established by U.S. and coalition forces. However, in addition to stopping and looting food convoys, the bandit groups in Somalia also preyed on normal Somali citizens and civilian traffic. In spite of the fact that the escorted convoys were safe, banditry continued to flourish. When UNITAF forces came by, bandits would simply hide their weapons and become indistinguishable from normal Somalis. So commerce continued to suffer. As a result, we began conducting counter-bandit operations in the lower Shabele valley region. These operations would follow the four "nos" to the letter. That is to say, armed individuals were disarmed and anyone caught in the act of banditry was apprehended.

Checkpoints, which were roadblocks made up of debris and maybe an old board to act as a gate, and bandits went hand in hand. Most banditry in the Shabele valley revolved around the roads and the commerce taking place. Typically, the bandits would set up their checkpoints after dark, then stop traffic for the remainder of the evening, taking money, weapons, and property, but rarely food, which was too heavy to carry and of which they already had plenty.

Our counterbandit operations consisted of both overt presence—mounted and dismounted patrols—and clandestine operations involving platoons and squads. The nature of these operations was largely low-intensity combat. Most did not result in contact. A few did, and even then results were mixed. The ROE, although fairly liberal for force protection, did require a threat to U.S. forces before engagement could commence. U.S. personnel were cleared to shoot if at any time they felt in imminent danger of lethal violence. Otherwise they had to challenge the Somalis before they shot. This little caveat required our forces to attempt to halt or capture Somalis with weapons prior to shooting them. Only if a Somali was clearly involved in robbing or endangering the lives of Americans or others were we clear to open a surprise engagement. Otherwise we could engage only if a Somali's weapon was not dropped on command, or if it came up in a threatening manner.

Complicating this even further was the nature of the enemy. The bandits of the lower Shabele valley region were unlike any previously encountered by U.S. forces. There was no Viet Cong–like infrastructure that could be destroyed, and no real chain of command. Unlike the highly organized forces of the warlords and political groups in Mogadishu, most bandit groups ranged from three to ten men, all related by blood or having come from the same village. Each bandit group had its own identity, character, and personality. The groups did not work together and, indeed, robbed one another if given the chance. They operated in the same area, normally along stretches of road. Here they would halt all traffic at scratch-built checkpoints. They were normally armed with small arms from any one of a dozen countries representing fifty years' worth of military weapons development. Some weapons were well maintained; most were poorly functioning junk. Many bandits had only a single magazine of ammunition. None encountered had more than a hundred rounds per rifle; most had less than thirty.

They would rarely initiate contact with UNITAF forces. When encountering them, they hid their weapons, then stood around looking like any other Somali. Their standard action, if surprised, was to fire a few shots and try to break contact. As opposed to some of the more organized warlord forces engaged by the battalion later in Kismayu, the bandits of the lower Shabele always tried to break contact when engaged.

To sum it up, the tactical problem faced by Task Force 2-87 infantry was as follows:

- Bandits operated in small groups, on whom it was hard to build an intelligence base.
- They became active only when we were not around.
- They hid their weapons if they knew or thought we were coming. Then they looked like everyone else.
- They broke contact if surprised, so we had only a brief window of opportunity to engage them.
- The ROE often prevented us from engaging without warning. We had to challenge them first unless we were fired upon or actively threatened.

Add these factors together and it made for some frustrating nights. Still, counterbandit operations were our mission. Without even breaking stride from our occupation of Marka and establishment of security there, we set out to provide a safe environment in the lower Shabele valley.

We had an inauspicious start. We began by extensive patrolling of the forests along the Afgoi-Kismayu highway. We reasoned that because this was where most of the robberies and relief supply hijacking incidents happened, the bandits must be based in the forests. We sent out numerous squad-sized patrols to saturate an area to try to make contact with the bandits. We didn't find a thing. This was puzzling, because the patrols were thorough in their sweeps of the area and bandit activity was still being reported. After a few days, we realized why we weren't finding anything by beating the bushes looking for bandits. To put it succinctly, we were ap-

Weird sights in Somalia were commonplace; even so, this guy carrying a fish on his head on the beach outside of Brava was strange enough to warrant a snapshot.

Soldiers on a sweep in the lower Shabele Valley. Notice how the "chocolate chip" desert camouflage blends nicely with the surrounding vegetation.

Morgan supporters out in force to show their non-hostile intent during the "peace" marches of late March 1993. Some of the boys and young men have their slings wrapped around their foreheads as a gesture of peace.

Members of the Marka police force. At first they were armed only with truncheons; later we gave them captured AK-47s. They never let us down.

Awards ceremony in Condor Base for soldiers who had distinguished themselves in firefights during the Kismayu fighting.

Weapons captured in the sweep of K-50 airfield south of Afgoi. In the picture are a 75mm recoilless rifle, a Russian 12.7mm DHSK machine gun, 7.62mm rifle ammunition, and several hundred mortar bombs.

TAC-2 driven by Specialist Terry Henry on the beach at Marka. The beaches in Somalia were absolutely beautiful and (at Marka, anyway) safe to swim.

Our dog, Bull's-eye, leaning against a two-quart canteen at Brava. He flourished on MREs and stayed the entire time we were there. We gave him to the 1-22 when we left.

The author with Somalis at Kurtenwary. "Standing around and watching" was the great Somali preoccupation, so anytime we came to town it was a good show. Kurtenwary was not a hostile town like Brava or Kismayu.

The aid station at Condor Base. The engineers put up a new roof on the building (barely visible), and the medics cleaned it up pretty well on the interior. Doc Alexander and WO-1 Sandhammer worked out of here. I don't know who made the Club Marka sign.

Crowd in Brava watching as we brought in the captured bandits from the "cattle rustling" firefight.

The sign reads "UNICEF Feeding Center 3. With education for future generations & domestic beneficiary studies. Please decorate your house before you die." Just another weird thing in Kismayu. Captain Tom Hollis is standing by the sign.

A street sign in Brava. The streets in Kismayu and Marka were similar. Lieutenant Colonel Sikes is to the left.

Crowd scene in Kismayu during the peace marches of late March 1993.

The only photograph I took during the Kismayu riots. We had just come through the crowds in the background and temporarily stopped in the open space. You can see the rock throwers in the middle distance. Shortly after this we captured the grenade throwers.

Major Joe Occhuzzio, the battalion officer and second in command. Never at a loss in the most exasperating circumstances, his calmness in a crisis and professionalism helped hold the battalion together.

The best tactical intelligence officer I have ever known, Capt. Mike Klein, the battalion S2. His imaginative and innovative approaches to intelligence collection, combined with plain hard work, gave us the best intelligence picture possible.

My brilliant operations NCO, Sfc. Scott Hardcastle. He often ran the battalion command post when all the officers were otherwise engaged. We couldn't have succeeded without him.

Lieutenant Colonel James E. Sikes Jr. cleaning his rifle. Although the authorized weapon for a battalion commander is a 9mm pistol, Sikes carried a rifle. This wasn't an affectation. Sikes always led from the front, and he used his rifle at Brava and Kismayu.

Ahmed Omer, our interpreter, the only man in the battalion who could tell the Somalis apart. An American citizen of Somali descent, he was a civilian volunteer working for the Department of Defense. He was also an exceptionally brave man on whose advice we relied heavily.

Captain Gordy Flowers, the A Company 2-87 infantry commander. A five-foot-eight-inch human dynamo and our most aggressive company commander.

Captain Steve Michael, our brilliant S4. He kept the battalion supplied in an area as big as Connecticut and Rhode Island combined.

Building with $20,000 rental fee at Marka.

A sign in Kismayu that was made after the Jess forces were thrown out of town.

The hole we blew in the ship at Brava. The things we did to keep amused.

The author on the beach south of Marka. Beachfront property as far as the eye could see—and no people.

Soldiers on patrol in the lower Shabele Valley. Constant patrolling day and night was necessary to suppress banditry.

UH-60 helicopters inbound to Condor Base to pick up soldiers for a counter-bandit sweep of the Shabele Valley.

Lieutenant Colonel Sikes, Ahmed Omer, and the author on the beach at Marka. Note the derelict pier in the background.

Operation Condor Tow Truck. A five-ton truck dragging a derelict car away from the streets of Marka.

Condor Tow Truck. We were the best show in town that day. Everyone was clapping and cheering at our efforts. It was one of the happiest experiences during our deployment.

Relief supplies on the beach at Marka. They were unloaded off barges and stacked in the open. The supplies consisted mainly of cooking oil and large sacks of lentils and rice. Protecting this from pilferage was one of our main tasks.

proaching the problem as if we were looking for the opposing force (OPFOR) at the JRTC.

There, the superbly trained OPFOR breaks down into small guerrilla cells that U.S. forces have to search out and eliminate. The JRTC OPFOR uses every hiding trick and subterfuge of field craft ever thought of by any guerrilla group. Our tactics there were designed to find guerrillas hiding in the forest, then pile forces onto them once contact was made. Unfortunately, in the lower Shabele valley we weren't fighting a dedicated guerrilla group that was politically motivated; we were fighting bandits—loosely organized groups of yahoos who were out to rob people. We weren't finding them in the forest because they weren't there. They were living in towns among their families, fellow clansmen, and the people whose commerce they robbed. They came out only to set up their checkpoints at night, always where there was traffic. While we were out beating the bushes, they'd walk down the road, set up, and rob people. Clearly a change of operations was in order.

Our goal was to catch the bandits whenever possible but, more importantly, open the roads to commercial and relief traffic. After our initial lack of success patrolling the forests along the major roads, we shifted tactics. We still conducted patrols, both vehicular and on foot, but only along the roads and in the more populated areas. Thus our operations became almost policelike in nature. We immediately became more successful. Robberies and raids on commerce became much less frequent, and the continuous presence of the soldiers along the road became a welcome fact to much of the valley's population.

After the delivery of food to Quorleey, we sent our first food convoy to Brava on 13 January. This was another step into the unknown for us. Brava was supposedly deep bandit country, but then we'd been told the same thing about Marka. We put together an escort force under Kirk Haschak, with Gordy Flowers's company providing the majority of the escort troops. Our plan for clearing Brava was a simple one. Gordy and his men would sneak in at first light and seize the intersection of the road at Mundun that led to Brava. This is where Mike Klein said that most of the bandit activity was reported. Then they would secure the town itself. Kirk and the relief supply trucks would follow when they received word that it was safe. The plan worked. Alpha 2-87 stole into Mundun without warning, surprising and disarming several gunmen and capturing a stock of mines in an old police compound near the intersection. A subsequent sweep of the town revealed all was clear, and Captain Haschak brought up the food convoy.

The decrepit, overloaded trucks were barely able to climb the steep coastal ridge. As they crested the top and started down, disaster struck. The brakes on two of the old trucks failed, and they went hurtling off the steep, winding road and down the hillside in wrecks that were as spectacular as anything in a Hollywood movie. The drivers managed to jump out just in time. The vehicles and their loads were total losses. Almost as bad, a humvee swerving to avoid the trucks hit a rock and was immobilized. Fortunately for us, just as Joe Occhuzzio and I were wondering how we'd get this humvee back, who should fly in but the 10th Mountain's aviation brigade commander (Colonel Dallas) on a familiarization flight of the area. Joe explained the problem to him and Dallas was happy to help. While we were giving him the necessary radio frequencies, the support platoon quickly loaded the slings necessary for the UH-60 to carry a humvee. Within twenty minutes of Kirk's first call, we had a UH-60 en route to him, and less than an hour later Colonel Dallas had the humvee dropped off at Marka and was gone with a wave. Kirk told us later that he was impressed with such a quick turnaround on a request for a recovery—and by a full colonel too. Joe Occhuzzio played it with a beautifully straight face and said it was nothing special; he did stuff like that all the time. Once the humvee was recovered and the food unloaded in a warehouse, the escort returned to Marka, arriving just before dusk.

Besides the stock of mines captured at Mundun, Alpha Company also captured a wheezing armored car of the Italian Oto Melera 6614 type. The Somalis had managed to keep it in operation through all the chaos, and it had become sort of a "Mad Max" battleship in the hands of the SNA chief of Brava. Or at least it had been, until Alpha Company 2-87 captured it from its snoozing crew without a fight. The SNA chief of Brava was hopping mad about it. The vehicle's presence had allowed him to exact tribute from the buses that infrequently took the road from Mogadishu to Kismayu. Even a bus with armed guards would not argue with an armored car. Now, in one fell swoop, we made a major dent in his business. Gordy and his boys rode triumphantly back into Condor Base, with the old armored car gasping along at the rear. A few hours later, the SNA chief of Brava came, bold as brass, to demand his armored car back. Lieutenant Colonel Sikes listened to his demands impassively, then politely told him that the vehicle was a "technical" and therefore subject to confiscation. I was for blowing it up right in front of the son of a bitch. However, Sikes correctly pointed out that if we ever did reestablish a Somali government, they might want their military property back. So we would hang on to the armored car, keeping it in our motor park. The SNA chief left in a huff, muttering darkly that we'd better not come down here again.

Our next convoy was to Kurtenwary, a town in the boondocks about halfway to Brava but farther into the interior of the valley. There had been a report of bandits looting the food distribution warehouse there, so we wanted to replenish it and at the same time show the flag. The drive out was long and boring. It took us through the town of Goobyene, a nasty little village along the road to Kismayu. Although we had transited this far south before to take relief supplies, this was the first time I personally had come this way. Goobyene looked like the African version of an Old West village—one main street with buildings on either side. It had the added attraction of several waist-deep holes in the street brimming with foul water. From one of the holes, the legs of a donkey in rigor mortis protruded. The place stank. Children jumped and splashed in the puddle with the dead donkey and the adults just sat listlessly in front of the buildings. It was dismal but, fortunately, fairly brief; soon we were past Goobyene, back on the open road. Kurtenwary itself was a small village on a secondary road west of the main Afgoi-Kismayu highway. It had a few modern buildings and another large red and white radio tower. The people were friendly but skittish. The robbing of their food warehouse had been a blow to them, and the bandits had terrorized the villagers, killing a few of them. There was an ICRC hospital in Kurtenwary, run by Somali staff and a small refugee community. When we got there, many told us that others had fled due to bandits. All we could do was turn over the food to the ICRC representatives, who would put it in a large, modern warehouse on the outskirts of town. They had a few armed guards, but I had no doubt that the bandits would return. I made a mental note to tell Lieutenant Colonel Sikes that we had to do a sweep through this area and increase our presence. It was little tragedies such as the looting of the Kurtenwary warehouse that brought home the frustration of trying to create a secure environment in an area as large as HRS Marka with one understrength infantry battalion. We couldn't keep a permanent presence in places such as Kurtenwary, so the bandits were always in business.

In addition to security operations in Marka, counterbandit patrolling, and convoy escort, the battalion also did several cordon and search operations. These were conducted when the battalion obtained intelligence of bandit operations in a certain area. This information was normally in the form of human intelligence (HUMINT) based on interrogations or volunteered by locals. Much of this information had to be taken with a grain of salt. Locals would often inform on one another in order to have us go in and disarm their neighbors. These newly disarmed people would then be easy prey for the people who had informed on them. Over time we developed a good intelligence base on where selected bandit groups were operating in the valley.

Mike Klein would go out with patrols as often as he could, particularly if the intelligence for a specific operation looked promising. These operations did not always succeed, but he felt obligated to share firsthand in the efforts that his intelligence produced. Sometimes this was rewarded by weapons caches found and bandits captured; sometimes it was an empty search and a long wait for nothing. A small operation that we had particularly high hopes for was based on information that bandits were going to raid a small village near Jannelle and rob a particular man who lived there of his truck. Because the intelligence came from a Somali informer who had been correct in the past, we sent out a platoon, which set up three squad-sized ambushes on the routes in and out of Jannelle. Mike himself and the platoon command group, along with the reserve, spent the night in a swamp near the house, being eaten alive by mosquitoes while waiting for the bandits to show up. They never did, and everyone was bummed out. Any number of things could have gone wrong. Whatever the cause, the stakeout was a dry hole. On the other hand, no one had stolen the man's truck by the time we left the valley three months later.

K-50 Airfield Operation (14 January 1993)

One of the areas of frequent bandit activity was the airfield south of Afgoi near the small village of Lantabur. This was one of the main khat delivery sites in Somalia. Khat was a mildly narcotic stimulant chewed by virtually everyone in the country. It does not grow in Somalia and is imported from Kenya. The traffic in khat is hugely profitable. Many bandits in the valley were either involved in the khat trade or preyed on the traders. Unfortunately, they also preyed on normal commerce in the valley. The airfield was a constant hub of activity, and our HUMINT about the banditry that occurred around it was fairly consistent. We decided to conduct a cordon and search of the area in order to catch the bandits in the act. In order to catch as many of the bandits and search as many khat traffickers as possible, we decided to clandestinely emplace an observation post (OP) to watch the activities at the airfield. This way we could develop a confirmed intelligence base on the periods of maximum activity.

The plan for the cordon and search of K-50 came from Gordy Flowers, the Alpha Company commander. He maintained that we would have to keep surveillance on the airfield in order to get an idea of peak operating hours. Once this was done, we could move quickly and establish the cordon and catch the greatest number of bandits at the airfield. Keeping a constant "eyes on" from OPs that we'd emplaced earlier would allow us to do this. Lieutenant Colonel Sikes and I at once saw the logic in Gordy's plan, and we made it the battalion scheme of maneuver with few modifications. The challenge was to establish surveillance on the place without tipping our hand.

The reconnaissance plan for the operation called for Alpha Company's antitank section to be inserted clandestinely. They would observe the airfield for up to three days, cataloging flights and numbers of people and vehicles present at any given time. Due to the relative openness of the terrain, a single OP, able to observe from the tree line to the east of the airfield, was deemed sufficient. Because of the distance between the OP and the battalion headquarters, a retransmission (RETRANS) signal site was set up to ensure communications with battalion headquarters. A reaction platoon would be approximately five kilometers away, co-located with the RETRANS team should it become necessary to reinforce the OP.

If the pattern of daily activity held true, on 16 January the battalion would conduct a cordon and search of the airfield. Because it was Gordy Flowers's idea, Sikes figured it was only fair that Alpha 2-87 would provide the majority of troops. The cordon would have three blocking positions, one inserted by air and two by ground. The western flank of the cordon consisted of mainly open ground and would be secured by helicopters. We left Gordy to execute the insertion of his observation post team under Staff Sergeant Evans, the AT section leader. Although we had the skeleton of a plan, I figured that we'd get at least two days of observations with which to refine it.

Unfortunately, the humvee inserting the antitank section

got stuck in a conspicuous place along a trail in the early morning hours of the fourteenth. Although the section was camouflaged, we did not wish to lose the element of surprise. Alpha 2-87 immediately launched along the beach to link up with the reaction platoon and get into position east of the OP. Meanwhile, the resupply convoy to Baledogle airstrip, under Joe Occhuzzio, was dragooned into providing the southern blocking position. Coordination was made for aircraft, but all there was available was the daily logistics flight of two UH-60s. These were quickly attached to us until 1200. While everyone was scrambling to get into place, the OP called in a tremendous amount of activity at the airfield. Lieutenant Colonel Sikes decided to execute the operation at 1100 because this was the earliest that all ground elements would be in position and the aviation elements could be used.

The adjusted scheme of maneuver that was developed for the operation was fundamentally the same. Alpha 2-87 would provide the balance of the forces, with the XO's resupply convoy providing a blocking position along the main road south of the airfield. Alpha would move along the coast in humvees and approach the airfield along the dirt track until it was short of the OP position. The Baledogle convoy would hold in the vicinity of Mundun, then move up the road until the blocking position was reached. Simultaneously, Alpha's air assault platoon would set down on the road south of Lantabur and north of the airfield. Upon discharging the troops, the helicopters would move off to loiter positions to the west of the airfield in order to discourage flight over the open ground. Once the air insertion went in, Alpha Company would move in from the east and sweep through the airfield complex, searching all vehicles and huts for weapons and detaining any bandits who offered resistance.

The operation went off almost flawlessly, with the helicopters dropping off the air assault platoon at the same time that the convoy rolled into position to set up a blocking position to the south. Alpha moved in from the east and began its search of the airfield and the few vehicles that stayed. The establishment of all key blocking positions in the cordon was nearly simultaneous.

As soon as the Somalis saw the helicopters fly in and disgorge troops, the airfield literally became a boiling mass of vehicles frantically leaving as fast as they could. Most traveled north and were stopped and searched by the northern blocking position. A few tried to go west, away from the troops. The helicopters performed their blocking role brilliantly, pursuing the odd vehicles that tried to escape in this direction and herding them back to the road and our checkpoints. The helicopters were assisted by elements of the 3-17 Cavalry who had been conducting familiarization flight operations in the area. After hasty face-to-face coordination on the ground, the 3-17 commander, Lieutenant Colonel Kelly, quickly agreed to provide a one-gun ship and two scout helicopter teams to assist the battalion in maintaining the western end of the cordon. The five helicopters were intimidating and were successful in keeping the Somali vehicles on the road. They were also a key factor in removing any inclination to fight from the Somali bandits. No vehicle inside the cordon escaped without being searched.

The vast majority of the Somali vehicles searched contained nothing but khat, which we let them keep. We confiscated about a dozen discarded rifles found on the road leading to the checkpoint. A much bigger haul was found in two abandoned Mercedes dump trucks at the airport. These trucks were filled to the brim with box after box of small-arms ammunition and hundreds of rifle grenades and rocket-propelled grenade (RPG) rounds. In addition, there were three heavy machine guns, an RPG-7, and a 75mm recoilless rifle. Apparently we had interrupted a major weapons shipment from an arms cache in our area of operations to the warlord forces in Mogadishu (whose forces, we never found out).

The Somalis were relieved that we had not taken their khat and even mentioned that it might not be a bad thing if we kept a permanent presence at the airfield—fewer thieves around that way. Considering this, I mulled over the law of unintended consequences, because I was sure that we hadn't been sent to Somalia to protect the drug trade. At any rate, the search of all the vehicles stopped by our checkpoints concluded around 1400, and all elements returned to the battalion base site at Marka around 1530. This was the battalion's first big arms haul in Somalia. There would be others.

The Big Cache (23 January 1993)

A few days after the K-50 mission, Alpha Troop of the 3-17 Cavalry, the one ground troop of the divisional cavalry squadron, was doing a sweep of the area south of the airfield. They were accosted by a Somali who said that he could show them the location of a large arms cache. The Somali man took them to a sand quarry, where two semi-tractor-trailer vans were dug into the side of the pit. The troops immediately secured the area and notified 2d Brigade. Brigade detailed us to take responsibility for the cache site, and Bravo Company 2-87 was given the mission to secure the vans and conduct an expanded search of the area. The search revealed seven more vans, completely buried in a manner similar to the others that were half exposed. Inside the vans was a bounty of weapons and ammunition. I went out the next day to look at it with Lieutenant Colonel Sikes. It seemed as though we had found the mother lode of recoilless rifles, mortars, and machine guns. The troops just kept pulling more weapons and ammo out of the vans. Soon, almost a twenty-five-meter swimming-pool-sized portion of the sandpit was covered with weapons, all laid out according to type. There were also literally thousands of rounds of mortar and recoilless rifle ammunition, as well as a large amount of small-arms ammunition for the machine guns. Apparently the vehicles we had seized at K-50 airfield a week prior had been a shipment from this site to Mogadishu. Fortunately for us, their drivers had been unwilling to pass up an opportunity to trade in khat and had subsequently abandoned their vehicles when we'd sprung our trap. Here was the rest of the arsenal. It was a truly impressive haul, enough to completely outfit a brigade-sized infantry unit with mortars, machine guns, and heavy antitank weapons. The final count on what we'd captured was twenty-six 106mm recoilless rifles, thirty .50-caliber machine guns, twenty mortars (82mm and 120mm), more than a hundred small arms of various types, thousands of rounds of recoilless rifle and mortar ammunition, and several hundred mines.

This was the biggest single haul of arms ever found outside of Mogadishu. The 3-17 Cavalry could be justifiably proud in finding it. The problem now was what to do with it. We couldn't leave a guard on it indefinitely, and we didn't have the trucks to drag it back to Marka, or the storage space to keep it even if we did. Everyone from JTF, division, and brigade came to visit the site and gawk at the number of weapons. Finally the word came down that an explosive ordnance disposal (EOD) team would supervise the demolition of the entire site.

The team that looked at it was enthusiastic. They wanted to get rid of a bunch of aerial bombs that they had collected at Baledogle. They could see no better way than to truck them down to the weapons cache site and blow them all at once. So they did. Truck after truck of old Soviet bombs arrived at the sandpit. The EOD guys put the weapons in the bottom of the pit and placed the mines, shells, bombs, and rockets on top of them. They just kept piling stuff up. Everyone was getting more and more excited. The sense was creeping into all of us that this would be one of those big bangs rarely experienced in one's military career. This would be a virtual Haley's comet of a demolition.

Sadly, when it was ready I wasn't there. I was back in the TOC planning our next operation. (Life goes on.) But even thirty kilometers away I heard it distinctly—*BANG!* Then the ground quivered slightly. Men who saw the explosion used words such as "awesome," "breathtaking," and "cool." A few weeks later, out of curiosity, I went to look at the crater made by the demolition. I am reasonably certain that it could be seen from space.

Shabele Valley Regional Council

Not everything happening during this period involved counterbandit operations. Concurrently with the tactical side of operations was the political and humanitarian effort going on in HRS Marka. After the Marka town council was first established on 14 January, the civil affairs team's next step was to go out into the surrounding towns and contact the elders and leaders. Their goal was a grander-scale version of what was happening in Marka: to reestablish the authority of the elders and set up the HRS regional committee, with representatives from each major town. At first, the civil affairs team and Lieutenant Colonel Sikes did not make much headway, but as Marka improved and became more prosperous and autonomous, the elders of the surrounding towns began to be more receptive. By February we had town councils established for Quorleey, Kurtenwary, and Soblaale. In addition, we attempted to bring other villages, such as Lantabur and Aw-Degle, into the fold.

The constant patrolling was beginning to have an impact, and by the end of January the number of bandits was not nearly as large around Quorleey and Shalamboot as it had been. The roads were safe to travel in the daytime, even for unescorted Somali vehicles.

Afgoi (30–31 January 1993)

The next big operation was a cordon and search of the town of Afgoi. There had been a lot of bandit activity on the roads near Afgoi; for example, on 24 January, an Irish Concern worker and two of her Somali assistants were killed at the Afgoi bridge. The town was reported to be the place where the bandits lived and worked from. In addition, caches of arms from various warlord factions were reported to be stored there, in violation of UNITAF rules.

Military traffic ran through Afgoi to get to Baledogle and

Baidoa in the west and Marka in the south. It was an important road junction, with a bridge across the Shabele River. After the incident described above, an MP platoon was assigned to protect the bridge. No other UNITAF troops were permanently encamped there. Still, enough traffic went through that American soldiers, Marines, and UNITAF military personnel were a common sight.

The problem with conducting operations in Afgoi was the same as in most Somali towns: no maps. This made it hard to plan operations. Therefore, Sikes thought it would be a good idea if the battalion's leaders reconned Afgoi. On 29 January, we loaded up the company commanders and selected personnel on humvees and drove into Afgoi. We turned onto the road leading to the marketplace, near a palatial white villa with tall iron fences and big, shady grounds right out of Faulkner's Mississippi. It appeared completely untouched by the civil war and was clearly under someone's protection. We traveled slowly along the main road running from the villa near the bridge to the market. The road became narrower as we proceeded, and the throng of Somalis thickened as we neared the market. I tried to memorize as many landmarks as possible, such as stores with signs in English or unique buildings, before we came back to do an operation. The Somalis looked perplexed by our presence but weren't unfriendly, just curious. We came to a crowded area near the actual market. I was uncomfortable with the closeness of the crowd to the humvees, and was to the point of recommending to Lieutenant Colonel Sikes that we stop and walk beside the trucks when we took fire.

At first the *pop! pop! pop!* sound didn't seem like much, but instantly there was pandemonium. Everyone dove out of their vehicles and took cover either behind the trucks themselves or on the sides of the streets while the crowded Somalis scattered. Lieutenant Colonel Sikes, Mike Klein, and the men from the lead vehicle charged down the street through the panicked crowd after the gunman, who they'd gotten a glimpse of.

I yelled at Henry to stay with the vehicle while Kirk Haschak and I peeled off to the left. My reasoning for this was that, with the river to the right, the only way the gunman could run was straight or left. Lieutenant Colonel Sikes and his group were already running directly after him. Kirk and I would parallel their pursuit and hopefully catch the gunman if he cut left. A couple more shots off to our right spurred us on. The chase led us through open-air markets right out of *National Geographic* magazine. People scattered in every direction as Kirk and I thundered past. We ran past the camel souk with maybe a hundred camels milling around and testy. At the corner was a camel butcher, with camel heads in a row on a wooden table. The Somalis pointed down the road frantically in a gesture of he went that-away. Finally Kirk and I came to the edge of town near a small building. We searched the building, then stood around for a few minutes. No frantic gunman came bursting out in our direction. After exchanging shots with Lieutenant Colonel Sikes and his group, he probably ditched his weapon and watched us run by. It was fast becoming apparent to us that these gunmen were hard to catch. I began to wish I'd brought a squad radio, because we were out of contact with Sikes and the vehicles. The whole thing took about twenty minutes. Unfortunately, when we got back to the trucks' location, they were gone. We later found out that they had moved out on the assumption they'd meet us on the edge of town.

Haschak and I found ourselves in the middle of the market with no other Americans in sight. Everyone was looking at us curiously, and for a moment I was reminded of the scene in the movie *Animal House* where the fraternity brothers and their dates walked into the bar and quickly realized that they were the only white people there. Kirk and I were like two grains of rice in a glass of chocolate milk. Fortunately, no one was threatening, and little children swarmed around us—a good sign; the kids could be guaranteed to leave at the first sign of trouble.

The nearest Americans were the MPs at the Afgoi bridge, half a mile or so away. I figured that we should join them. So

Kirk and I walked along the road with our entourage of children in tow, pursued by the ribald but good-natured comments of the Somalis (who recognized fools when they saw them). The MPs were surprised to see us but generally nonplussed. We called Lieutenant Colonel Sikes, and the recon party came and recovered us. The whole episode brought home to me the danger of going off half-cocked. Kirk and I got off cheap. Anyway, we'd gotten a good look at Afgoi.

The cordon and search operation for Afgoi was set for 30 January. The plan for cordoning off the town came from 2d Brigade, which would be in charge of the operation. Besides Task Force 2-87 infantry, Tom Wilk's Echo Company; the MP Company; and Alpha Troop, 3-17 Cav would be involved. The line companies would conduct the actual search; the other elements would set up the cordon around Afgoi. The plan was developed by Dave Wood, the brigade S3, and was a good one. It had Wilk's Echo Company, Alpha 3-17 Cav, and the MPs moving into position and establishing the cordon just a few minutes before the rifle companies of Task Force 2-87 conducted a heliborne insertion to the outskirts of Afgoi. Once they landed, the two companies of the 2-87 would begin to search the town for weapons and technical vehicles as well as other bandit-useful equipment (military radios, ammunition, et cetera). It was a simple plan and easy to execute because each unit basically had only one mission to perform. If executed properly, it would give whatever bandits or gunmen there were in Afgoi almost no chance to escape. The brigade order the day before the operation was straightforward. All players worked out their assigned roles and coordinated with one another. Helicopter availability would not be a problem, because this was the only major operation occurring at the time. Our drive-through leaders' recon was not as big a tip-off as you might think. A lot of military traffic went through Afgoi, and occasionally the MPs and other units drove into the town proper. There was nothing to indicate that we'd selected the town for special attention.

The battalion operations order was given later in the day. We would enter the eastern side of town along the main road.

Both companies would sweep toward the river, searching all the houses, with Bravo 2-87 taking the northern half of the town and Alpha 1-87 taking the southern half. My TAC-2 vehicle would travel between the two companies and ensure no gaps were created between them. This would be easy to do, given the built-up nature of Afgoi, which was different from either Wanwaylen or Marka. Unlike Marka, more of the houses in Afgoi were of traditional native construction—mud and sticks—and the streets were more confined in many places. Keeping command and control there at night without maps would be a real challenge.

During this operation, Lieutenant Colonel Sikes would be traveling with Bravo 2-87 initially with his radiomen. He could quickly shift to where the action might develop. Our mortar platoon was emplaced south of town to be able to fire illumination on call and have the illumination canisters—hollow metal tubes, which were the residue of the illumination round and potentially lethal if they fell on a person—impact away from the town and the troops on the cordon.

The battalion CP would set up near the old jail east of town and co-locate with the battalion trains under the overall control of Joe Occhuzzio. All members of Task Force 2-87 understood their missions, and Sikes gave his last-minute instructions. Lieutenant Colonel Sikes, Joe Occhuzzio, Mike Klein, and I sat down and tried to think of anything we'd missed, but we couldn't. I talked briefly with Frank Kirsop and Sergeant First Class Hardcastle on moving the TOC and command and control issues, but they'd already covered all the bases like the pros they were.

The operation began without much fanfare. Everyone was in position and knew his job. The companies were on the pickup zone, and all the elements of the cordon were prepared to go in. As a precaution, Sikes told me to make sure no reporters were on the landing zone, because they might tip off the operation. The brigade S1, Maj. Frank Hannon, was holding them about two miles up the road toward Mogadishu. I joined them there until the first lifts were inbound. The public affairs officer (PAO) and Frank were put out that I wouldn't let them go forward in time to see the first lift go in, but I was still under the illusion that we might get some element of surprise. As it was, there were so many humvees full of public affairs and PSYOPS types driving around on the outskirts of Afgoi that I needn't have bothered. (I found out later that JTF PSYOPS had done a leaflet drop earlier telling the people of Afgoi that we were coming and not to resist. Frank Hannon had been right after all.) The only good press we'd get out of this one was a well-executed air assault. Still, the reporters got to film the second and third lifts, which was something. Soon we had all our troops on the ground and ready to go. It was just about dusk when Lieutenant Colonel Sikes gave the go-ahead.

The actual search was a bust, which of course it would be. Imagine the police in any large city telling the drug dealers by leaflet that they were going to search their houses the next day. In addition, the search was hard to control, because of the rabbit warren of houses and the lack of maps. Initially I tried to create a boundary line between the companies by turning on TAC-2's lights, pointing down one of the main streets. Unfortunately, this interfered with the troops' night sights even several rows of houses over, so I quickly turned off the lights. The two companies proceeded slowly and carefully to keep from crossing over into each other's sector. I traveled between them to ensure they did not get ahead of each other. We painstakingly searched each house, with sleepy and bemused Somalis staring at us blankly. There were a few incidents during the search, such as the couple of shots fired at the circling helicopters. Elements of Echo Company on the cordon and Bravo 2-87 in the search took sniper fire, which was returned by the Bravo 2-87 troops. They chased and captured the sniper. On another occasion, Alpha 1-87 soldiers took several rounds of small-arms fire. The gunmen were seen running and dropping their weapons by the cav helicopters with the night sun infrared spotlight. The weapons—a rifle and an AK-47—were recovered, but the gunmen escaped. On the whole, though, the search had few incidents. The "night sun" infrared searchlight on the helicopters was a big hit. Wearing your night vision goggles when it was flicked on surrounded you in a surreal green daylight that was so strong you could read by it. The scout helicopter from the 3-17 Cav that was equipped with it was much in demand throughout the search.

After a couple of hours it became clear we weren't going to find much. The reporters walked around with the troops and were generally well mannered, although some hid their amusement better than others. By the time they left, we had captured only a couple of weapons. When Sikes called off the operation at about 0300, we had confiscated a total of nineteen, only half of which were in operational condition. The troops moved into assembly areas on the outskirts of town and waited for the trucks and helicopters to pick them up after dawn. The cordon was pulled from around the town shortly after the first lift of troops headed back to Marka. For what it was worth, we had shown our presence in Afgoi. In fact, we'd presenced the hell right out of them.

The troops had been given a little Somali phrasebook, and a few of them began trying to learn the language. The next morning, while we were pulling out of Afgoi, I stopped by some Echo Company vehicles to ask them how the cordon went. As I was talking to them, some young Somali women carrying laundry to the river came walking by. The gunner behind the machine gun on the humvee waved at them and smiled as he spoke what sounded to me like pretty good Somali: *"Etoos Naasa Haaga,"* or something to that effect. The girls giggled and hurried along. The soldier shrugged and said to his buddy, "Didn't work this time." Interested, I asked what the words meant. The gunner, who hadn't noticed me before, hesitated for a second, then grinned. "It means, show us your tits, sir," he said. I had to laugh. It was as good a way as any to end the Afgoi mission.

Afgoi in Retrospect

The Afgoi operation was typical of the schizophrenic nature of the objectives that were being set at that time. On the one hand, UNITAF wanted massive shows of force to intimidate and disarm the bandits, gunmen, and factional forces. On the other hand, we didn't want to provoke fighting. The Afgoi operation failed because UNITAF hadn't decided what was wanted. If we were going to do a straight-up cordon and search, we should have put the cordon in before dawn and started the search at daylight. Needless to say, we should have made no leaflet drops or done anything to tip our hand, such as leaders' recons or unusual vehicle activity. If we were going only for a show of force, we should have come in the early afternoon and been gone by dusk. In retrospect, the night search was a dumb idea. It surprised no one, made it harder to search, and increased the chance of fratricide in the rabbit warren maze that was Afgoi. All that any of us got out of it were a few more gray hairs.

Nonetheless, it had been good practice in many ways. The cordon had been established quickly. A Troop of the 3-17 Cav, the MPs, and Tom Wilk's Echo Company moved into position with dispatch and had their sides of the town sealed just as the air assault elements went in. Had we not warned them, assuming they were there to begin with—a big assumption—we would have trapped any gunmen there were in the town. Furthermore, we gained even more appreciation for how difficult it was to search Somali towns, particularly at night. It also broadened our experience, because Afgoi was different from other Somali towns we had worked in, such as Wanwaylen or Marka. Keeping command and control in such a place, at night, without maps was a challenge and kept everyone on their toes. Although the troops were naturally disappointed at having come up with a "dry hole," their confidence in conducting such an operation was increased. In addition to that, we'd gotten another battalion air assault, and anytime we got to practice that type of complex operation was for the good.

Brigade had controlled the operation well, and neither Lieutenant Colonel Sikes nor I had the impression that we were being jerked around by higher headquarters at any time. Both Colonel Ward and Dave Wood did a good job of

preventing possible screw-ups. The 3-17 Cav troops also offered valuable assistance with their OH-58s and night sun
infrared searchlights. It was a pity there wasn't anything in
Afgoi to find.

After the Afgoi operation, the battalion moved back to
Marka. We soon began the process of renovating the deserted
police compound to accommodate the battalion. Sikes told
me that it looked as though Marka was to be our home for
some time to come. I remember feeling cheerful as we crested
the hill and saw the ocean and the deserted barracks. We were
all looking forward to a saltwater bath and a good night's
sleep.

Condor Caravan (1–20 February 1993)

After the Afgoi operation, we conducted a series of minor security operations in the vicinity of Marka. Squads would
stake out houses and bits of road for bandits reported to be
operating in the area. We also conducted sweeps of specific
villages, searching for weapons. Captain Klein and the scout
platoon spent another long, mosquito-bitten night outside
one village, waiting for a bandit group that never came. Intelligence was rumor, and there was no way of evaluating it. We
were still in the inception stage of building our intelligence
base. Like a cop in a new neighborhood, we didn't know what
was rumor and what was true. Over time we developed a
database of who was trustworthy and gave accurate information and who was not. In the learning process we engaged in
our share of fruitless operations. Now and again a few bandits
would be caught on the road or weapons caches would be discovered. We were making an impact, and the people in the
valley knew we were out there. Bandits didn't roam as freely
as they once did. The NGOs and civil affairs people had a
more secure environment within which to work. However,
this safety applied mainly to the central valley. A higher degree of banditry still occurred in the southern valley around
Brava, where our old friend the SNA chief still held sway.

Further operations were needed to suppress banditry and violations of the "four nos" in these areas.

In addition to the continuous patrolling of selected areas in the valley, we developed a system of what Lieutenant Colonel Sikes called "flying checkpoints," usually consisting of one or two humvees and an infantry squad. They'd be given a series of locations within their company's designated area of operations to move to and set up. The checkpoint itself would consist of the vehicle drawn across the road and one fire team positioned to search anyone who approached. The second fire team would be stationed in overwatch near the road. A checkpoint could be set up in less than a minute. Flashlights and reflectors were made available for night operations.

Placing the checkpoint required judgment. A patrol leader didn't want to place it in such a manner that approaching traffic could spot it too far out and turn off to avoid it. Neither did he want to put it where a vehicle would see it too late to stop. Keeping in mind the poor state of most Somali vehicles, brake failure was much more likely than a cold-blooded attempt to run the roadblock. Having chosen his place, the patrol leader would set up the roadblock and overwatch position and wait for "customers."

In the first few weeks of flying checkpoint operations, we surprised a number of bandits who were going to set up their own "checkpoints" and found themselves relieved of their weapons before they knew what hit them. The flying checkpoints also searched commerce for arms and other military contraband, but never khat; we left the drug trade alone. Sometimes the searches became quite involved; it could be a half-hour proposition to get all the passengers off a dilapidated school bus, search the vehicle and the people, then get them and all of their belongings back on the bus. Normally, a flying checkpoint stayed in one place for only two to three hours. By then, it was reasoned, word would be out and the people we were looking for would start avoiding this particular stretch of road. After about three hours, the checkpoint would pick up and move to another side stretch of road, set up, and wait. The unpredictability of the flying checkpoints was a great hindrance to those bandit groups who relied on vehicles as their prey. They might be able to hide their arms from us, but they were no longer able to range up and down the valley at will. They never knew when they'd run into us.

During this period we continued to suffer from "administrivia" and "minutiae," proving that the army had not yet made the mental transition from peace to war in dealing with Somalia. We continued to lose people to normal permanent change of station/end time of service (PCS/ETS), schools, and questionable reassignments within the division. This led an exasperated Lieutenant Colonel Sikes to include the following in his 4 February 1993 situation report:

> By 15 February, based on current projected losses, TF 2-87 will begin to disband one platoon in each rifle company and use the soldiers for fillers if replacement leaders and soldiers are not provided. The average rifle strength of the squads is six men. This will bring the battalion's combat power potential from nine platoons to six.
>
> The task force was short personnel prior to the deployment (122 soldiers) and has steadily redeployed soldiers for mandated requirements. Red Cross messages, PCS [permanent change of station] and ETS [end time of service] demands cannot be adjusted. PLDC [Primary Leadership Development Course] and BNOC [Basic Noncommissioned Officers' Course] are now in question. Currently the battalion will curtail the redeployment of soldiers as follows:
>
> a. Only Red Cross, doctor requirements, for medical illness of family members
>
> b. PCS: Previous redeploy 60 days prior to PCS. Change to redeploy 30 days prior to PCS
>
> c. ETS: Previous redeploy 90 days prior to PCS (due to ACAP transition). Change to redeploy 30 days prior to PCS
>
> d. TF 2-87 will not participate in Ranger competition
>
> Further, the battalion will identify critical MOS shortages for further operational deletion. PLDC and BNOC soldiers will be deferred until after the battalion redeploys.

A 75B E-7 was sent to DISCOM [Division Support Command] and a 75B E-6 was sent to 2d Brigade (reported to Fort Drum as a change of orders on post). We have been without these personnel and have had critical shortages in PAC [Personnel Action Center] personnel for seven months. In addition, two Ranger-qualified soldiers from Fort Benning light fighters school originally slotted to the battalion have been reassigned by post to the 10th MTN Div light fighters academy.

I urgently request senior officers to review the personnel situation of this battalion and provide guidance to this command. The battalion continues to take great risks in assigning missions to severely understrength rifle platoons in a contingency deployed hostile fire area.

Unfortunately, this rather stark message had only minimal effect. We got a few replacements in, but deploying additional forces (such as Charlie Company or our own scout platoon, both left in Fort Drum) was verboten under the troop ceiling. More importantly, the hemorrhaging of personnel for PCS, ETS, and schools slowed but never stopped. Task Force 2-87 personnel should have been frozen for the duration of the deployment, as units were in Desert Storm. Instead, we always had to keep an eye on our end strength. We hadn't lost a man to enemy action or disease, but we were gradually getting smaller.

Our support arrangements in Marka were maturing. After our move to Marka, the battalion received most of our logistical support from the 210th Forward Support Battalion (FSB), the dedicated support battalion for 2d Brigade, located at Baledogle. However, this necessitated a long turnaround in supply runs. The FSB got all of its supplies out of Mogadishu, and it didn't make much sense to truck them to Baledogle, then down to Marka, if we didn't have to. Because the 548th Corps Support Battalion was coming on line in Mogadishu early in February, Capt. Steve Michaels, the battalion S4, arranged to send our supply run directly to Mogadishu every four days. Subsequently, as more transportation units arrived in country, the 548th transitioned into a "push" system and sent supplies to us. Thanks to these efforts, the supply system got consistently better. Toward the end of March we were even able to open a small post exchange for the soldiers.

In addition, we received assistance from the 43d Engineer Battalion in improving the buildings on our base camp. They worked like beavers on overdrive, putting roofs on the buildings and removing a lot of the debris. They also shored up walls and built permanent latrines. They built showers for the time we would get a shower unit. They hit Condor Base like a tornado that built things instead of destroying them. After three days they had transformed our camp. They brought their field kitchens with them and gave us our first hot meals since we'd arrived in country. They left the next day—an engineer Robin Hood off to do other good deeds. We were all very grateful for their efforts.

The next big operation was Condor Caravan, a two-company sweep through the Shabele valley to suppress banditry and provide a show of force. The first objective was the town of Kurtenwary, where bandit activities and raids on the ICRC warehouse were reported. The Kurtenwary sweep stands out to me mainly because it was an example of those rarest of occurrences, an operation executed exactly as planned. The plan was to encircle the town of Kurtenwary and disarm any armed groups we found there.

Encircling the town was harder than one might think. We didn't have enough helicopters available to put people on all four sides simultaneously. If we couldn't do that, the gunmen would run out the other side into the bush. It was obvious that we would have to send in a ground element as well without exciting the suspicions of any gunmen who happened to be there.

Kurtenwary was about twenty kilometers from the main road running the length of the Shabele valley from Afgoi to Kismayu. The track that led to Kurtenwary was barely one vehicle wide in most places and extremely rutted. It was the only avenue of approach into Kurtenwary that was at all trafficable to wheeled vehicles. Kurtenwary itself was a nondescript place of about twenty permanent cinder-block buildings with sheet metal roofs. A large warehouse on the outskirts was the ICRC local relief supplies depot, and a tall radio tower painted red and white loomed forlornly over the shabby little place. On the other side of town was a feeding center and a hospital run by NGOs. In normal times there would have been, at best, a few hundred people around Kurtenwary. Now there were thousands.

Our scheme of maneuver for Kurtenwary was simple. There would be a ground echelon—the mortar platoon, an antitank platoon, and the PSYOPS guys led by me in TAC-2—and an air echelon, consisting of Lieutenant Colonel Sikes with his TAC-CP and Alpha Company 2-87 and Alpha 1-87. The ground echelon would leave Marka the night before the operation, pass the turnoff to Kurtenwary, and keep going along the Kismayu road, camping about ten kilometers from the turnoff. The next morning, the ground element would backtrack and travel down the Kurtenwary road, blocking all traffic attempting to pass us and detaining all persons traveling from Kurtenwary to keep them from warning the bandits. The column would stop about two miles from the town and wait for the aircraft to give a ten-minute inbound notice. They then would begin moving to assume blocking positions on the north and east of town. The airlifted forces would land to the south and west to establish the remainder of the cordon. Then Alpha Company 2-87 would move in a south-to-north sweep and search the entire town.

We were not expecting any trouble. Searches of this sort normally resulted in finding abandoned weapons or weapons in the possession of persons who claimed to be ICRC guards. However, if there was trouble to be had, we were more than prepared for it. More than two hundred soldiers and a dozen vehicles would surround Kurtenwary from out of nowhere in a matter of minutes.

The ground echelon under my command left Marka in the late afternoon and moved past the Quorleey turnoff to Goobyene (the putrefying donkey was still in the receding waters of the hole in the middle of the road). Thankfully, soon we were past the town and on our way down the deserted road to Brava. We passed the Kurtenwary turnoff and continued for several miles. When we were well away from all known habitation, we pulled about a mile off the road and set up our perimeter for the evening. I wanted to ensure that we had enough light left to get a good defense put together. I had everyone dig in, including the PSYOPS loudspeaker team (much to their annoyance). I wasn't going to take the chance of anyone surprising us; we kept a quarter of the troops on watch throughout the night. It passed without incident, save for those odd animal sounds you really do hear in Africa, just like in the movies.

The next morning we were moving down the Kurtenwary road. The asphalt soon gave way to dirt track, which got worse and muddier as we went on. Off to the side we could see warthog families—daddy, momma, and little babies—running through the bushes.

We detailed the few people who came down the road. Those who left Kurtenwary were not allowed to return and warn the others. We reached the outskirts of town and set up our portion of the cordon just as the air assault of Alpha 2-87 began into the southern side of the cordon and Alpha 1-87 into the western side. Echo Company and the battalion TAC-CP were already in place and the town was sealed off. Lieutenant Colonel Sikes disembarked and joined the headquarters section. It had been a perfect insertion, the best we ever did in Somalia. Now all that remained was to search the town. We took a couple of stray shots as Alpha 2-87 entered the town from the south, but Gordy Flowers's people couldn't see where they were coming from, so they held their fire. The search itself was unavailing, netting only one rifle. People we questioned said that the bandits had moved out a few days previously, so the whole thing was a bust. But we had at least impressed the Somalis by appearing suddenly and sealing off the town. Major General Arnold flew out during the operation to confer with Lieutenant Colonel Sikes. Sikes told General Arnold of his plan to continue to sweep up and down the valley for a few more days, and Arnold approved. Then the general was back in his helicopter and returning to Mogadishu. I think Arnold found Mogadishu frustrating and tried to come out and see his units whenever he could, just for a breath of fresh air.

We set up the battalion CP under a big tree in the field across from Kurtenwary. Sikes, Joe Occhuzzio, and I reviewed our options. We could go up around Aw-Degle to the north or move south to Brava. For me, there was no comparison. Aw-Degle was quiet, whereas Brava was a well-known den of thieves whose chieftain had warned us not to come there again. In my opinion we couldn't let anyone in the valley get away with threatening us. I was all set to make an impassioned plea to go to Brava when Lieutenant Colonel Sikes decided upon just that course of action. So much for mentally preparing my arguments.

The operations order for Brava was typical of how our troop-leading procedures had evolved. The problem with the "traditional" deliberate planning process was that it was too lockstep and time consuming. It was not realistic for the environment we operated in. The abbreviated decision-making process as taught by the infantry school at Fort Benning was just a cut-down timeline version of the deliberate decision-making process. Had we followed all the steps, it still would have taken hours to produce an order. Sikes began the deployment trying to adhere to approved doctrine; the Belet Uyene operation, the Marka occupation, and the Afgoi operation were all orders for which we followed the deliberate decision-making process, but increasingly we didn't have the time. Our orders process by necessity evolved into something much simpler and more abrupt. Basically the boss and I, the XO, the S2, and the S4 would discuss and war-game courses of action based on what we knew about our mission and the enemy. This was normally done in the TOC but also happened on the hood of a humvee. From this discussion, Sikes would outline his chosen course of action and I would develop the scheme of maneuver to support it. The XO and the S4 worked on the logistical plan. Because we had an ROE that basically precluded the use of mortars, fire support—normally an important part of any operations order—was almost never mentioned, and the mortars just moved with the battalion. We could produce a battalion operations order in two and a half to three hours. Instructors at Benning and observer controllers at the NTC and JRTC would have pursed their lips in disapproval, but it worked.

The plan for Brava was simple. We would upload the TOC and form the battalion in march elements. At night we would strike out across country for the valley road and from there move south to Brava. We would sweep the town for a few days with a rifle company, the scouts, and the TOW platoon, really making our presence felt. So much for the SNA chief's threats.

We left Kurtenwary that night and moved eastward overland, beating the bush until we reached the main highway. The movement itself was fun. We spooked a lot of animals who were not used to crazy Americans driving through the bush at midnight with no lights on. From a land navigation perspective, the movement was a no-brainer: just keep going east until you hit the first paved road, then turn south. I giggled to myself when I thought of the SNA chief and how he'd come to our camp at Marka demanding his armored car back. We'd give him a nice wake-up call.

We went through Mundun at dawn. Not a person stirred. Only a few dying fires showed any sign of life in the little town, which, like Goobyene, had houses on either side of the road. On the turnoff to Brava was a large, white-walled compound, which had been a police post. There were some derelict pieces of engineer equipment around the station as well. No doubt the facility had been a combination of road maintenance and law enforcement activities. Both functions of government were long defunct in this area. We turned left and climbed the coastal ridge toward Brava. At the crest of the ridge was a radio tower similar to the one at Kurtenwary; it was another impotent link in the country's communications network. We crested the hill and began weaving our way down the turns leading to Brava. I could see where losing your brakes here would cause a spectacular crash and could only marvel that the truck drivers in Kirk's convoy had not been killed a few weeks earlier. Coming down the hillside, we had a good view of Brava.

The Lonely Planet guide says the following about Brava: "This is a beautiful old Arab town five KM off the main Kismayu road. Take a visit to the leather tannery where you can get cheap leather sandals for 80 to 150 Somali shillings. A cheap place to stay is the Kolombo Hotel on the right at the entrance to town. It has large airy rooms for 150 Somali shillings a double. There are no good eating places in town."

It was a pretty place, with white houses and buildings set against the pearl blue water, with the deeper blue of the ocean behind it. It seemed in better shape than many places we'd been. Most of the houses still had their roofs, and only a few buildings showed any damage. After the stifling heat of the valley, the fresh, breezy salt air was cool and invigorating. We passed the wreck of an armored car similar to the one we had captured earlier. There was yet another one just visible at the bottom of a gorge (probably another victim of brake failure).

We established the battalion CP in a walled compound at the beginning of town in front of the Kolombo Hotel. The compound was abandoned and had a decent gate. There was one apartment building with its roof still on and two more buildings without their roofs. More importantly, the hotel had good fields of fire and was separated from the town. Geoff Hammil's company went off to the south and established its base camp around another walled compound.

While these base camps were being set up, we began our patrols. Brava was a small town, and a company-sized element took only about an hour to cover it completely. We weren't really looking for anything, just wanting to make our presence known. Lieutenant Colonel Sikes met with the SNA chief of Brava and told him that we'd be in the area from now on and any bandit activities would no longer be tolerated. The SNA chief was a bit flustered to see all the troops in Brava, but he tried to make a show of bravado, saying that he could not be responsible for the activities of bandit groups and that Americans "were not safe." Our response to this was to stay for two days and patrol the town. We had to be careful. We were not going to stay permanently in Brava. It would have been a good place to set up a company, but we did not have the troops (that old "troop ceiling" showing its effects again). Anyone who overtly supported us would no doubt suffer the wrath of the SNA chief once we left. So we just patrolled day and night and had a good laugh at his discomfiture.

The second day in Brava we had a bit of action. Some Somali men coming in from the valley claimed that their cattle herd had been taken by bandits. Sikes and a platoon from Alpha 1-87 immediately gave chase, guided by the victims. They caught up with the cattle herd, and when the bandits saw the troops, a running gun battle ensued that lasted for about five minutes. Many shots were fired by both sides, and a grenade was thrown by one of the bandits. Fortunately it did not explode. Lieutenant Colonel Sikes's radioman wounded one of the bandits, and four others were captured. The rest got away. The thankful Somalis departed with their cattle, and the wounded bandit was brought back to the headquarters compound, where he was treated by Chief Sandhammer and the medics. The captured bandits were later taken back to Marka and turned over to the Marka police (who subsequently let them go). I kidded the boss about chasing cattle rustlers.

The environment in Brava was not at all like that of Marka. We were not getting any cooperation from the SNA/USC chief. On 18 February, Sikes wrote in his daily sitrep the following civil affairs summary for the past twenty-four hours.

The civil affairs team has been in the lower Shabele River valley since 12 February conducting operations in the towns of Kurtenwary, Shabele, and Brava. The following is a summary of operations to this point with operations scheduled to continue through 21 February. USC/SNA has control of Brava. The current ongoing situation in Brava is:

• Traditional leadership has been suppressed and replaced by the local district commissioner [card-carrying member of the USC] and his representatives. Any traditional leader who is outspoken is paid a "visit" during the night. Leaders who have had dealings with coalition forces have been beaten or have had a "visit." This list includes private citizens of the community. A special "tax" has to be paid to the USC when individuals talk to coalition forces. This tax is also paid as a course of life within the community.

• Beatings and intimidation are a fact of life within the community. After nightfall, window shutters and doors are locked and people await another night of violence. Little night activity occurs.

• The commercial market has few vendors for a community of this size. A special tax must be paid. The sultan has stated that the current situation is not life and death; however, coalition forces are much needed because the entire community and its activities are not under any legitimate control. The traditional leaders have stated that when the coalition forces leave Brava, they will leave also because they fear that they will be beaten or worse when the coalition forces are not around to witness the acts by the USC.

• The local ICRC guards (thirteen) are from two clans (Hawiye and Habr Gedir) and seem to be the quick reaction force for the USC. They do not guard resupply trucks, and kitchen trucks never make it to local kitchens without being looted by USC, bandits, or local clans. The local sultan has stated that he has directed his clan to rob the trucks for two reasons: to get food for his people and to get a coalition force presence in the area.

• The DOD-hired civilian translator working for the CA team has been threatened by the USC in the presence of the CA team: "If you come back to Brava we will get you." Informants in Marka have stated that four Brava USC members were sent to "get" the translator following the earlier confiscation of an armored car from Brava. CA is continuously under the watchful eye of the USC. The USC members in Brava have stated, "Who are you? We are the USC and have fought against Barre" and "Who is more powerful than the USC?"

• The sultan has stated that he will incorporate leaders from all the clans into a community council and police force (if these two organizations get off the ground, which is doubtful considering the choke hold the USC has on this town). He also stated that each clan would be free to select its own representative.

Of course nothing came of attempting to set up a Brava town council. We didn't have the troops to dedicate to a permanent presence. Without them, the bad guys would just bide their time until we left. The best we could do was roust the SNA chief's men when they engaged in banditry on the road. This impotence was yet another example of the far-reaching ill effects of the troop ceiling. A single infantry company or artillery battery could have secured Brava and broken the power of the thugs. As it was, all we could do was sweep through the area when the banditry on the road got too bad and help succor the refugees from Brava in Marka.

After a second day of patrols, Lieutenant Colonel Sikes took the majority of the battalion back to Marka, leaving me with Alpha 1-87 and a cross section of HHC under Kirk Haschak consisting of an antitank platoon, the scout platoon, and a small support section. We would stay in communications with Brava by means of the TACSAT team from 18th Airborne Corps, which would be attached to us. My mission was to keep our presence in Brava for a few more days, then come back on 20 February. After two days in the little town we already knew it well. I sent the scouts into the town to map it and had the infantry patrol every few hours day and night. The antitank platoon I sent out on recons of the surrounding area, back over the ridge and into the valley. Soon things were running along in a comfortable routine. The SNA chief and his men were sullen but resigned. We set good security at night and stayed alert.

The first night of my little independent command, the antitank platoon brought in a tidbit of information. After Sikes left, a roadblock was constructed on the main road leading to Kismayu for the first time since we'd come to Brava. This was the first act we had seen of outright defiance to our presence. No doubt about it, the bandits had taken our lessening of presence in Brava as the cue to resume their activities. Clearly the game was afoot. Rather than react, though, we would just watch. It was hard to sneak up on the bandits, harder still to catch them. I decided we'd keep up our present activities and wait for a chance.

In the meantime the patrols went on, and by the end of the second day things were boring. The TACSAT guys adopted a puppy. I was not too keen on this because the local animals were in pretty bad shape, with mange and other diseases. I told them they couldn't take the dog back to Marka and would have to leave it here. I told them it would probably starve, so we'd have to shoot it when we left. Brilliant psychology on my part; I'd thought that it would make them give it back to the Somali they bought it from. Instead, they named it Bull's-eye, and he continued to flourish on corned beef hash MREs. They set to work building a little parachute for it. Their intent was to drop it from the big derelict microwave tower on the hill above Brava. I thought about ordering them to get rid of the dog, but it wasn't hurting anything. They had a few days to think it over, and I had a few days to come up with a better solution than just plugging the little guy.

On the second morning while we were alone at Brava, we test-fired our weapons by shooting at the crabs on the beach. It was quite a test of marksmanship, because after the first rounds the crabs scuttled like crazy across the wet sand where the beach met the water. They moved at such great speed that it took some skill to pick them off. When a crab was hit, it just exploded in a shower of blood and legs. Then its buddies would run over and start eating the eviscerated remains and in turn be rendered by further bullets. We all test-fired our weapons for about half an hour, plinking crabs with the thoughtless, bloodthirsty enthusiasm of thirteen-year-old boys with their first .22. The radios were quiet, and I sat in the vehicle for a while on radio watch and let the boys go out and shoot. I listened to the radio for a few minutes. Nothing. I did communications checks with everyone. Everybody answered right away. Show of force patrol in the town—no problem. Scouts preparing for a night mission—okay. It was the same with the antitank platoon off on its sweep of the highway— nada, mafi, oop-so, zero, zip. We picked up and cleared our weapons, leaving about forty crabs as food for their brothers. The rest of the day was spent monitoring the activities of the patrols, getting the night patrols ready, cleaning weapons, pulling maintenance on vehicles, and doing general house-keeping duties. The TACSAT operators continued to work on their little project and played with Bull's-eye. The night patrols were uneventful, and when security was posted we settled down for a good night's sleep. The stars were as beau-tiful and close as ever, and I lay on TAC-2's hood and listened to the surf in the distance. Peaceful, restful, uneventful— another boring day in Somalia.

The day after our crab target practice, we did the same thing: show of force armed presence and mounted patrols. No one bothered us. We had a small flurry of excitement when we discovered and confiscated some mortar rounds and mines in one of our numerous sweeps around Mundun. Com-bined with the mortar rounds we'd already found, we had a good deal of captured ordnance, and I decided to have it de-stroyed. Normally we would just blow the stuff in place or take it somewhere in the middle of nowhere and blow it up. But I had an idea. When the command group had been out shooting crabs, we saw a large ship beached on the shore about five miles south of Brava. I'd thought, why don't we take those mines and the mortar rounds we've already cap-tured and see how big a hole we can blow in the ship? Exactly why I did this is now beyond me. All I can say is I was really bored and it seemed like a good idea at the time. The men went at it with a will. The chance to blow something up is one that most troops will jump at. There's something viscerally satisfying about it. Like a kid with a cherry bomb on the Fourth of July.

The ship was an old tanker that must have washed up on shore years or even decades before, when Somalia was still a country, maybe even when it was an Italian colony. The tanker was hard aground and at low tide sat entirely stranded on the sand with only the very tip of its stern touching the water. It was rusted and derelict; everything usable had been stripped by the Somalis long ago. It sat mute and lifeless, cast off from the civilized world, just the thing to blow up. We piled up the mines and mortar rounds next to the ship. This took a while because we had to walk up and down the bluff to reach it. We placed some C4 plastic explosive on the pile, and the whole charge was primed with an electrical and a backup nonelectrical fuse.

We spent about a half hour making sure that no one was near the ship and that nomads traveling along the beach were well clear. Finally everything was secure and safe. Everyone backed off and we all yelled, "Fire in the hole! Fire in the hole! Fire in the hole!" The engineer sergeant turned the handle on the electric blasting device and *KABOOM!* Pure nirvana. Everyone stood up and admired the cloud of smoke enveloping the ship and the clutter of falling debris. Cool, way cool. We all drove up to take a look at the hole. It wasn't as big as I would have thought. A lot of the force of the explosion had gone out from the hull instead of into it. But it was still a very satisfying "bloody great hole," as the British would say. We all took pictures of it and giggled. It looked for all the world like a torpedo hole. So here we were, the 2-87 Infantry, otherwise known as "Das Boot," as Hans Lothar Buchiem would have said, "frigging around." I felt slightly foolish, but the people were happy and it occupied a few hours and we went back to our base camp outside of Brava well pleased with ourselves.

That evening we killed some bandits.

The antitank platoon's morning patrols discovered roadblocks near the Mundun intersection that had not been there the night before. This meant that the bandits had been waiting for our mounted patrols to go up the hill in the evening before establishing their roadblock checkpoints to rob people on the road. I had purposefully told the antitank platoon to come

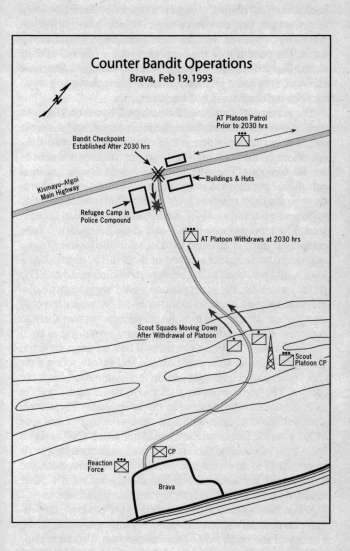

Counter Bandit Operations
Brava, Feb 19, 1993

AT Platoon Patrol
Prior to 2030 hrs

Bandit Checkpoint
Established After 2030 hrs

Buildings & Huts

Kismayu–Afgoi
Main Highway

Refugee Camp in
Police Compound

AT Platoon Withdraws at 2030 hrs

Scout Squads Moving Down
After Withdrawal of Platoon

Scout
Platoon CP

Reaction
Force

CP

Brava

back and go out about the same time each day. Each day when they went out, they tore down the roadblock. It was still down when they returned, but the next morning it would be up again. The bandits took the humvees going up the hill as their signal that it was safe to begin robbing people. Lieutenant Harvey of the scout platoon wanted to sneak down and try to surprise the bandits—my thoughts exactly.

The scheme of maneuver I developed, based on Harvey's idea to surprise the bandits at the intersection, was a simple one. The antitank platoon would conduct normal patrolling operations on the main highway, stopping vehicles and searching for weapons. The rifle company would conduct normal patrolling operations in town with two platoons and one in reserve as the team reaction force. Every effort would be made to present a normal show-of-force, business-as-usual appearance. The scout platoon would wait in the headquarters base compound until after dark, then move to the vicinity of the large microwave antenna on top of the hill. The antitank platoon would pull back to the headquarters compound at 2030. At the same time, the scout platoon would begin to move dismounted through the trees to the intersection, where it would set up observation. The plan for our deception was that the departure of the antitank platoon would signal the normal end of the main highway patrol, as it had on previous days. The bandits, upon seeing this, would feel safe to set up their checkpoint and start operations. In this assumption, we were correct. The scout platoon leader sent two squads, one on each side of the road leading to the intersection. These were standard scout squads with five men—four rifles and one M203 grenade launcher. Each squad had two PVS-7 and two PVS-4 night vision sights. It took the squads until approximately 2145 to reach the intersection. During movement, the north squad fell about a hundred meters behind the other squad. As it turned out, this difference was significant.

When the southern squad reached its OP position, they almost immediately spotted three men walking together in the vicinity of the north side of the intersection. Two were definitely armed. The scouts saw that the checkpoint had been put back up only an hour after the antitank platoon's patrol had passed. Obviously, the bandits were back in business. The three Somalis left the intersection and began walking toward the scout's position. It appeared that they were going toward the refugee camp in the compound behind where the scouts were positioned. When the bandits were about ten meters away from the scout's position, they were challenged by the two lead scouts. When the lead bandit attempted to raise his M16, the scouts immediately opened fire, killing two bandits. The third bandit fled into the small group of houses and ditched his weapon. A subsequent search by the reaction platoon of the area revealed one M16 rifle, one large knife, and a few loose AK-47 rounds. Had the second squad been in position, the third bandit would have run right into them. As it was, he narrowly escaped.

The two dead bandits (six hits in one, nine in the other) were subsequently identified by the town elders as two serious bad guys; one had slashed a woman the week before and the other was a known murderer. The SNA chief said nothing but was plainly taken aback by the loss of two of his gunmen. It made me particularly happy to see the bastard's face when we handed their bodies over to him. I wasn't naive enough to think we'd stopped banditry around Mundun, but I like to think we had a chilling effect on it for a short while. At any rate, one stretch of road was probably a little safer.

Radio traffic was intense after I reported the contact and the dead bandits. As was normal, there were dozens of questions from 2d Brigade and JTF on the nature of the contact. I patiently explained the whole thing several times. We knew it was a righteous kill. We had recovered weapons that had chambered rounds in them. Those guys hadn't been walking around out there at night for after-dinner exercise. They had tried to fight after being challenged and were hosed for their troubles. Lieutenant Colonel Sikes backed us up, and once the initial flurry of questions died down, no attendant hysteria followed. It was becoming clear to all of us that this sort of thing was going to get more frequent over the next few weeks.

We left the day after handing over the dead bandits to the chief of Brava. We had been going to leave the same day, but Sikes and I both thought that we had better stick around another night, to drive home the point that we could come and go where we pleased in the valley. Besides, I thought, if we're really lucky these guys will take a poke at us and we'll get to finish the whole thing right here. We kept a higher degree of alert that night, but the SNA chief didn't bite. Too bad. So we formed up the next morning and returned to Marka. Bull's-eye kept jumping around the TACSAT operator's feet in the back of the humvee. Terry Henry had a grin a mile wide but didn't say anything. Okay, so I'm a sucker for puppies.

When we got back to Marka, everyone wanted to know about the contact and the bandits the scouts had killed. I gave basically the same report that I'd given over the radio. I checked the TOC to learn what we had planned for the next day—just security patrols and convoy escort. We were already back to normal after the extended foray into the valley. Mike Klein updated me with the latest intelligence on bandits in the valley and activities of the political groups in Somalia. I was amazed at the amount of work that had been done on Condor Base in my absence. With roofs on most of the buildings and other amenities, such as sit-down latrines, we had gone a long way toward making the place livable. Best of all, there were four packages from home—one from Donna, one from my parents, and two from my sister. She'd hit upon the ingenious idea of packing what she was sending in little ketchup and condiment packets instead of Styrofoam peanuts. I soon became the battalion's point of contact for ketchup. Anything that made the MREs less monotonous was a relief.

That night I thought about the bandits we'd killed. I didn't feel bad then and don't now. Given the ultimate pointlessness of the whole Somali venture, I suppose you could say that it wouldn't have mattered a great deal if we hadn't done our counterbandit operations in the lower Shabele valley. We couldn't have known that then, of course. Our mission was to suppress banditry, and this we did, sometimes by just sheer presence and sometimes by outfoxing them. The bandits at

Brava had been predictable and had allowed us to sucker them by creating a false pattern of activity. Everyone had clicked that night: the antitank platoon, scouts, and the reaction force all did their jobs well and the result was success. If anything I was satisfied with a plan well executed and felt proud in being associated with the men who executed it.

At the same time I didn't kid myself about any lasting impact this little operation would have. It made the bandits around Brava cautious for a little while, that's all. In terms of numbers, it was like trying to bail a leaky ship with a spoon. Two down, two hundred thousand to go.

After Brava, Gordy Flowers had another idea with great potential to capture or kill the bandits that plagued the Shabele valley. His idea was as old as World War I naval warfare. A Q-ship was a merchantman that looked ordinary but actually concealed a naval crew with large cannons behind false sides and decks. When a submarine came up to the surface to use its deck gun at close range on the "helpless merchantman" in order to conserve torpedoes, the naval crew surprised and sank the submarine before they knew what hit them. We would do the same thing. Flowers proposed that we use one of the captured technicals as a "Q-truck." We would take off the weapons mounts and fill it with relief food bags, which also would make excellent sandbags. Two African American soldiers would go in the front dressed as Somalis, and a fire team of five men would be in the back ready to spring on the bandits as soon as they stopped the vehicle. Further improvements would allow for firing ports to be cut into the side. The Q-truck would operate at night when the bandits normally operated their roadblocks. The idea was greeted enthusiastically by the troops, and there was no shortage of volunteers to either drive the truck or be in the back. Lieutenant Colonel Sikes had reservations about it because of the danger it put on the drivers. As it turned out, however, it was all a moot point. Before we could actually put our Q-ship idea into practice, major trouble erupted in Kismayu, and Task Force 2-87 headed south.

Twelve

Kismayu: Part 1 (20 February–1 March 1993)

Kismayu is the second-largest seaport in Somalia and the largest city in the southern part of the country. It has an excellent deepwater harbor that can accept large merchant ships and is connected by paved road to both Jelib and Mogadishu. Its value as a center of commerce and a pivotal hub of communications made it a key objective during World War II, when the British launched their 1941 offensive out of Kenya, under General Cunningham, to seize what was then Italian Somaliland. One of the few pitched battles of that campaign was fought just to the north of Kismayu at the Juba River. In the present crisis, Kismayu was a place where humanitarian supplies could be brought in by bulk as opposed to being flown in. The proximity of so many relief supplies brought refugees, who almost doubled the city's normal population of thirty thousand, and warlord forces who came to receive spoils and tribute from the NGOs.

The city of Kismayu was shaped like a backward "L" along the waterfront. Its houses were similar to those in Marka—mainly adobe and cinder-block structures—with none of the mud and stick dwellings that could be found in other locations, such as Afgoi and Wanwaylen. The streets were constricted except for the main road through the center of town. Most buildings were one or two stories high, although a few were three and four stories. In the elbow of the inverted "L" was an abandoned food-processing plant bearing the cryptic name of "meat factory." This complex held the largest number of refugees, who lived in incredible concentration and squalor within the factory buildings. Beside the plant was a large antenna—at more than three hundred feet the tallest structure in all Kismayu. In the center of town, lining the square, was a clutch of government buildings. Of Italian origin, built before Italy lost its colony in 1941, the buildings were large and brown with an air of fading patrician authority. Years later, reading a book on the 1941 campaign, I saw a picture of the King's African Rifles parading through the square they had just captured. The buildings looked exactly the same in the grainy black and white photograph as they do now. It was as if time had stood still in Kismayu. Next to the town square was the makeshift Red Cross hospital, which had been operating since the beginning of the crisis. Farther along the waterfront was a derelict navy yard with looted shops and offices and a patrol boat mounted on the stocks for repairs, its ribs showing through the sides. Past the navy yard were the beginnings of a man-made causeway that led to a long, thin peninsula and the Kismayu port proper. The peninsula, more than a mile long, served as a natural breakwater for the harbor. The port facilities, with their offices, cranes, warehouses, and harbormaster's building, were at the end of the pier, next to the berthing facilities. Moving north from the turnoff to the port, the town ran on for about another three kilometers before gradually becoming thinner and petering out right before a small rise. To the north on the other side of the rise was the former main airport for Kismayu in the 1930s. Bombed by the British in 1941, it had been abandoned and probably not used since. Only with difficulty could one make out the tarmac runway through the grass. The current airport was on the south side of town, about ten kilometers from the outskirts of the city. It had a large and fairly well maintained airstrip, from which the largest military transport and commercial airliner could fly. The facilities had been trashed, but not as badly as those in Baledogle. There was a terminal building with a sign that read, "Welcome to Kismayu." There was one hangar and a few smaller service buildings, which had no roofs. Numerous derelict Somali air force

training planes sat beside the hangar, and there was one for-
lorn, old Canberra bomber, with its undercarriage half collapsed, in a corner on the ramp. None of the lighting worked,
so the air force control team had brought its own.

When UNITAF intervened, Kismayu was secured in mid-
December 1992 by a landing force of U.S. Marines, who stayed
just long enough for elements of JTF Kismayu to arrive before returning to Mogadishu. The main components of JTF
Kismayu consisted of elements of the 10th Mountain Division built around the division artillery headquarters and Task
Force 3-14 infantry, which had initially been supposed to join
us in Baledogle but had been diverted. Other units included a
troop from the division's air cavalry squadron and logistical
assets from the division support command. There was also a
Special Forces detachment co-located with the JTF Kismayu
headquarters; it maintained close contact with the leadership
of both major Somali political factions.

The other major unit in JTF Kismayu was the Belgian
parachute battalion task force. This elite unit was about the
same size as a rifle battalion from the 10th Mountain (three
rifle companies and a headquarters company). But like the
Canadians, it had been augmented to almost twice its normal
size with a company-sized squadron of Scorpion light tanks,
an aviation section with Allouette scout helicopters (of which
you will hear more later), and a robust logistical base. This
last included a medical detachment with some pretty nurses.
In addition to that, the task force had a support ship—the
Belgian warship *Zinnia*, docked at the port of Kismayu. The
Zinnia supplied the Belgians with many important creature
comforts, such as fresh bread.

The overall command of JTF Kismayu was under Brigadier
General Magruder, with Colonel Gaddis and the DIVARTY
headquarters serving as his staff. Outside the forces in Mogadishu, JTF Kismayu possessed the single greatest combat
power of any organization in UNITAF. On 28 December,
HRS Kismayu was officially activated. It consisted of all the
land south of the Juba to the Kenyan border and as far north
as Jelib. The JTF would assist NGOs in the security of their

operations in this vast area and stop warlord violence by enforcing the "four nos."

The JTF based its operations out of two locations, the airfield and the port. The airfield supported the aviation assets and provided a landing strip for resupply flights. The port had its wharves and logistical infrastructure. These facilities had sustained a good deal of damage in the anarchy preceding the UNITAF intervention, but after being cleaned up they provided sufficient space for JTF Kismayu HQ to operate. Situated as it was on the peninsula forming the breakwater for the harbor, the port offered an ideal and easily secured location for the JTF headquarters. The airfield was another matter, and required a company full-time to keep it secured.

Initially it didn't seem that there would be trouble. Of all the HRSs in those early days, Kismayu was one of the quietest. Indeed, one of the more exasperating things was the inordinate amount of time that JTF Kismayu spent in reporting mundane occurrences on the TACSAT radio while the rest of us were waiting to report the daily ration of arms cache findings, firefights with bandits, and general mayhem. JTF Kismayu seemed to be a jump ahead of all of us in terms of bringing normality to their HRS. They restored the local police authority before anyone else in the country and largely eliminated banditry along the main thoroughfares. A truce of sorts had been worked out between the two warring factions of Mohammed Hersi Morgan and Omar Jess. This was thanks to the efforts of the special operations forces (SOF) detachment and the UNITAF negotiator, Col. Mark Hamilton, a brilliant officer who had a tremendous reputation from conducting previous negotiations in El Salvador. JTF Kismayu was also successful in restoring infrastructure, particularly at the port and airfield but also in repairs to the roads. The crowning achievement was a pair of Bailey bridges across the Juba River built by U.S. Army engineers. This bridge site was named the Freeman Bridge after Sergeant Major Freeman, who had been killed by a mine a few weeks earlier at Belet Uyene. By early February, HRS Kismayu looked stable enough that the decision was made by JTF to hand over responsibility for the HRS solely to the Belgian paratroopers.

However, there was an undercurrent to all the progress in HRS Kismayu. The two major factions fighting for control of Kismayu prior to UNITAF intervention were still present. Although the conflict had been brought to a temporary halt, it was by no means resolved. Both sides jockeyed for position within the town and continued to smuggle in arms and militia fighters. To exacerbate matters, disturbances in Jelib caused JTF Kismayu to send the bulk of Task Force 3-14 to that town to restore order, leaving only one company to secure the NGO sites in the town. This effectively cut the combat power of UNITAF troops in Kismayu by almost half, just as things were beginning to heat up. Incidents between Morgan and Jess followers increased, and UNITAF-sponsored negotiations between the two elements went nowhere despite the best efforts of Colonel Hamilton. UNITAF headquarters decided that a show of force was necessary to disarm the two sides and help defuse the situation. On 23 February we got the call to deploy Task Force 2-87 to Kismayu. Along with us would go the 2d Brigade HQ from Baledogle, an MP company, and support assets.

What made this deployment awkward was that the crisis took place just as JTF Kismayu was closing up shop and turning over the whole HRS to the Belgians. Task Force 3-14, except for one company, had already displaced from Kismayu to Jelib, and DIVARTY headquarters had already sent the majority of its equipment home. So in addition to sending down extra combat power, the UNITAF headquarters had to send down a JTF headquarters to command it. Colonel Ward and the 2d Brigade HQ came down from Baledogle to act as the JTF headquarters. For a short time we would have the outgoing and incoming (temporary) JTF staffs together; then 2d Brigade would have the ball. The overall plan was to have the brigade in charge until the crisis died down, then disband the JTF, send us back to Marka, and leave the Belgians in charge, as was originally intended—not too complicated.

The preparation to go to Kismayu was pandemonium in

the best sense of the word. Lieutenant Colonel Sikes and Joe Occhuzzio were away from the battalion in Mogadishu when the warning order arrived. I called the battalion orders group together and filled them in on the situation as I understood it. I alerted Alpha 2-87, Bravo 2-87, and Alpha 1-87 (minus one platoon) that they would be going along with most of the battalion's command and control and logistical assets.

We couldn't leave HRS Marka entirely uncovered for all the time we were gone. At the same time it was clear through reports that we would have to bring the majority of our combat power to Kismayu. Sikes decided that we would leave a detachment under Frank Kirsop consisting of an infantry platoon from Geoff Hammil's company, the air defense section for convoy escort, and the attached MP platoon, as well as a small support base. This would give Frank enough assets to perform the basic site security mission that we were responsible for and the capability to support a reduced convoy security schedule. That was all. Leaving this skeleton crew was a risk. If there was any serious trouble in Marka while we were gone, Frank would have to be reinforced from Mogadishu.

The battalion would move to Kismayu by air and ground. The rifle companies and the battalion TAC-CP would move by helicopter. The rest of the battalion would move in convoy from Marka down three hundred kilometers of haphazardly paved road. Joe Occuzzio would be in charge of the ground movement. I didn't envy him the ride. He walked back to the TOC to continue his preparations for the next day's movement. Lieutenant Colonel Sikes, Mike Klein, and I, along with our RTOs, piled into a Black Hawk and lifted off for Kismayu. Below us the convoys were beginning to stage.

For the most part it was a boring flight. The only variation in the monotonous scenery was Brava, and I looked with interest at the compound we had based out of, the tower at the top of the hill, and the winding road leading down the other side. I thought about the bandits and how lucky the scouts had been. A minute later we flew over the beached ship, and I looked back to see the big hole we had blown in its side (the things we do to keep amused). Presently we flew over the

Juba estuary—a wide, muddy ribbon spilling into the Indian Ocean—and Kismayu came into view. It had been a while since we'd seen a town that big, and the thought of sweeping it was a daunting prospect. Eat all elephants a bite at a time, I chided myself. We'd obviously have to do it in phases, but it could be done. The helicopter flew on to the airfield, where we were met by representatives of Task Force 3-14 and the Belgians.

While the line companies were settling in to the airfield and relieving the security detachments there, the planning team went to JTF Kismayu HQ at the port, where we met with Brigadier General Magruder and the outgoing JTF staff as well as the Belgians. The overall plan was to wait for the arrival of the convoys from Marka and Baledogle, and while doing so continue with negotiations between the Morgan and Jess factions in the hope of averting bloodshed. Once all the forces were in Kismayu, the JTF control would pass to 2d Brigade, with General Magruder remaining as the overall commander. The JTF forces would then conduct a detailed cordon and search of the city to confiscate weapons and separate the factions. It was agreed that we would spend the next day conducting leader recons and developing our plans for a cordon and search. The companies would then spend one day patrolling the streets to establish presence and familiarize themselves with the area. The operation would begin on 27 February.

We returned to the airfield later that night and spread out our sleeping rolls in the abandoned control tower. It was a cool night with many stars. I reflected that I seemed to be spending a lot of time on the roofs of trashed airport facilities, but I was too tired to take the thought any further.

I was at the port the next day doing coordination for the upcoming operation when one of the JTF Kismayu soldiers came running into the office saying that the lead convoy, led by Kirk Haschak, was in a fight near the old abandoned airfield to the north of town. The next hour was damnable; I kept trying to raise the convoy on the radio and get its status, but it was just out of range and its transmissions kept breaking up.

Nor did it come up on TACSAT. Attack helicopters were alerted from the Kismayu airfield and vectored to the north of town. They reported that the fight was over and we had sustained no casualties. This was a relief, but the inability to communicate with a unit in contact was hardly reassuring. When I saw Kirk at the airport later that night, he told me what had happened.

They were driving by a large assembly area of Jess forces, including numerous technical vehicles, when the outposts of that force opened fire on the convoy. The lead security element, under Lieutenant Harvey, along with Kirk and other soldiers, instantly dismounted, returned fire, and began maneuvering on foot to close with the ambushers. The Somalis withdrew and soon the soldiers began taking fire from machine guns. The Americans went to ground and returned the fire. Just as suddenly as it began, the firing stopped. A representative of the Jess forces gingerly came forward and explained that it had all been a mistake, and he apologized for the incident. He explained that they were in the assembly area for their technical vehicles that had been designated by UNITAF and had no intention of fighting U.S. forces. The Jess officer said that all of his personnel would stand down in place. He promised that no further hindrance to U.S. convoys would take place. Miraculously, no Americans had been hurt by the large volume of Somali fire. Lieutenant Harvey stated that he saw three Somali gunmen dead on the ground and had no doubt that several more had been hit. The forces cautiously backed away from one another, and the convoy continued on its way, driving through Kismayu without incident and arriving at the airfield in midafternoon.

Kismayu by now was an extremely tense place. The Morgan faction soldiers had succeeded in infiltrating into friendly portions of the town. The Jess people were gearing up for a major counterattack to the north of the town. The firefight we had with them was inadvertent, but it did show that Jess was going to make a fight for Kismayu. Many people wanted only to be left in peace, and they were already hunkering down waiting for the blowup. Much of the population, though, was in active support of either Morgan or Jess. The NGOs we talked to were not at all optimistic, saying that this was as tense as they had seen the city for some time. The stage was set for a major confrontation. To stop or control it, we had two companies of Belgians and two and a half companies of Americans plus assorted supporting elements. Between us we could put about six hundred troops on the streets. Not much to control a city of fifty thousand people bent on self-immolation.

I had no doubt the Belgians would do well, because they had a long history of intervention in Africa. The battalion had jumped into the Congo in 1964 to rescue the Western hostages being held by the Simbas in Stanleyville. A few senior NCOs had actually participated in that operation. Since then the 1st Belgian Parachute Regiment had sent troops back to Africa on numerous occasions. Their staff was professional and easy to coordinate with. The officers and NCO knew their business. The two battalions got along well, and a brisk trade in rations soon developed. All in all I was impressed and put much at ease by the professionalism of the paras. You never know what another nation's army is going to be like when you work with them for the first time. The Belgians would be just fine.

There were some professional differences of opinion and different tactical approaches between us. At the brigade back brief held at the port, our battalion's scheme of maneuver for the upcoming cordon and search raised a few eyebrows from the Belgians. They wanted to do a simple on-line sweep through the city, the kind of operation we'd done in Afgoi and come up empty. Lieutenant Colonel Sikes knew that this is what would be expected and that people would merely move and hide their weapons ahead of the advancing troops and smuggle them back in when it got dark. Instead, Sikes opted to do the unexpected and cordon off an area in the center of town, then work north from it. The Belgians would sweep to the south and east of us in the neighborhoods that bordered the beach and old naval base. Our scheme of maneuver had two companies abreast searching south to north and one platoon as the task force reserve. Colonel Ward listened to Lieutenant Colonel Sikes's rationale and approved the plan.

Our tactical dilemma was that even if we managed to achieve surprise, the Somalis could quickly react, grab their weapons, and slip through the cordon. We did not have nearly the right number of troops for the spacing of men to be tight enough to prevent escape from the search area. Our solution was a simple one—concertina wire. Our plan was to slip in the engineers under escort at 0300 while the whole town slept and establish a hasty double concertina fence around the entire search area. This would be done by paying out spools of concertina wire from trucks, then linking them together. The engineers called it speed wiring. Other teams would follow the trucks paying out the wire and pound pickets to anchor the wire on the dirt roads. Tom Wilk's Echo Company would block all exits from town and guard the teams emplacing the concertina fence. The engineers reckoned they could have the entire search area surrounded before anyone inside it woke up and saw what was happening. Once the wire was in place, teams of soldiers would be positioned within sight and mutual support of one another, ready to apprehend anyone attempting to flee through the wire.

The other big factor in everyone's thoughts was the prevention of fratricide incidents if the cordon and search did involve fighting. No one was worried that the Belgians or Americans would mistake one another for Somalis, but there was the fear that, in the maze of streets, fire from one side or the other against an armed opponent might miss the gunman, continue into a neighbor's sector, and endanger friendly troops. The key to preventing this was liaison officers down to company level and a special liaison cell to be formed at battalion level. Lieutenant Colonel Sikes suggested that a liaison cell consisting of an American and a Belgian operations officer be formed to fly in one of the Belgian helicopters over the operation. His reasoning was that we would certainly be able to talk to everyone involved and could deconflict movements and lessen the chance of fratricide by being able to see into the town and tell the search forces exactly how close they were to one another. Flying a helicopter low and slow over potentially dangerous neighborhoods entailed some risk. But considering that the threat to helicopter operations consisted of mainly small-arms fire, it was a risk worth taking. Anyone who stayed to shoot at the helicopter ran the risk of being run to ground by nearby Belgian or U.S. troops.

The only snag was, who would be the U.S. officer in the helicopter? I'd have recommended Frank Kirsop except he was back in Marka. This left Lieutenant Colonel Sikes looking at me. I tried to dodge it by suggesting Mike Klein, but Sikes was adamant. I'd written the plan and knew it better than anyone, so what better person to deconflict any maneuver issues between us and the Belgians? Joe Occhuzzio would take TAC-2 and be the alternate CP on the ground, Mike Klein would manage the TOC. The helicopter assignment left me frustrated. This operation looked as though it might turn into a good fight, and I wanted to be in the middle of it. Instead I'd be orbiting around like the morning commute helicopter reporter. I rationalized that it was only for a few days, and after that I'd be back with my guys in TAC-2.

My apprehension increased markedly the next day when the Belgian helicopter arrived to pick me up. U.S. Army helicopters, such as UH-60s and CH-47s, are huge, brutish, powerful machines. Even the little OH-58 scout helicopters at least have the interior space of a smallish family sedan. The Belgian Allouette that would carry me and my airborne liaison teammate was a small, toylike machine that almost seemed as if it belonged at a show of radio-controlled aircraft. It had four seats that would hold midgets in comfort and absolutely no fuselage or body to speak of. A bubble, an engine, and a metal frame. Add a few rotor blades and that's an Allouette. It had a single door gun sticking out the left side. To shoot at anything, we'd have to do a slow, slightly tilted, left-hand circle around the target. It had no extra radio, so I'd have to bring a PRC-77 and a headset in order to communicate with the troops. Coordination with my fellow liaison officer would be done by screaming over the noise of the engine, which was right behind us. Charming. The helicopter was

flown by a chubby, oldish warrant officer, who grinned at me
with a universal facial expression used by every helicopter
pilot I've ever flown with—a demented leer that says this guy
is going to do his absolute best to make you lose your lunch.
It's probably the undercover recognition sign of helicopter pilots, like a secret handshake. No safety briefing, just a quick
snap of the safety belt, a casual discard of the cigarette that
had been dangling from his mouth, being careful to miss the
growing pool of hydraulic fluid that was forming under his
machine, and we were off.

I have a confession to make. I've always disliked flying
in helicopters. The vibration and noise are unsettling, and
they're usually flown by people who take great delight in
swooping all over the place. U.S. Army helicopters were bad
enough, but this little thing was like being up in the air with
nothing at all. Visibility out of the bubble canopy was unlim-
ited, and so was the sensation of height. There's nothing like
being in a small aircraft at two thousand feet to give you the
feeling of being really high up. The equatorial sun beat down
on us through the clear Perspex bubble, and even with an
eighty-mile-per-hour wind and the altitude I began to get hot
after only a few minutes. We puttered over the city instead of
taking the direct line to the Belgian HQ out on the port of
Kismayu. I thought the guy was just giving me an aerial view
of the maneuver area. I should have known better. Suddenly
he grinned to himself and did a vicious ninety-degree turn
out toward the port, descending steeply and sharply toward
the beginning of the little peninsula that the Belgians used as
their HQ and staging area. He pulled up at about fifty feet,
and we screamed over the water toward a small beach, where
I could see several women in next-to-nothing bathing suits
lying on towels, sunbathing. I gawked and blinked; I couldn't
believe my eyes. The pilot laughed and said in broken English
that this was where the Belgian nurses and female medics
sunbathed. We roared over them, and our rotor wash caused
one unhooked top to go flying before being grabbed by its
owner. The pilot giggled and did another low, fast pass over
the now waving women *("Oooo la la! Est Marcel, la grande*

fromage c'est un bon aviator formidable, n'est-ce pas?"). We jumped the peninsula and went screaming down the length of it about ten feet off the deck at 120 miles per hour, flared up briefly, dumping speed, then floated onto the helipad next to the Belgian headquarters like a naughty dragonfly. I stumbled out, a little green around the gills. I could see already that this would be a long day.

We picked up a Belgian captain, my liaison officer counterpart, who looked as tough and fit as Gordy Flowers. He was thankfully only slightly larger; two of me would have probably maxed out the aircraft. We flew over the city, comparing our notes and envisioning the control problems we would have with the upcoming operation. Communication with the ground was no problem. I could talk to everyone in the city and could act as a relay between searching elements. This would be important, because previous experience in Kismayu showed several dead spaces for radio transmission.

We landed in the port late in the afternoon. I did not even want to think about two full days in this helicopter as the airborne liaison. We finished our review of the plan and went back to the airfield to conduct final preparations for the next day. Thankfully, we drove home. I'd had quite enough of the Allouette for one day.

Returning to the airport, I received the unwelcome news that we were going to lose Capt. Kirk Haschak. Kirk had dodged reporting to school for some time now, but the army had finally tracked him down. Apparently it was more important for Kirk to attend a staff school at Fort Leavenworth than be a company commander on a combat deployment. Not only that, we were to be given no replacement. Kirk would have to leave no later than four days from now. Lieutenant Colonel Sikes's protests about this proved fruitless. Everyone in the chain of command all the way up to Major General Arnold had tried to get it turned off. The army's personnel weenies were adamant. Kirk had been selected to be a foreign area officer and was going to Russian language school, but first he had to spend six weeks in Leavenworth. Crazy. I would have to find someone else to play Pigs with.

The battalion went to sleep that night with a sense of anticipation. I think we all knew that there was a real potential for violence this time. For most of the people, it seemed almost a relief to be doing something different. This operation was going to be more interesting than patrolling in HRS Marka or doing convoy escort.

The next morning, everyone got up early. The engineers and their security teams went out first, to emplace the fence around the search area while it was still dark. The companies left by truck and got into position on the outskirts of town, waiting to start the search at the crack of dawn. Echo Company and the MPs established their blocking positions on the routes out of town. Chief Sandhammer, along with the battalion aid station, moved to their position behind the companies. Every unit got to its start location without a hitch. I went over some last-minute details with Lieutenant Colonel Sikes and Joe Occhuzzio, then they both left to be in position. The airfield was almost deserted. For a few minutes it was lonely. I went out of the TOC and sat down to eat a quick breakfast of MRE crackers and cheese, hoping I could keep down the bland food. The sun was just creeping over the horizon. In the distance I could hear the insect sewing-machine buzz of the Allouette. Apprehensively I picked up my radio and my weapon and went to meet the helicopter.

We reached the town shortly after the search began, flying low and slow along the boundary, each of us looking to ensure that the troops were in the right place. The Belgians and Americans were easy to tell apart. We had desert camouflage helmets and body armor; the Belgians had green uniforms with tan body armor and red berets. I could see the soldiers entering houses and covering one another. The occupants were sometimes led outside while the house was searched. Everyone was being thorough, searching the yards as well as the houses themselves. This sometimes involved digging through piles of garbage and refuse. The going was fairly slow at first but picked up after the troops got into the swing of things. Periodically we would have to tell one side or the other to slow down or coordinate with units to their flanks when one or the other looked as though it might be moving into another unit's path. We lazily crisscrossed town and flew up into the 2-87's sector. The view was spectacular. Hovering over the meat factory, I could almost make out the entire American scheme of maneuver from a single location. We were able to give good directions to the troops on the ground.

The U.S. search was going well. The speed wire fence laid by the engineers completely surprised the Somalis. Some had to be cut out of it after they ran into it full tilt to escape the searching troops. Others, seeing that the fence was guarded, turned frantically into the search area to ditch their weapons. Soon reports started coming in to the helicopter of weapons caches found as well as Somalis who had been wounded in the previous factional fighting being discovered and brought to the ICRC hospital. We flew lazy circles around the city, moving here and there to check out a particular piece of the action. After the first flurry of coordinations and corrections, we were used mainly as an aerial observation post. TAC-1 with Lieutenant Colonel Sikes, TAC-2 with Maj. Joe Occhuzzio, and the company commanders with their liaison officers coordinated most of the action without our getting involved. The rising sun beat into the bubble canopy, and I was beginning to get nauseous. Periodically we would pull off station to get more fuel. In the time it would take to refuel, I would run over to get a cool drink and find a place to take a leak. I was ravenously hungry but didn't dare eat anything. After the second refueling I looked at my watch; I'd been flying for three hours. It seemed a lot longer.

There were a few incidents. A man shot at troops from Geoff Hammil's company in the vicinity of observation post three. The troops pursued the gunman but couldn't get a clear shot at him and eventually lost him. The house searches went exceptionally slowly, as we knew they must. It takes time to search a house, especially if you're doing it right.

The Somalis didn't make it easy for us either, hiding their weapons under dung heaps, in open-air latrines, down wells, and in piles of garbage. The toll of captured weapons continued to grow, however. Occasionally we'd relay radio transmissions or adjudicate a boundary issue between units, but mostly we just flew around and around over the city. The news of the search appeared to have caused quite a stir. Many people outside the search area were either hiding or moving their weapons on the chance that they might be next. The search continued and the hours crept on. It was blazingly hot and the troops suffered considerably in their body armor and helmets. The heat and physical exertion caused them to drink prodigious amounts of water. Humvees continuously provided water to the search elements and the security teams on the cordon. We continued to find small caches of weapons as well as people wounded in the factional violence holed up in their houses. We also found the bodies of a number of people killed in the violence as well, some of whom clearly had been mutilated by torture. The details of the atrocities as they came over the radio sounded jarring and out of place to me on this sunny day. A few of the torture victims were still alive. We got medics to them as quickly as we could and rushed them to the ICRC hospital, but all subsequently died. The search continued, and the helicopter flew and refueled and flew and refueled.

Around 1800 the search was called off. It had already been decided prior to execution that we would not risk searching houses in the dark. The line companies assembled and returned to the base camp at the airport. Echo Company and the MPs kept the checkpoints at all main road exits from town. In addition, they conducted mounted patrols in town to prevent the mass movement of people on the street after dark.

Back at base we went over the day's actions in the TOC. Everyone was beat. I was wobbly and a bit deaf from the Allouette. Fortunately, Mike Klein and Sergeant First Class Hardcastle had most of the work done on the orders for the next day. After a short conference with Lieutenant Colonel Sikes, I briefed them on the scheme of maneuver for the next day and left them to finish the plan. I sat down and closed my eyes for a few minutes, happy not to be hearing any helicopter sounds. Later we had an after-action review in the TOC with the key leaders, company commanders, specialty platoon leaders, and staff, in which the day's events were examined in detail. The concertina fence had been a great success, entrapping a few people trying to flee with weapons and turning the others back into the search area. A cautionary lesson learned was that we would have to increase the number of soldiers dedicated to guarding the fence if we were going to do it in more restricted parts of the city. Each company commander went over some of the weapons-hiding techniques their companies had encountered.

The other disturbing thing we'd found was the injured and tortured people from the previous fighting. Evacuation and treatment of them had used a surprising amount of our medics' time. If things got worse, I wasn't sure we could keep treating Somali casualties without jeopardizing our ability to quickly treat any of our own casualties. We next briefed the order that gave out assignments to units for the next day's search. We were about halfway through the town. The next day should complete the sweep of the town if we kept up the same pace. Near the end of the operations order, Echo Company reported that one of its patrols had just taken several rounds of rifle fire near checkpoint number one. No casualties or damage were sustained and they could not find the gunman. This made me nervous. Sooner or later a gunman was bound to get lucky. There wasn't much we could do about it in the short run, though, and Echo Company troops continued to patrol.

Leaving the TOC, I told Joe Occhuzzio that being over the town during the search had been most interesting, and I generously offered to switch places with him. "Really, Joe, it's a blast," I said. Being far too clever to be taken in by such a transparent (and desperate) ruse, he declined. I was in for another day in the dragonfly. I went over to Lieutenant Colonel Sikes, and we discussed the day while we cleaned our weapons. It had gone well and we had every confidence for the morning. I was dismayed to learn that he'd found our airborne liaison cell most helpful; I hadn't thought we'd done all that much. He said he wanted us above the search as much as possible tomorrow. *I just hope you're not underneath us when I heave,* I thought. I bid the boss good night and walked back to the TOC to check on our mounted patrols in the town, but so far no more incidents. I told the TOC shift to wake me if a patrol in the town had contact, then I went to bed. I looked at my watch: six hours to wake-up. I stretched out and soon fell asleep despite the mosquitoes buzzing around my head like tiny Allouettes.

There weren't any more incidents during the night, so the next morning we were hopeful for another good day. Unfortunately, the engineer trucks had gotten lost moving into position to emplace the wire, so there was no physical barrier to slow escape from the search area for the first two hours. As it turned out, this was not as important as we had first thought, because few people were moving toward the outskirts of town. Instead, most residents of all ages and genders seemed to be taking to the streets to confront one another. We kept searching and continued to find weapons. Bravo Company found rifles and mortar rounds buried in fresh graves, and the Belgians found an unexploded grenade near the hospital. However, as the morning wore on, we became progressively distracted from the search. Incidents of violence, mass demonstration, rock throwing, and gunfire became more prevalent. Shortly after refueling we heard the first grenades go off as what seemed like the entire population of Kismayu was out in the streets. The explosions were audible in the helicopter, and I turned my head to see the little puff of grenade smoke below with a few still figures next to it and others running away. All of a sudden I had the feeling that searching houses would be a low priority for the rest of the day. Like a pair of beat cops in the middle of a domestic disturbance at a Mafia wedding, Task Force 2-87 and the 1st Belgian Para were caught up in the chaos. The tensions of the previous days boiled over completely, and the rioting in Kismayu had begun in earnest.

It's not the kind of tactical problem you're normally given at Command and Staff College. The tasks, conditions, and standards of the problem facing us might have looked something like this.

Situation: A small African port city of about fifty thousand with two opposing political militia armies vying for control. Mobilized power base for each army includes several thousand—exact number undetermined—active unarmed supporters who will use street riots to screen the movements of their smaller groups of armed militia fighters. General rioting between the two factions is taking place. Also a large refugee population exists.

Task: Restore order in the town by disarming or apprehending all gunmen. Displace all armed political groups from the environs of the city and into holding areas. Facilitate the conduct of negotiations between the factions to establish a peaceful solution to the crisis.

Conditions: Given—Two understrength infantry battalions from two different armies, assorted smaller units, a rules of engagement (ROE) in effect that does not allow you to lethally engage unarmed rioters except in the defense of your life, and no place to detain prisoners. Your force does not have the release from JTF to use riot control agents such as tear gas.

Standards: Apprehend, disarm, and take into custody all gunmen. Disperse all rioting crowds, treat all wounded people you find, and ensure that the forces of the opposing warlord factions return to their designated areas outside the town. At all times stay within the ROE and use deadly force only if threatened by or attacked with deadly force.

There are easier ways to make a living.

The only saving grace in the whole situation was that the Somalis in Kismayu did not seem genuinely interested in fighting us directly. They'd shoot or throw rocks at us and the Belgians if we were in the way, but they were much more interested in getting at the opposing militia and its supporters. By midmorning the search had been called off entirely, and both battalions were fully engaged in trying to keep the rioting factions apart.

I, of course, had a bird's-eye view of the mayhem, and it was fascinating to watch. As soon as the soldiers would separate one group and quiet one street, the riot would flow like water onto an adjacent street and start all over again. The rioters (men, women, and children) seldom actually came to blows with one another but instead hurled rocks at one another, many using slings that could launch stones with killing force. Two sides would exchange massive volumes of rocks, alternately surging forward or subsiding back up and down a street. The true unfortunates were those who were hit and off their feet when their side was retreating and the other side was surging forward. If they were overrun by the opposing side, they would literally be torn limb from limb. The crowds of rioters provided cover for the movements of gunmen. Periodically a gunman would step out and spray the opposing crowd with fire or throw a grenade, which just added to the chaos and the number of casualties. Soldiers would arrive and attempt to chase the gunman and disperse the crowd, shoving them roughly and hitting them with rifle butts. The crowd, like a malevolent, viscous fluid, would go to another street and the mayhem would begin all over again.

Trying to aid command and control from my vantage point was futile, because there was just too much going on. I tried to help where I could. The Belgian captain tugged frantically at me and pointed to a small knot of Belgians trapped shoulder to shoulder in a large, rioting crowd. Our troops were the nearest to them, and I called Lieutenant Colonel Sikes to send relief to them. Soon after this I saw one Somali man (who was cut off from his own side, I suppose) being chased into an alley and savagely attacked. I was going to call for someone to break it up, but in the time it took me to make the radio transmission the crowd had already torn him to pieces and left him squashed and broken in a large pool of blood. Sickened, I canceled my transmission and watched the group return to the main fray. From the air they seemed quite happy, skipping and jumping and slapping one another on the back while tossing pieces of their victim in the air. All morning and into the afternoon, the radio was an endless chatter of incidents.

Gordy Flowers's troops encountered a firefight between two

groups of gunmen and had a grenade thrown at them. They responded by suppressing both groups with fire and capturing one gunman. Lieutenant Colonel Sikes in TAC-1 was fired on by two Somalis. Returning the fire, he and the TAC-1 crew gave chase, capturing one gunman after he had thrown down his weapon. Joe Occhuzzio in TAC-2 had a grenade go off nearby but was not injured. Bravo Company took a burst of automatic weapons fire, which miraculously went between soldiers and hit nothing. The TAC-2 crew chased the gunman but lost him in the crowd. The 3d Platoon, Alpha 2-87 took fire from three Somalis, immediately returned fire, and captured two of them. A Belgian soldier was shot and evacuated by Alpha 2-87 medics. All the while we kept finding bodies of people killed in the rioting as well as wounded people who were either active rioters or just unfortunates who were in the way of one faction or the other. The wounded were evacuated to the ICRC hospital, which was receiving a steady stream of casualties. The rioting went on, with the factions falling back, regrouping, then filtering forward around us to strike at each other.

The time in the helicopter seemed interminable. The sunlight coming through the bubble canopy made me feel as though I was boiling; everyone in the helicopter was drenched in sweat. I felt even more nauseous than I had the previous day. About 1400 I couldn't keep it down anymore and threw up into a plastic bag. I tied it shut and dropped it on a group of rioters, where it exploded with a most satisfying splat. A few minutes later I was sick again, so I had to have the pilot quickly land on the outskirts of town while I barfed up my guts. The Belgian captain was all grins as I staggered back to the helicopter, with another grenade going off in the distance. Back to the riot we went.

We found even more people who had been tortured and disemboweled. This occurred with depressing frequency. The victim had his or her abdomen slit open, then the intestines yanked out and dropped in the dirt beside the still-writhing victim. Most people found this way were already dead, but a few were still alive, kicking feebly. We'd send them to the

ICRC hospital as quickly as we could, but they all died from their injuries.

Some Somalis tried to help us. Realizing that we were after gunmen, they pointed out locations to us and a fight would invariably ensue. This assistance was less from public spiritedness than a desire to rat on the other side in order for us to pursue and disarm them. Nonetheless, it did produce results as the day wore on. In one incident, Bravo Company surprised ten gunmen in this manner, and in a sudden, confused flurry of fire ended up capturing three of them, with the rest dispersing back into the city. The gunmen were exceptionally hard to capture, because the crowds would instantly surge around to protect them, and the ROE prohibited us from firing on a crowded street unless the source of the fire could be clearly identified. Several gunmen who had been wounded by U.S. and Belgian troops in the exchanges were taken to the ICRC hospital along with everyone else. I worried about the presence of the rioters from both sides in the hospital, but the soldiers from Task Force 3-14 who had remained to guard NGO sites in Kismayu ensured there were no incidents.

The riot finally began to run out of gas around 1630 that afternoon. Just as people started trickling back to their houses, troops from Alpha 2-87 reported coming under fire from the meat factory. Gordy Flowers's people took cover but could not ascertain exactly where in the meat factory the fire was coming from. There were too many refugees in the building to return suppressive fire. Sweeping through the factory, Alpha Company troopers found spent casings but no gunmen. An hour later Wes Bickford's people also came under fire from the meat factory.

Around 1800 the streets of the town were finally quiet. Lieutenant Colonel Sikes and the Belgian commander established patrols throughout the city and pulled the majority of the troops out to rest. My little Allouette finally deposited me back at the port of Kismayu, and on unsteady legs I wobbled into the port building reeking of vomit like an inner city wino. I cleaned up as best I could, then went to meet Sikes and Joe Occhuzzio, who were coming to discuss the next day's course of action with General Magruder, Colonel Ward, and the Belgians.

We had known that the town was tense, and incidents of violence had been a regular occurrence, but the sheer size of the day's violent outbreak had been a surprise. I personally doubted whether or not we could contain it. Obviously, we had to keep a strong presence in the town overnight, in case the fighting flared up again or one side or the other tried to infiltrate groups of gunmen into new positions. Just as important were our dispositions for the next day. If the rioting began again in earnest, how could we array ourselves to be ready? It was critical that we pace ourselves. The troops had already gone through one full day of exertion, and most of them would get little sleep this night. A few more days of rioting at this pace would see us asleep on our feet. Lieutenant Colonel Sikes decided to trade out Alpha 1-87 and Bravo 2-87. This gave Bravo Company the airfield and reserve mission after tonight's patrolling cycle and used Geoff Hammil's two fresh platoons in the town the next day. Alpha 2-87 would unfortunately be in for another full day tomorrow, but Sikes and I both had no doubt that Gordy Flowers's people could handle it.

For want of a better idea, we decided mainly to keep on doing what we had been doing: continue to separate rioting groups of people and actively pursue and apprehend all gunmen and grenade throwers. All those apprehended were turned over to the Belgians, who had made a sort of impromptu detention camp, which was ostensibly guarded by the Kismayu police. These last had been of no assistance in the day's events other than to help secure the ICRC hospital. They definitely were not as reliable as our own Marka police.

The whole approach we took to the Kismayu riot was, at best, a short-term solution. As has been pointed out already, UNITAF had no long-term facilities for keeping prisoners. In a week or two at the most, we'd just have to let them go. Meanwhile, the SOF and the negotiating team under Colonel Hamilton continued to work, trying to bring some sort of cease-fire between the Morgan and Jess factions. The only good news was that the Allouette needed maintenance and would not be ready before tomorrow afternoon, so at least I would be spared another day in the traffic watch–upchuck helicopter. The meeting broke up and we all went back to our respective units.

We had captured a large number of weapons over the past two days. They were all laid out in front of the port headquarters for a photograph. The haul looked impressive, but in reality it had become unimportant. We had a full-blown riot to contend with. The Somalis weren't hiding their weapons anymore; they were fighting with them. In the next few days, confiscating weapons would be the least of our problems. I took a couple of pictures for posterity's sake, then gratefully got into TAC-2 for the return trip to the airfield. The Belgians had given me one of their rations and some fresh bread from the *Zinnia*. I was ravenously hungry and munched contentedly as we drove through the town's now almost deserted streets. Darkness was falling as we reached the airfield.

It had been quite a day and it wasn't over yet. Everyone was tired, but the battalion had handled it well. In truth, as fatigued as they were, the troops were excited from the day's events. Gordy Flowers's company took up position in an abandoned walled compound in the center of the town near the meat factory. There he could rest his troops and send out patrols on shifts to keep a presence in his sector all night. At 2130 a patrol from Alpha Company again took fire from the meat factory. Lieutenant Colonel Sikes ordered Alpha and Bravo Companies to sweep through the meat factory again. I went down to watch it in TAC-2 but didn't find anything. Finally around 2300 we settled down to patrolling and gave the troops as much rest as we could.

Lieutenant Colonel Sikes, Joe Occhuzzio, and I discussed the day before we went to sleep. Sikes told me to take TAC-2 the next day, while Joe was to stay by the TOC and be prepared to come in with the reserves. I was almost giddy with gratitude for not having to go back up in the Allouette. Twenty hours in the air over three days had been quite enough, thank you. In comparison, the thought of going into the middle of a riot was a relief.

The next day we were up before dawn as the troops got ready to move into the town and resume their sectors for patrolling. A quick wash combined with the joy of being able to eat breakfast had me feeling like a new man. Everyone was eager to get into the town. In TAC-2 I had Terry Henry for a driver, Mike Klein in the back seat, and Higgenbotham and Hugley in the back of the vehicle as security. We pulled up outside of town at checkpoint three, near the medics. Around 0700 the first demonstrations started and by 0800 we heard the first grenade explosions. Grenades were going off with greater frequency than the day before, and fragment-wounded along with dead bodies were already being taken to the ICRC hospital. Today's festivities had definitely begun with a bang. I moved TAC-2 behind Alpha 2-87, and Lieutenant Colonel Sikes was behind Alpha 1-87. This way, one of us could be close to any contact that was made and get a quick appraisal of the situation while the company commander fought his platoons. This was the theory anyway. In reality, the sheer chaos of the riot made any command and control problematic.

The fighting followed the pattern of the previous day, with rioters attacking one another and troops trying to keep them apart. Gunfire and grenades were, if anything, even more prevalent than on the previous day. The armed fighters of both sides became bolder, or more desperate, and some resorted to unique tactics. Echo Company intercepted a beat-up blue and white van from which men were throwing grenades at random into the crowds of people. The occupants were captured and turned over to the Belgians.

I arrived at Alpha 2-87 just in time to see Gordy's people break up a firefight and capture several gunmen. There was still a lot of turmoil there, and a small rock bounced off my helmet. A little later TAC-2 came under fire. We couldn't determine where from, so we just moved. A platoon from Alpha 2-87 got a glimpse of the gunmen as they ran away and gave chase, but they escaped.

Lieutenant Colonel Sikes came up in TAC-1 and we hastily

conferred. The bulk of the riot seemed to be drifting back and forth along the main road going north, in a place the troops called "the arcade." Sikes was telling me that we would concentrate our efforts there when another flurry of firing began. We both crouched low, and a Somali near Sikes went down. Again we couldn't see where the fire came from in the confusion. *We're going to lose some people today,* I thought. I didn't see how the gunmen could keep missing us.

We separated and I took TAC-2 farther down the street to see if I could link up with the rest of Gordy's people. We stopped at one point in a clear space, only to find ourselves between two groups of rock throwers a few seconds later. We dismounted and took up a defensive posture around the vehicle. A platoon from Alpha 2-87 joined us a few seconds later. I remember one man in his fifties who looked a bit crazed running right up at me with a big rock in his hand. I pointed my rifle at him and screamed "stop." The word he didn't understand but the rifle he did. He dropped the rock and held both hands palms up, pleading with me. I kept him covered, motioning for him to go away, and he took off. For the others, we fired a few warning shots in the air and they kept their distance again. Seconds later we heard more shots close by, and I saw a Somali rioter stagger and fall. A few of us ran through the scattering crowd to see if we could catch the gunman, but he had disappeared. A man hit me with a large stick like a pick handle. I took the blow on the shoulder pads of my body armor, then butt-stroked him to the head. He was just leaning into his second swing, and instead of catching him in the temple I got him full in the mouth. His head snapped back with teeth flying like white pebbles in a red spray. Feeling oddly guilty, I left him on the ground. As we turned to go back to the vehicle, we were approached by a frantic Somali man, with his shirt torn half off, pursued by a crowd of rioters with clubs, spears, and farming implements. Just some other poor bastard on the wrong side of the riot, I thought. He ran past the nearest two soldiers and literally grabbed me around the waist, gibbering with fear, huge tears running down his face. The rioters checked when Higgenbotham and other soldiers pointed their weapons at them, but I couldn't get the terror-crazed fool to let go of me. Finally I had to hit him in the head with my rifle butt, knocking him to the ground. He was up in a flash, and we held off his pursuers while he disappeared around a corner. Looking disappointed, they ran off to rejoin the riot.

We hadn't gone fifty meters back to rejoin Captain Flowers when Higgenbotham was screaming "stop" and banging the top of the vehicle. We all piled out and Hig shouted that three men he was pointing toward had grenades. We ran after them and cornered them against a wall. One had a grenade in his hand, and Hig was yelling at him to drop it. With our men in front of me, I couldn't get a clear shot. I was yelling at Hig, "Shoot the motherfucker!" but the man lay down on the ground before Hig could fire. The man still had the grenade in his hand, and now I could see why he hadn't let go. The pin was pulled. We managed to find a small length of wire to render the grenade safe, but I didn't trust it. I was glad when the Belgian EOD men showed up later to take possession of the captured grenades and our prisoners.

It was a good action on the part of the TAC-2 security detail, especially Higgenbotham. I mentioned something to him about his wish to me a few months ago when he had wanted to transfer to Special Forces in order to be where the action was. Was this enough action for him? He grinned at me.

A most discouraging thing about the riot was the number of women and children being killed and injured. TAC-2 was moving to link up with Echo Company around 1300 when we heard shots in our vicinity. Not knowing whether they were aimed at us, we dismounted and took up defensive positions. Some Somalis came out and started pleading for help. Apparently some of their family members had just been shot by gunmen. Other soldiers arrived on the scene, and we went into the thatch houses. I was nervous that the gunmen were still around and that if people started shooting, bullets could go right through the walls. A woman who had been shot in the abdomen several times lay on the floor in a growing pool of blood, her eyes dull with agony and despair. Outside the building I could see the crumpled bundle of a small child lying on the ground, obviously shot by the same gunman. I quickly did what I could for the woman using my field dressings, but I couldn't stop the blood oozing out of her. I called for medics, and they showed up in a few minutes and took the woman away. I rubbed the blood off my hands with sand and went back to TAC-2. The others had been pulling security or checking other casualties. No one mentioned the child. I felt wretched and useless. I was glad that Donna and John couldn't see me then.

Meanwhile, throughout the town, Task Force 2-87 and the Belgians continued to separate rioting groups and chase gunmen. Several were wounded by our return fire, and even more were captured unharmed after they threw down their rifles when it became clear to them that they could not escape us. Lieutenant Colonel Sikes continued to be in the thick of it, alternately exchanging shots with the gunmen and vectoring troops to new outbreaks of violence. On one occasion his command group chased down three bandits, wounding and capturing one of them.

It was an infantryman's fight. Helicopters could fly over the big rugby scrum happening in the streets, but they couldn't affect it. The Belgians brought their Scorpion light tanks onto the streets as a show of force, but this didn't help much, because the Somalis just ran around them. The tanks were more useful on the cordon around town along with the MPs and Echo Company. There they could help keep more of the warlord forces from entering the town. The PSYOPS loudspeaker trucks were ignored by all as they plaintively broadcast their appeals for calm. All the power of UNITAF came down to the four hundred (give or take) American and Belgian riflemen in the streets moving nonstop from one crisis to the next.

The weapon that would have made life easier for us, we couldn't use. We could not obtain permission from UNITAF to employ riot control agents (tear gas and pepper spray) to disperse the crowds. This was the result of a well-intentioned concern at the beginning of the deployment that these agents could have severe and perhaps even fatal health consequences for people who were debilitated by starvation. It was no good trying to make the point to JTF in Mogadishu that none of the thousands of people who were rioting in Kismayu looked the least bit starved; most of them were downright frisky. Only after riots started in Mogadishu next to UNITAF headquarters was permission given to use riot control agents. Until then, we did riot control the old-fashioned way, with rifle butts and bayonets.

The rioting began to subside earlier than the day before. By 1700 the streets were mostly deserted. It had been a wild day. The medical platoon evacuated numerous wounded and tortured Somalis. The battalion was in more firefights than the previous day, killing and wounding several gunmen and capturing a dozen. Miraculously, for all the fire we had received, not one Task Force 2-87 soldier was wounded by rifle fire or shrapnel. The only injuries we had were minor cuts and abrasions from the hand-to-hand scuffle of rioting. The Belgians had not been as fortunate, losing three wounded.

Returning to the airfield, we had an even greater surprise in store for us. The commander of Task Force 1-22 infantry (the unit that was projected to replace us), Lieutenant Colonel Martinez, and his S3, Maj. Jeff Baughman, and some of the 1-22 staff were there. They had been flown out to Somalia to gain an appreciation of what they would be facing in less than two months. We would take them out on patrols that night; it was to be quite an initiation.

In the TOC that night before darkness fell, we learned of the rioting that had begun in Mogadishu. The UNITAF headquarters expressed concern that the entire reaction force for UNITAF remained down at Kismayu, leaving HRS Marka minimally manned and no other reserve available. The 2-87 was directed to prepare to move back to Marka and resume the UNITAF reaction force mission. This didn't make much sense at the time. The riots in Kismayu could well start again with equal fury the next day. But UNITAF was out of forces. This was yet another upshot of the shortsighted policy that did not allow the 10th Mountain to deploy the 2-14 Infantry and the 2-7 Field Artillery with the rest of 2d Brigade. There were literally no forces to spare, and we had two major riots happening in different places simultaneously. Oops. Another triumph in planning.

We decided that we would return to Marka in stages. In the morning I would accompany the lead element, consisting of Alpha 1-87 and TAC-2. We would stop outside of Brava and conduct a counterbandit sweep of Mundun that night. Hopefully we'd catch some of our buddies at work. Doubtless they'd been having an easy time of it in our absence. Because we expected to be called out for Mogadishu contingencies shortly after returning to Marka, this would probably be the only chance to do this kind of operation around Brava for some time. The rest of the battalion would redeploy later that day, and we'd all be at Marka by 4 March. I gave Geoff Hammil and the support platoon the warning order for the next day's movement, then went to join Lieutenant Colonel Sikes for the night's activities. The 1-22 operations officer, Major Baughman, rode with me. We reached observation post three at dusk. From there we went into town to link up with Captain Flowers's people. Before we could do that, Captain Flowers was involved in an incident from which he and Staff Sergeant Evans were lucky to escape with their lives.

Captain Flowers was with a patrol from his antitank section when they came under fire from a group of gunmen. Returning fire, they chased some of them into a house. As they started to go through the door of the building, AK-47 fire erupted from the inside, and the door splintered around Gordy and Sergeant Evans. It was like a Road Runner cartoon in which the coyote's body is outlined in bullets. Surprised, Gordy and Evans tumbled back and everyone started firing into the building, only to stop when they heard screams from women inside. A few seconds later a gunman came out and surrendered. For all the firing that had occurred, no one had been hit. It was a miracle; our luck still held.

There were other small firefights and contacts that night. The most successful contact was a patrol from the scout platoon under Sergeant Zimmerman, who had a fight with three gunmen at close range in an alley, killing one of them. The other two staggered off, leaving their weapons and patches of blood. Again, we were incredibly fortunate that no gunman managed to hit any of our soldiers, although all had fired. After Lieutenant Colonel Sikes and I arrived on the scene, another pair of gunmen stumbled into us and there was a second flurry of firing; one man was shot. It was only Major Baughman and Lieutenant Colonel Martinez's second night in Somalia and their first night with the battalion. I could only imagine what they were thinking. No doubt something along the lines of, what the hell have we gotten ourselves into? We took the dead gunmen to the Somali police at the town square.

After we got back to the airfield a little after midnight, I went over the plan for the next day. I would take Alpha 1-87 and do the sweep of Brava. Lieutenant Colonel Sikes and Joe Occhuzzio would follow with the rest of the battalion a day later. I said good-bye to Kirk Haschak, who would be leaving for America the next day. What a time to be losing a good man. I went to sleep that night remembering the regret I'd felt the moment I'd knocked the man's teeth out. I remembered thinking that I hadn't meant to do that. *No, I was just trying to fracture his skull,* I told myself. It had been a strange day any way I looked at it.

The next morning we were up early and I checked with Geoff Hammil to ensure that all was in readiness with the convoy. I loaded into TAC-2 and we moved out shortly after dawn, traveling through the town before anyone was up. Behind us the Belgians, along with Bravo Company and Alpha 2-87, were getting into position for another fun day. Less than an hour out of town, while I was still in radio range, I heard that Alpha 2-87 had already killed an individual who attacked a soldier with a knife and that Bravo had captured and disarmed three gunmen. Leaving Kismayu made even less sense to me than on the previous night.

Later I learned that the single bloodiest incident during the entire riot happened that morning. Two grenades were thrown into a crowd of people near the ICRC hospital, killing fourteen and wounding more than twenty others, including a Belgian soldier. Troops who had responded to the scene told me later that blood had splashed on their boots and formed in puddles around the mass of bodies. The rioting continued for a short while but then, inexplicably, ran out of steam. Later I was to learn that while we were involved in the city, Colonel Hamilton and his negotiating team had managed to get both sides to agree to a cessation of hostilities and pull back to their respective areas. In the late afternoon, most of Task Force 2-87 returned to the airfield to prepare to go back to Marka. Only Echo Company continued to conduct mounted patrols to keep a presence in the streets.

We would not be bringing Bravo Company back to Marka, however. It would stay and take over the security mission around the key sites in Kismayu currently being done by a company from Task Force 3-14. Task Force 3-14 would return to Kismayu and, if things continued to be quiet, go back to Fort Drum in about a week. JTF Kismayu was dissolving. The responsibility for HRS Kismayu would fall to the Belgians alone. The redeployment of Task Force 3-14 seemed to me premature, given that we still had two large groups of armed maniacs in the area who had only been recently dissuaded from attacking one another. Lord knew how long this truce would last. But there it was. The U.S. government couldn't wait to divest itself of this tar baby, and the thrust of everything was to stand down UNITAF and stand up UNISOM as quickly as possible.

None of this was on my mind as we went north toward Jelib before turning toward Brava and the Shabele valley. I was enjoying the view and the relative peace and quiet after six hectic days. We stopped in to see the 3-14 in their base camp, a large, modern farm complex outside of Jelib. I talked for a short while with Lieutenant Colonel Bero, the commander, and my friends Mike McKinnon, the XO, and Joe Patykula, the S3. I briefed them on what had just occurred. They were all incredulous. After all, they had worked in Kismayu for more than two months and nothing like that had happened to them. They told me that Jelib was as quiet as the proverbial grave and they looked forward to going home. Lucky bastards,

I thought. After about a forty-five-minute visit, we hit the road again and traveled north.

I told Geoff that I didn't want to come up on Brava and Mundun while it was still light because the bandits would see us and head for the hills a long time before we got there. No traffic had passed us on the way up the valley, so we halted about fifteen kilometers short of the Mundun turnoff to Brava. We went about five hundred meters off the road, hid our vehicles behind bushes, and waited for dark. Around 2000, we started moving to a dismount point about five kilometers short of the town. Geoff was to take his people in from west to east, hopefully surprising the bandits at the intersection by not coming from the direction of the road. I almost went with him but then stopped myself. Let the man command his company, I thought. I stayed with TAC-2 on some high ground where I could talk to the rest of the convoy as well as Geoff and Kismayu on TACSAT. It was a peaceful night, balmy and cloudless; the stars seemed near and were beautiful.

After a few hours Geoff called me. They'd surprised and captured four bandits in the process of robbing a bus. I grinned; the Brava bandits were nothing if not predictable. Calling for the vehicles, I went in to meet Geoff. He was miffed. When he'd come up on the scene, the bandits were too close to their victims to get a clear shot. He had to take the riskier course and go up to challenge them at close range. The poor fools never knew what hit them as a platoon of troops looming out of the darkness disarmed them before a shot could be fired. We let the bus go, with everyone on it clapping, cheering, and waving to us. We tied and blindfolded the bandits and took them with us to Marka, where we turned them over to the Marka police. They held them for about a week, then let them go. We went to a compound outside the main part of town that offered good security. The operation, although a success, had taken much longer than we expected. It was almost 0300 before we posted security and bedded down for the night.

The next morning around 1000 we were about to resume

our march to Marka when I got a call from Joe Occhuzzio, who wanted to know where I was. He and the lead convoy were already at Mundun. They must have gotten started about the time we'd gone to bed. I told him it would take us about an hour to get ready, and he laughed and told me to pick up the rear. Jesus wept, sleep six hours and I'm Rip Van Stanton. We left Brava and picked up the line of march again. In the late afternoon, we hit Shalamboot and turned to go over the ridge. It felt like coming home to see the old police barracks and Condor Base again. It had been only eight days, but what an eight days it had been.

The stay-behind detachment was naturally elated to see us. They'd had a few incidents of their own. Sergeant First Class Bellis and the resupply convoy going to Mogadishu had been attacked by bandits south of Afgoi. In a well-fought reaction to contact, the convoy members killed one bandit and captured three more. No Americans were hit, but Sergeant Bellis's truck and several others had bullet holes in them. The angels were still on our side.

There had been a more serious incident when the port security platoon exchanged fire in Marka with unidentified snipers. The Marka police were actively looking for the culprits, but so far no one claimed responsibility. It was not good news, because we had generally thought ourselves to be free of this sort of thing in Marka. Other than these two incidents, things had been quiet. Food convoys kept going out, and there was a general equanimity about the place.

Later that evening I sat down with Lieutenant Colonel Sikes and Joe Occhuzzio and talked about our operations in the valley and Kismayu, concentrating on tactics—what had worked and what hadn't. Over the next few days I talked to many people who had participated in Kismayu and our cordon and search operations. From them we came up with lessons learned and documented them for further use. Some of the major lessons learned were as follows:

• A key advantage enjoyed by American forces is that of night vision equipment. Few of our potential opponents in Africa will possess other than rudimentary first-generation passive infrared night vision devices, and even many of these devices will not be working due to poor maintenance and lack of parts. Our ability to conduct twenty-four-hour operations and see people and vehicles at night will give us a decisive edge.

• Military police and TOW vehicles with spotlights are useful for armed presence and show of force patrols. They can also be used to deceive the gunmen, because they can make the gunmen believe that the UN forces are patrolling only by vehicle at night and can thus be easily avoided. While this obvious show of force is going on, squad-sized dismounted patrols can be infiltrated into the areas that the gunmen will use to avoid the mounted patrols.

• The use of squad-sized elements, moving slowly and stealthily into ambush or overwatch position, is essential in this type of environment. Think small. In the beginning of the Somalia deployment, Task Force 2-87 sent out platoon- and company-sized elements on sweeps and had no success. We were afraid that a squad did not have the firepower to survive a contact with bandits, but this was unfounded. A squad with two SAWs and its other organic weapons is sufficient to deal with any bandit threat. Even a five-man scout squad was more than up to the threat. A disciplined group of soldiers who maintain security can engage larger numbers of bandits. (Remember, though, warlord and political forces in the cities are another situation entirely.) Bandits will try to break contact if contact is made, and they will probably have no idea of the number of soldiers they've made contact with. So squad-sized operations are the way to operate in places such as the lower Shabele valley. Your squads must practice moving as independent units with rear and flank security designated, pace man, compass man—all the patrolling skills. Practice the battle drills until they are instinctive.

• Most engagements in Task Force 2-87 took place at

less than twenty-five meters, some at ten meters. All but a few were at night. Units must practice firing with night observation devices (PVS-4s and PVS-7s), point firing techniques, and the old Vietnam "quick-kill" range. Contacts should be quick, close, incredibly violent, and over in a matter of seconds. Troops must be trained to shoot while wearing a flak vest and helmet. Train your soldiers to run a hundred-yard dash in full LBE, helmet, and flak jacket, then stop, aim, and hit a target in three seconds. This is normally all the time they will have.

• Task Force 2-87 developed what was called "stalking uniform." This comprised a helmet, flak vest, weapon, five magazines (four in the flak vest pockets, one in the weapon), a two-quart canteen on a strap, and first-aid pouches attached to the flak vest. Leaders carried a PRC-126 radio in a flak vest pocket and carried only three magazines, or carried the other two in their pants pockets. SAW gunners carried four hundred rounds. M203 gunners carried a six-round bandoleer. This light load could be justified, because dedicated support vehicles with supplies (water, ammunition, first aid, et cetera) were always close at hand. The lighter load gave our soldiers a better chance of dealing with the fleet gunmen.

• The bandits watch you and your patterns. They can figure out quickly when it is safe for them to operate. You can bait them by being predictable while planning to do the unexpected (for example, sneak people back down to the roadblock position after doing the predictable mounted patrol, as we did in Brava).

• Another good technique for catching bandits at night is simply to walk down the road as stealthily as possible— if it's paved you might consider wearing sneakers— using your night vision devices to acquire the bandits at their hasty roadblocks before they see you. This worked on several occasions for Task Force 2-87.

• Use of M203 illumination rounds is effective in helping to search an ambush area after you have secured it with the reaction force. This technique allows a more thorough search of the ground than using flashlights or night observation devices (NODs). This can also serve as a signal for the reaction force to deploy if radio communications fail.

• Night identification devices such as bud lights and glint tape are lifesavers and prevent fratricide. Each soldier needs one or the other. Also useful are infrared flashlights and spotlights.

• Water resupply is critical in this equatorial environment. All vehicles need to carry extra water cans, and the support platoon needs to continuously run water to troops engaged in the physical exertion of riot control or house searches.

• The reaction force in a local patrolling and ambush operation has the challenge of being close enough to quickly affect the action but far enough away not to tip its hand. Terrain is always a factor—that is, how fast can you traverse it in humvees—as is the ability to easily communicate. As a rule of thumb, the reaction force should be no closer than three kilometers. In the case of the Brava action, it was four kilometers away. The reaction force should be at least of platoon strength in order to effectively cordon the site of the action.

• Search the site of an action thoroughly. The bandits can quickly blend into the scene simply by discarding their weapon. (If you do it right, they won't get the chance.) Even if they get away, you can at least recover their weapons and equipment and by doing so make it harder for them to operate.

• Troops need to learn to look for concealed weapons: in roofs, under floors, broken down and hidden in pieces in wells and water cisterns, wrapped in plastic bags, in latrines, fresh graves, et cetera.

For the most part, that first night back in Marka was one enormous sigh of relief. Not a complete one, because Wes Bickford's Bravo Company was still down there and things could get ugly again, but a tangible sigh of relief nonetheless.

After three days of almost constant rioting, it was still hard to believe that we hadn't lost anyone. Later that evening I went out and offered a silent prayer of thanks for our good fortune. I'm sure Jim Sikes and almost every other man in the task force did something like that when they thought no one was looking.

Thirteen

The Valley: Part 2 (March–April 1993)

We once again found ourselves in Marka, only this time it was different because we knew who would relieve us and when. It was an odd feeling knowing that we were to be going home in about six weeks. Much had been done, yet there was still so much to do. I had a vague sense of guilt that I was getting ready to quit a job not really finished. It was nonsense, of course. Many of the problems before us were insoluble, but I couldn't help it. Donna and John were distant and somewhat unreal to me. All that mattered was the job at hand.

The job mission was going well. Although we still patrolled Marka, many of the day-to-day policing functions were being taken over by the Marka police and the town council. Walt Wojtas and Lieutenant Colonel Sikes continued to work exceptionally well with the elders, and commerce was flourishing and expanding. It was getting to the point where Marka was boring. One company had responsibility for the Marka operation and another remained on UNITAF reaction force duty. This company was usually maintaining its equipment or conducting training in the local area. If called, we had to have them ready for helicopter pickup within the hour. The other combat elements—mortars, the air defense artillery section, and Echo Company—were used mainly for convoy escort missions. MPs would normally work out of Mogadishu, and only infrequently would we get a platoon to help with the escort mission. This was unfortunate, because with their many humvees they were a natural escort force in the low-threat environment of the Shabele valley.

Supply runs were made every few days to Mogadishu, where the great American military logistics machine had finally kicked into high gear. For we who had been concerned about rationing drinking water in the opening days of the deployment, this cornucopia of supplies was most gratifying. Condor Base had a fully functioning mess hall now and a working reverse osmosis water purification unit (ROWPU). Water was no longer a problem, and neither was food. We finally had our own field kitchens functioning and had T rations twice daily. We were even given fresh fruit supplements, manna from heaven after more than two months of straight MREs. The ultimate, however, was the opening up of a small PX, although it didn't sell much, just cookies, Coke, chips, razors, soap, stationery—that sort of thing.

People scoff at the need for the U.S. Army to supply amenities on an active deployment. But in a situation such as Somalia, you'd be amazed what a few amenities can do for the soldiers' morale. The PX gave another link with normality in a decidedly abnormal place.

The troops generally spent what little free time they had catching up on sleep or playing cards. Many worked out on the weight sets brought in with the battalion's MILVANs of equipment. Paperback books and magazines were popular, as was the battalion's unofficial "smut library," run by the support platoon. This was a footlocker full of sublimely dirty books lent out to any and all. In the politically correct army of the 1990s, this was a shaky thing to do, but we were forward deployed and there were no women soldiers permanently with the task force, so we got away with it. I contributed several magazines mailed to me by one of my friends who never got over being a nineteen-year-old tanker in Vietnam. One of them featured grossly overweight women doing all sorts of imaginative things with their genitalia. Lieutenant Van Hoesen, upon being presented this, scanned it and whispered in a reverent voice, "Sir, you are a *god*." It became the most popular magazine in the library—yessir, real highbrow entertainment. Lieutenant

Colonel Sikes did not give any official permission for it; he simply ignored its presence. It improved morale.

After we returned from Kismayu, we received a representative from Brown and Root contracting. He was attached to the battalion to facilitate troop support issues with the local economy. He hired a laundry, so soon all of our clothes were being washed by Somali women from Marka. In addition, he hired labor for waste disposal and any minor construction or excavation we required. The people of Marka were grateful for the pay, and the troops were happy not to have to do their own washing. Brown and Root fit right in with our logistics team. Another thing to make life more bearable.

Patrolling Marka continued to be a mundane chore. Most people were friendly toward the soldiers on their walks through the streets and marketplaces. We still conducted three patrols through Marka each day, varying the times and routes to avoid setting a pattern. Several Marka policemen went with the patrols. The fact that the Marka police were increasingly being asked to adjudicate mundane occurrences such as theft and domestic disturbances was another sign that life had reached a sort of equilibrium. Members of the Ali Tihad for the most part stayed on their best behavior. They kept to themselves and didn't bother us or anyone else. Produce was starting to come into Marka, and relief supplies were not the currency they once were. Things were looking up.

This improvement in the overall situation also extended to the way we worked with NGOs. The tensions evident earlier between their lack of organization and our penchant for control had largely dissipated. Now all aid to NGOs was handled through the UNITAF headquarters coordination cell. Convoy escort and NGO support missions progressed from the "hey you, drop everything to support this" chore that it had been to a series of organized taskings. Working with JTF headquarters, we knew each day how many NGO convoys we had to escort, along with linkup time, destination, and points of contact. We could look at the destinations and tailor the escort according to the level of threat, then make our internal taskings. The staff knew when we were overtasked and could turn back or defer relief supply convoys that we could not adequately cover. The whole process was tracked by Sergeant First Class Hardcastle and the shift NCOs on a big status chart. Convoy escort assignments and destinations for the next day were briefed at the 1600 meeting.

A typical escort mission began with the troops assigned to the escort assembling in their billet areas about two hours prior. Precombat inspections were held, as well as final weapons and equipment checks, ammunition accountability, and a patrol briefing. If the escort was not from a unit that had its own organic vehicles (such as Tom Wilk's Echo Company with its TOW humvees, the 81mm mortar platoon with its cargo humvees, or MPs with their hardtop humvees), then linkup with designated vehicles happened at this time. Normally, the designated vehicles were from the battalion's support platoon or the attached Stinger section. A typical escort mission was made up of four humvees with a platoon-sized infantry element mounted on them. They normally had two M60 machine guns, four to six SAWs, M203 grenade launchers, and M16 rifles. The escorts were more than adequate to overpower any bandit groups they might encounter. After the vehicles had linked up, communications checks with man-carried radios and vehicle-mounted radios were conducted. The troops mounted up, with one squad per vehicle. The platoon leader and platoon sergeant rode in different vehicles. The escort commander then called the TOC and reported he was ready to move to the port to link up with his convoy.

The lieutenant or sergeant who was the escort leader had been given his mission the night before. He then coordinated with the TOC the route he would take and the checkpoints he would report over the radio. There were standard routes to each of the major food distribution warehouses in HRS Marka. This made our movements predictable but also made it easier for us to find and get to convoys in trouble. I approved of this because at this time satellite location ground receivers (SLGRs) were still a novelty, and there were not enough of them in the battalion to provide one for each convoy. Lieutenant Colonel Sikes concurred. We never had a convoy seriously attacked while we ran HRS Marka, although a few received sniper fire. The familiarity with the route did on one occasion allow us to vector in a medevac helicopter and evacuate a soldier who had succumbed to heatstroke. Escort leaders taking a convoy to a location unfamiliar to them were always given at least one subordinate leader who had been there before. After a period of time, though, we'd repeated enough convoys that everyone knew where to go by rote. We'd restock a food warehouse on an average of once or twice a week. Soon it was a rare lieutenant or squad leader who hadn't visited every warehouse in the 2-87 area of responsibility.

The escort pulled out of Condor Base and turned left, heading down the coast road toward Marka. The Somalis they passed on the way might wave and smile, or might not. Some tried to thumb rides, and sometimes escort commanders accommodated them. This was a violation of security, but it helped our relations with the townsfolk. The humvees transited the checkpoint, and the troops bullshitted briefly with the guys on duty. The escort leader mentioned that his convoy would be back through in a little while. If anyone had seen anything suspicious, the news would be passed on.

Approaching town, the escort passed the first house on the left, then a clump of houses, and then reached the outskirts of the town proper. On the right, children were playing naked in the surf, with the rusting relief ship sitting looted and helpless aground in the harbor. The humvees passed Sister Anna's hospital and entered the port of Marka proper, the gates being opened by two Marka policemen in green uniforms with blue berets and AK-47s, which they always seemed to hold upside down by their ammunition magazines.

The troops were shown the vehicles they were to escort. The trucks were preloaded the night before and lined up in a column of twos inside the port secure area. The drivers were sitting in the cabs conversing or sleeping and had to be made to check the maintenance status of their vehicles. The trucks were usually dilapidated, and no two were of the same make. Dented and bruised, held together with rope and tape, their gaudy paint faded and lights more often than not smashed, they looked like automotive lepers. Their condition was exacerbated by the general lack of care they received from their drivers. At first the truckers we worked with had a tendency to overload their trucks. It was common in the early days for an escort commander to delay starting for hours while many of the food bags on a truck were taken off. At first we tried to apply some U.S. Army standards to the truck checks, but we quickly learned to go for the lowest common denominator (Did they all have enough fuel? Were they overloaded? Did any have flat tires? Were any on fire?)

The escort commander confirmed the number of trucks in his charge with the ICRC representative and the port security commander. Normally, food convoys were from six to twenty trucks, depending on where they were going. The escort commander spent a few minutes having his people run down the last stray drivers while the remainder sat in their vehicles and gunned their engines. It sounded like an asthmatic Daytona 500. Crowds of children and onlookers gathered at the gate to see the convoy depart. Although it was a sight they'd see often enough, they never appeared to tire of it. The convoy commander gave the word, and the police opened the gates and beat back members of the crowd with sticks. The convoy escort moved out with a point humvee, followed by the commander and then the food trucks wheezing and gasping and blowing blue smoke. The last two humvees brought up the rear.

The trucks began down the road at about thirty kilometers per hour and gradually gained speed as they cleared the town. The convoy slowed briefly to clear the checkpoint, then continued past Condor Base toward the coastal ridge. Climbing the ridge would be the first true test of the mechanical condition of the vehicles, and it was not unusual to lose one or two vehicles on the ascent. These were returned to the port by Condor Base as soon as they could run again. At the intersection in Shalamboot, the convoy went either north toward Jannelle or Aw-Degle or south toward Quorleey, Kurtenwary, or Brava. It was important not to let the convoy stretch out too much lest some unscrupulous driver take the opportunity to slip from the convoy and disappear. Once everyone caught up, the convoy increased its speed to about fifty kilometers an hour and headed down the road toward its destination. The roads were of packed earth, which stood up to wear and tear reasonably well. After prolonged rain, however, they had numerous muddy spots that could be negotiated only with difficulty. The first escort vehicle was charged with finding the most promising ways around these areas.

The scenery was invariably lush and green, with stands of trees and well-watered crops in evidence. The relative bounty of the valley made the humanitarian mission seem incongruous. Then again, as Kirk Haschak had said, maybe they just didn't eat corn. The troops continuously scanned out from their vehicles, each man with his sector of observation, weapon at the ready, rounds chambered, on safe. The lead vehicle kept a good look at the road as the convoy proceeded slowly along. We'd found only a few mines laid on the road since we'd been in the valley. I suspected that those were the result of previous interfactional fighting, but we never could tell. Troops talked and told stories to one another but never took their eyes from the side of the road and their sector of observation. It was serious business, and no one wanted to be caught unaware if something happened. Occasionally the convoy passed a truck or bus overcrowded seemingly to the point of bursting—proof that some entrepreneurs were still attempting to eke out a profit from the chaos. Imagine Greyhound bus lines trying to operate in Germany during the Thirty Years' War.

The miles and hours rolled by in a lazy, desultory fashion, the sun a continuous presence and the heat an enervating, all-encompassing shroud. Canteens of water were drained and refilled. Troops thought of ice and cold soda or beer. The road threw up dust or mud, depending on conditions. Sometimes the troops saw people working in the fields. A few waved, but most just stared dully at the convoy and returned to work. The convoy of sweating, bored soldiers continued on its slow journey down the Shabele valley.

Eventually, the convoy neared the environs of the town whose food warehouse was to be resupplied. Children started running beside the trucks hoping for a handout. The convoy passed goats being herded down the road and other animals being brought to market. Many people came out to watch the arrival of the supplies; we were the best show in town. If the throng of people was too great, troops dismounted to clear a way. Only rarely did a convoy get to a warehouse without having to do this.

As the convoy reached the warehouse, it was met by a harried ICRC "official" who either bemoaned the fact that we brought too little or berated us for bringing more than he could store. Off-loading proceeded quickly if the ICRC people were competent. If not, the escort commander paid an impromptu gang of stevedores with MREs. A few extra cases were always kept on hand for this eventuality. The troops established a security perimeter and faced out while the food was being off-loaded. An occasional glance back at the sweating Somalis off-loading bags of rice and lentils and tins of cooking oil was all they saw for their efforts. It was late afternoon by the time the food was off-loaded and the food warehouse was again put under local guards.

Unencumbered, the trucks moved twice as fast as the convoy commenced movement back. It retraced its steps in what seemed to be an amazingly short time, proving yet again that it's always quicker when you're going home. The escort dropped off at Condor Base, leaving the trucks to make their own way back to Marka. The troops dismounted and shook off the dust or brushed the mud off themselves. It was close to chow time (sometimes it was after hours, with food being held for them). After eating, the troops conducted recovery operations. Drivers refueled and performed maintenance checks on their vehicles. Other soldiers cleaned their weapons and equipment. The first sergeant dropped off the mail with the platoon, then the soldiers cleaned themselves up at the beach (later, they would use the showers erected at Condor Base). The escort leader stopped by the TOC to debrief Captain Klein on any unusual activity he'd seen. A few hardy souls started a game of cards after the recovery work was done, but most washed up and went to sleep. Another day down in Somalia.

With the heavy commitment for convoy support (up to six convoys to separate locations each day), we began to run short of vehicles and troops for escorts. Some of the smaller convoys of only a few trucks didn't require large escorts. The temptation to cut corners and send less than full platoon escorts was strong. Sometimes we were forced to do it, but I never felt good about it. My perspective was, our convoys never got hit because their escorts were big enough to discourage attack. I was certain that if we lightened the escort too much, sooner or later someone would take a poke at us. Still, the requirements for escort came at us so thick and fast that sometimes we had to send squad-sized elements on escort duty. I always scheduled these escort missions to the close-in destinations, which we could reinforce quickly, or the ones that went up the valley toward Afgoi, by now a relatively peaceful area. Anything that went south toward Brava or any other recognized injun country needed at least a platoon. In spite of these precautions, I fretted over the lightness of the escorts we were forced to send. The absolute worst was a two-humvee escort from the ADA section that we had to scrape together for some NGO bigwig going to Mogadishu who couldn't wait another day. He had gotten UNITAF headquarters to order us to provide an immediate escort, a whopping six troops. I worried all day, keeping close tabs on their whereabouts until they returned. It's not an enriching experience to put troops in harm's way just to meet some asshole's schedule. Nothing happened, but stuff like this wore on Lieutenant Colonel Sikes and me.

About this time we were ordered to begin planning to open a repatriation camp to hold several thousand people. It was to be set up outside of Marka and hold the demobilized gunmen of various factions who would now be going home. Shades of Appomattox.

Lieutenant Colonel Sikes told me to go and find a site, so I took TAC-2 and a security team and headed out. After much searching and casting, I located a space on the other side of the ridge from Marka, near Shalamboot. It had the remains of a house and looked as though it would drain well. Sikes approved it and we were in business. I was mentally calculating the number of tents, cots, and field kitchens we'd need to feed the demobilized people when I was hit with the next part of the tasking. Not only would we have to house the returning gunmen, we would have to assist them back into civilian life. One way to do this would be to give them back their herds so they could return to their pastoral lives. It appeared now that not only would the battalion be responsible for returning refugees and demobilized gunmen but livestock for them as well. I wearily made notes for the S4 to inquire about goat feed (and how much water does a goat drink a day anyway?), as well as materials for goat pens. I also made a note for Lieutenant Lavellie, the medical platoon leader, to inquire about possible veterinarian support from the JTF. I relayed the information about the goats to Lieutenant Colonel Sikes, who took it well; he just sighed and went back to cleaning his weapon.

I called together the staff NCOs to give them a brief update on what was being planned. They received it impassively. At this stage in the deployment, nothing surprised them anymore. When I got to the part about handing everyone a few goats as they left the demobilization site, there were a few giggles. Sergeant First Class Hardcastle correctly pointed out that not everyone was a goat herder before the civil war began, and what would we give those guys? I had the sudden mental image of a Somali certified public accountant being given ten goats and told to get on the truck. I didn't have an answer. Staff Sergeant Magnant asked, "What if the guy was a pimp before the war?" At that point I ended the discussion.

After two days of sketching and planning and gathering, we were suddenly told to put the whole project on hold. It was still on hold when we left.

The situation report for 11 March, found in Appendix III (Operations Summary, Marka), gives a good snapshot of operations during this period.

We subsequently got a new Marka police chief, Mohammed Omar Mohammed, and he did just fine. We didn't get any reinforcements or individual replacements for our shortage of communications personnel or additional units from JTF that could have relieved us from the Marka security mission in order to be as robust as the JTF ready reaction force (RRF). Oh well.

As March progressed, the weather became a lot windier. No rain, just overcast with incredible windstorms. I was worried about the roofs on our compound, but the engineers had done their jobs well. The wind wasn't cold, just bracing with a hint of sea breeze. Early one morning I awoke to the news that a ship had gone aground near the checkpoint outside of town. Apparently, a small Egyptian freighter about the size of a large trawler had lost its engine and drifted aground. The crew had scrambled ashore and now the hapless ship was being buffeted against the rocks right in front of us. What was amazing was that people from town were boarding the vessel and beginning to loot it before we even managed to get there. We shooed them off, pending evaluation of the ship by naval personnel from JTF. They confirmed the next day that there was water in the holds and the engine room was flooded. Although the ship looked good enough above the waterline, because it ran aground on a fairly even keel, if it was dragged into deep water, it would sink like a stone. I asked Lieutenant Colonel Sikes if we could have salvage rights on the ship and its cargo. He gave me one of his "now, Marty" looks and gave directions that nobody from the task force was to go near the ship. We abandoned the hulk to the Somalis. The Egyptian crew had been taken to Mogadishu for evacuation, and the good people of Marka looted the derelict with abandon. Within a week it was just another stripped, trashed wreck on the coast. The land of Somalia, with its roofless houses and bleak shoreline that malevolently ensnared still-working pieces of man's progress, itself seemed to reject civilization and delight in any small victory over it.

We had many high-ranking visitors in this time frame.

Marka was getting to be a showcase for how things could work in Somalia. Visitors took a certain amount of time away from Lieutenant Colonel Sikes, who was forced to take them on little tours of the site and give them briefings. Sikes did all of the briefings himself, because he was the boss and because it allowed the rest of us to continue to work with a minimum of outside interference. He was a blocker for Joe Occhuzzio, Walt Wojtas, and me. Our highest-ranking visitor was the then chairman of the Joint Chiefs of Staff, Gen. Colin Powell. He came with a large entourage, and I could have forgiven Lieutenant Van Hoesen for believing that Elvis had indeed arrived. General Powell contented himself with talking to soldiers who had been assembled to hear him speak. He spent about an hour talking to the troops. Then he was off, with his satellite communication people, aides, security men, dog robbers, and hangers-on following close behind. Each one of these visits was good for two to four hours' disruption of Lieutenant Colonel Sikes's day, not to mention its impact on others. Sikes would then stay awake at night catching up.

The boss didn't spare himself. He was forever answering mail and inquires from the rear and sending advice to his wife about how to handle family support group matters. This last seemed a waste, because Ruth Anne seemed to be doing fine on her own. My point of view was that we had a rear detachment commander, First Lieutenant Osteen, back from the JRTC (Charlie Company had been tasked to go to Panama), and Fort Drum could look after itself. There was nothing happening there that could not be put right when we got back. We sent a video back to the family support group of us getting our gamma gobulin shots. I painted a big target on my buttocks so they could all see it. Donna told me it was a big hit.

Many people, however, were worried about their families. My father was in a bad way; my mother's letters did not convey this, but my sister filled me in. She was concerned he wouldn't make it to my return, but there wasn't anything I could do. My dad, a retired sergeant major, would be the first to understand that I couldn't leave the battalion. I was far from the only one. Sergeant Hardcastle's wife had cancer and was undergoing treatment. Although it wore on him, he would not ask to be sent home. He knew how much he was needed by the battalion. Mike Klein's marriage was in trouble, and the thought of how a divorce would affect his little boy particularly bothered him. Many troops had worries and anxieties they had left at home, but none would ask to be exempted from deployment or ask to be relieved of their duties and sent back. Tough comes in many forms. The soldiers of the 2-87 bore their personal hardships well and without complaint.

Kismayu: Part 2 (March 1993)

After we returned to Marka and resumed the UNITAF reaction force mission, things continued to get dangerous in Kismayu. The truce between the Morgan and Jess factions did not last, and they were soon hard at it again. The Belgians did not have the strength to stop small groups of gunmen from infiltrating the city, although they did prevent larger groups on several occasions. Bravo Company was limited to site security of critical locations throughout Kismayu. Within a week of the battalion's return to Marka, we were getting reports of fighting from Kismayu. Wes Bickford reported numerous incidents of rifle fire hitting the locations guarded by his troops. He also reported the increase in rioting. We were all worried, but UNITAF would not commit us (its last reserve) until the situation worsened. The Belgians and Bravo Company were reduced to securing the port and the airfield as well as the key NGO sites in town. Patrols would chase and disperse large groups of warlord gunmen, but they were powerless to stop the constant trickle of infiltrators by both sides. In a short time Kismayu was worse off than when we left. At first the Somalis of both sides continued to avoid confrontation with UNITAF troops if at all possible, as they had done in the original riot. Soon, however, they began showing a more aggressive stance.

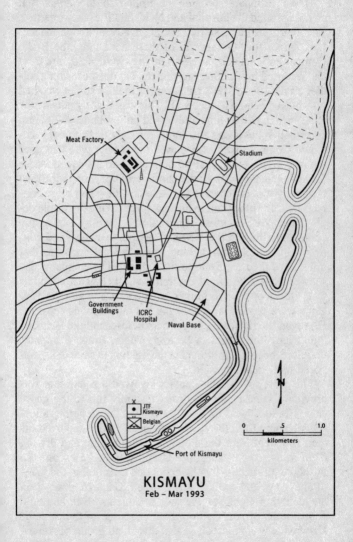

KISMAYU
Feb – Mar 1993

Bravo Company became embroiled in the fights that swirled around the hospital and NGO facilities they guarded. The guard positions started taking steady, although inaccurate, sniper fire. On several of these occasions, the Bravo Company soldiers observed where they were taking fire from and returned fire, killing the snipers. On one occasion a soldier used a 40mm M203 rifle grenade to kill a sniper who had just ducked behind a stone wall. This was slightly outside the ROE, which at that time authorized only rounds of 7.62mm and smaller, but it was absolutely the right thing to do. Lieutenant Colonel Sikes interviewed the soldier who had used the rifle grenade and praised both him and his squad leader for acting as they did. In the short period of time that Bravo Company was attached to the Belgians, they had more contacts than any other unit in the task force during the whole deployment. Wes Bickford came into his own as a company commander during this stressful period, keeping good control of his people and making sound tactical decisions that minimized their exposure to the fighting. The company also showed itself to be a tight, disciplined outfit that had found its feet. Our people were limited to site security, and the Belgians were supposed to keep the fighting factions separate. However, the riots were larger than before, and the Belgians didn't have the forces to be everywhere. Bravo Company, therefore, became embroiled in the fighting in spite of its supposed static guard mission.

The most spectacular contact involved a squad that was providing security for a normal resupply run to the guard sites. The squad was fired on from one of the numerous alleyways leading onto the road. The squad leader deployed his men and went after the gunmen, returning fire and driving them away; so far, so good. Unfortunately, he became so flushed with success that he continued pursuit into the maze of alleyways and walls that was urban Kismayu, away from the main thoroughfares. He soon became involved in a fight with dozens of Jess faction gunmen. None of the Somalis knew what was going on or that this small group of Americans was really on its own. Had the Somalis realized that this was just an understrength rifle squad that got carried away, I doubt that any of the squad would have made it out alive. As it was, the squad's sheer aggression in the attack and the individual proficiency of the soldiers carried them through a thirty-minute engagement in which they killed at least nine of the gunmen without suffering so much as a scrape. Confused by this miniature buzz saw that had literally burst into their midst, the gunmen eventually broke contact and fled. The squad leader belatedly saw that he had bitten off more than he could chew and withdrew in the opposite direction. When Lieutenant Colonel Sikes and I walked the ground a few days later, I was in awe of their luck. I just couldn't believe that they hadn't lost anyone.

So much was going on in Kismayu that Lieutenant Colonel Sikes resolved to go back down and appraise the situation firsthand. He took me and Sergeant Major Key with him. We arrived at the port and were briefed by the Belgians and the last DIVARTY members who were in the process of redeploying to Fort Drum (Task Force 3-14 had already departed). We learned that although the fighting in Kismayu was not as spectacular as the riots we had encountered earlier, it was constant and more decisive. The forces under Mohammed Hersi Morgan seemed to be gaining the upper hand over those of Omar Jess. However, there was enough fight left in them to make it interesting for the UNITAF forces. We spent most of the day reviewing security with Wes Bickford and going over the firefights that his people were involved in. Wes had a handle on things. His guard sites were as safe as he could make them. He shared our view that the resupply truck escort should have broken contact after suppressing the initial fires they had taken, as opposed to pursuing the gunmen. Kudos to the squad leader for a great fight but a general admonition not to try it again.

We spent the night on top of Bravo Company's headquarters at one of the NGO sites. Periodically throughout the evening we'd hear the *pop*, *pop*, *ziinnggg* of rounds going overhead as the two factions continued to fight. In the morning the Bravo Company troops said that it had been a relatively quiet night.

Sikes and I flew back to Marka the next day. We both thought that, as the JTF reaction force, we would be sent to Kismayu in a few days. We weren't wrong.

The Morgan faction pushed the Jess faction out of town the next day in a flurry of activity, which the UNITAF forces were powerless to stop. UNITAF headquarters alerted us to return to Kismayu to prevent any further violence. This was a bit late because the violence had already happened, but orders were orders. We left Geoff Hammil's company at Marka to continue patrolling and escort the convoy, and took the rest of the battalion back to Kismayu. Alpha Company 2-87 and selected personnel from the battalion staff flew; everyone else drove. Joe Occhuzzio controlled another long, torturous movement down the Shabele valley to Jelib and on to Kismayu. At Jelib there was some tension because the Jess faction had retreated to there. However, they were under the impression that we were going to Kismayu to eject the Morgan forces, so they made no attempt to hinder our movement.

We again set up our base camp at the airport and began patrolling Kismayu that evening. It was completely quiet; not one shot was fired. The next day we were treated to the first of several "peace marches." These consisted of groups of Somalis (Morgan supporters no doubt) marching, skipping, and dancing down the street while they sang and chanted. There were more than a thousand of them waving green branches and palm fronds. The marchers danced merrily among us, smiling and waving at the soldiers. Our men stood impassive and puzzled at the side of the street. Many younger boys had their slings wrapped around their foreheads in a symbol of harmless intent. We knew that these people were some of the same ones who had shot at us in the previous month, but because they had driven the Jess people out of town, there wasn't any point for them to fight UNITAF. We had the power to hurt them, if not defeat them in a final sense, and they knew we would leave sooner or later, so why pick a fight? Delegations from "General Morgan" assured us that there would be no further trouble in Kismayu, and he pledged full cooperation with UNITAF.

Because of this, the second trip down to Kismayu was an anticlimax. Bravo Company was relieved of the guard mission by the Belgians and rejoined Task Force 2-87. Although Kismayu appeared peaceful for the moment, we were directed to maintain security in the town for a period of time to ensure that the rival faction did not return and start the fighting again. Our battalion and the Belgians conducted the same extensive patrolling and sweep pattern as we had earlier. Alpha and Bravo Companies both did daylight sweeps. Squad-sized patrols at night did their best to ferret out armed gunmen. The battalion maintained its patrolling of Kismayu for a few days, and nothing at all happened. The town seemed to be under a self-imposed curfew. It became a metaphor for the overall Somali situation. Someone of the warring factions had "won," and because there was a "winner," some semblance of order and peace had been restored. The winner was no moral exemplar by any standard, but at the same time the peace and quiet was unmistakable.

Two days before we redeployed to Marka, we were witnesses to one of those senseless tragedies that occur from time to time in military operations. There were several derelict Somali air force aircraft on the Kismayu airstrip. The most intriguing of these was an old British Canberra bomber sitting stripped and broken a hundred meters from the terminal complex. One of the first jet bombers, the Canberra had been used extensively by the British in the 1956 Suez operation. As a history buff I took a look at it. The Canberra was widely sold all over the world, so it was not unthinkable that one would end up in the Somali air force. The aircraft was clearly in sad shape. All the windows were broken. The left side landing gear had collapsed entirely, so the plane tilted onto one wing like a broken toy. A cursory inspection showed that the Somalis had ripped almost all of the shell. The cockpit was almost stripped, although the pilot's seat was still there. God only knows how long the bomber had sat there— probably since the 1970s or 1980s. Our troops and the Belgians used to climb on it to get their pictures taken.

One day about a week after we got back to Kismayu, I was

coming out of the TOC when I heard a single loud explosion on the other side of the terminal. I remember thinking that we were being mortared and was about to yell for everyone to take cover when someone started yelling that the old plane had blown up.

Apparently during all those years, the cartridge in the ejector seat was present and no one had touched it—until one day in March 1993 when a young Belgian soldier sat in the pilot's seat and said, "What's this?" and pulled the lever. He was catapulted about a hundred feet into the air (witnesses said) and landed with a sickening thump, which caused numerous compound fractures. He was still alive when the Belgians put him on the helicopter, but he died en route to the Belgian aid station.

When I think of the number of troops who had poked around that old bomber, I still shudder. Needless to say, an immediate lesson learned from this was to have qualified EOD people check out each derelict whenever we occupied a place such as Kismayu airfield, no matter how old and harmless the derelict may look. Until you can do that, place the damned things off limits.

It was clear that the Jess faction did not have the strength to attempt to reimpose its power on Kismayu, and for a short duration, at least, the town would be stable and peaceful. JTF ordered us back to Marka to reassume the JTF reaction force mission. We were also informed that Task Force 1-22 from the 1st Brigade would come and replace us during the second week of April. This news was cheery, and we set off for Marka in high spirits. I commanded the convoy going north this time. I figured that three times for Joe Occhuzzio (down and back and down again) was enough and he could use the break.

Unfortunately, we had to drive back through the Jess faction at Jelib. They were not at all pleased that we hadn't ejected Morgan's faction from Kismayu. I went with the lead march serial of the convoy, because that was the one I thought would have the most difficulty. I was wrong. The lead serial got through Jelib with only a few dirty looks and the occasional rock thrown at us. The subsequent serials that passed through Jelib waited along the road for the last serial to clear in case they had to return and provide reinforcements. This precaution was well taken. By the time the last march serial went through the town, hundreds of people were jeering and menacing along the road. Many Somalis were throwing rocks; one of the soldiers in the convoy had his arm broken. Warning shots served to clear away the Somalis briefly, but several other soldiers were injured by thrown missiles in this short time. Injuries would have been worse had it not been for the old-style armored vests and Kevlar helmets the soldiers were wearing. The troops in the last serial responded well and cleared the Somalis away from the convoy without having to resort to lethal violence.

I was waiting outside the town in the first march serial. I decided to return to help the last serial commander with their fight and was in the process of turning my vehicles around when they radioed for us to stay put and keep the road clear. Presently they came out, a few dings and broken windows on the vehicles but no serious damage. I was more concerned about the people. A rock thrown hard enough to break an arm could as easily have killed. I was furious at the lieutenant in charge of the serial for allowing his people to be injured, but I held my tongue. I wasn't there and didn't see it, so there was no point in second-guessing the man on the scene, particularly after the fact. The kid had gotten through the serial without any major casualties. That was the important thing.

I thought about my initial anger with the lieutenant as we continued the drive north and was a little disturbed. I realized that, had it been my serial, I probably would have shot the rock thrower or throwers. This was in the gray area of the ROE and could have resulted in all sorts of complications for Lieutenant Colonel Sikes and the battalion. I was becoming aware of a gradual shift in my whole attitude. Even though this latest Kismayu mission was peaceful, I was still distrustful and on guard around the Somalis. I had little of the patience I'd had at the start of the rotation. I was ready to respond to violence or threat immediately. I was fatigued, cautious, and generally tired of fucking around. The mission looked increasingly chaotic, and I could not guess where it was going. I knew only that we did the best we could wherever we went. I didn't believe in anything but the battalion, and getting us home in one piece was all that mattered. The fact was that the lieutenant had probably handled the situation better back there in Jelib than I would have, given my frame of mind. I sucked on these thoughts as we drudged north at about thirty-five miles per hour.

Before I could get too introspective, we started having mechanical breakdowns. The miles we had put on our tortured vehicles finally started taking their toll. The column had to stop repeatedly to make repairs, change tires, or fix tow cables. The convoy speed reduced and time seemed to stand still. The troops kept at it, though, making me proud of them. It would have been so easy just to leave a vehicle to catch up, or not keep security at a halt, or take off the body armor and helmets and sleep, but none of that happened. The troops stayed alert and stayed hard. They kept security posted at halts and fixed the vehicles in the shortest amount of time. Throughout that whole interminable day and night, I did not have to tell a single man to keep his equipment on or his weapon with him. Discipline is easy to keep in moments of extreme peril. Maintaining discipline in the slow, dull grind is the true test of a unit. Task Force 2-87, the battalion and all of its attachments, was a disciplined unit.

The last element finally made it to Marka well after midnight. All personnel, vehicles, and equipment were accounted for. Joe Occhuzzio was waiting for me on the HQ building steps. I asked him how he had managed to pull off three textbook road marches. When I did it, the whole thing went to hell. He just laughed and said it was all in knowing how, or something of the sort. We went to see Sikes and had a cup of coffee. I was dirty and tired but felt strangely carefree. Yes, the trip to Kismayu this time had turned out to be unnecessary. Hell, the whole Somalia mission was a disorganized mess. Although earlier in the day I probably would have killed a guy if he'd thrown a rock at me, now none of that seemed to matter.

There was Jim Sikes with his sly grin shaking his head as I detailed our vehicle recovery woes. Joe Occhuzzio offered me some Cheese-Its from a box his wife had sent. I felt happy—and felt something else I couldn't put a name to right away. I guess the feeling could be summed up in one word: confident. I was with the battalion and we were good men. No matter what happened or what task we were given, we would do it well. This in and of itself was all that mattered.

Fourteen

The Big Picture: Operation RESTORE HOPE
February–April 1993

By the beginning of March, the complexion of the UNITAF effort changed considerably. The Marines had withdrawn from Baidoa and were replaced by an Australian infantry battalion. HRS Baledogle was taken over by a Moroccan battalion, and both of these as well as HRS Marka came under 2d Brigade and ARFOR control. After more than three months, 2d Brigade headquarters was finally commanding the same number of units it did at Fort Drum, only most of them weren't American. Both HRS Baidoa and HRS Baledogle were relatively quiet AORs. Most real action in country took place in and around Mogadishu and, to a lesser extent, Kismayu. UNITAF was still looking for a force to come to Marka and relieve us so we could act solely as the UNITAF reaction force, but so far there were no takers.

Meanwhile, the relief efforts were becoming a victim of their own success. The country was literally glutted with relief supplies, so much so that they actually started losing value on the black market. Confronted with an abundance of free food brought by eager relief agencies, many farmers did not bother to plant crops of beans and sorghum. Why eat that when there was relief rice all over the place? About the only part of the economy (or what passed for an economy) not affected by the glut of relief supplies was the khat trade. Khat grows only in parts of Kenya, so a steady stream of light aircraft continued to come into the country. Many of them flew to the K-50 airfield south of Mogadishu, the same one we had raided in January. These flights were flown mostly by white South Africans, who were paid in Somali shillings, which I guess they exchanged somewhere. Crazy. Khat trade was actually on the upswing in the lower Shabele valley because we'd done such a good job of suppressing banditry. So at the beginning of our fourth month in Somalia, we had managed to give the Somalis so much food that many didn't feel the need to farm and boosted the drug trade. Somalia was a laboratory for the law of unintended consequences. More relief workers continued to come into the country to set up hospitals and clinics, distribute yet more relief supplies, or work to restore the local infrastructure. The Somalis sat by the side of the road and watched this gigantic effort on their behalf with a detached and regal air. They came to regard it as their due.

The transition to UNISOM gathered steam. Although UNITAF still called the shots, it was clear that the U.S. government wanted to hand over this mission to the UN soonest, no matter what condition the UNISOM headquarters was in. This was unfortunate, because the Somalis sensed a weakening and uncertainty in our presence. Incidents in Mogadishu continued to increase. Somalis became more brazen in their thefts from U.S. vehicles and living areas. There were a few celebrated cases of Marines being tried for excessive use of force in dealing with thieves, notably one where a sergeant was court-martialed for shooting a Somali looter who had stolen the sunglasses off his face. The honeymoon period of Restore Hope was definitely over. The Somalis looked upon us as people to be gulled and taken advantage of. The troops looked upon the Somalis with suspicion and distrust (but never hatred; I never heard a single soldier express actual hatred for the Somalis). We couldn't deny, however, that the atmosphere was getting nastier.

The UN staff was less than enthusiastic about taking the reins, and they objected and delayed for the rest of the time that Task Force 2-87 was deployed. We could see their point. No one wanted to be handed a work in progress that looked like Somalia. Even worse, the United States was withdrawing many of the forces that had made Somalia stable initially. This presented an opportunity to the Somalis. They stole and agitated and generally stirred things up. This boded ill for UNISOM II. Strength is respected above all else in places such as Somalia, and the multinational force was getting weaker as the troop units withdrew. The word was getting out that the new sheriff in town was a mincing, sissy caricature of the old lawman. UNISOM II would not get the respect earned by UNITAF.

It looked as though Task Force 2-87 would be out of the country before the actual handover to UNISOM took place. I was happy at this prospect. The UN organization was unimpressive, the mission itself vague and undefined. I could see no clearly articulated end state or vision for what UNISOM II was actually supposed to do. I had the feeling that everyone was making it up as they went along. I sensed a bad ending to the whole mission and only wondered what form this ending would take.

Fifteen

Last Operations (March–April 1993)

Lieutenant Harvey and the scouts were doing a routine sweep of Marka when they took fire from an Ali Tihad member outside the main Ali Tihad compound. No one was hurt, but the man got away. Lieutenant Colonel Sikes wasn't about to let a group as organized as the Ali Tihad get frisky with us, so we quickly surrounded their compound and told them to leave without their weapons while we searched the building. We found more than a hundred small arms as well as machine guns and antitank rockets. The Ali Tihad took it stoically; they probably had more cached locally and could afford to let us take this batch without resistance. I had the impression that they were angrier at their man who had fired the shots than at us. I did not envy that sad-sack guard.

The confrontation with the Ali Tihad put us all on edge. If anyone in the area was capable of causing us casualties, it was them. Lieutenant Colonel Sikes increased the strength of the patrols and always kept the reaction company close at hand, but nothing happened. There were no more confrontations with the Ali Tihad, and Marka returned to normal.

There was another strange flurry of activity one night. Joe Occhuzzio was in Mogadishu coordinating the arrival of TF 1-22, and Lieutenant Colonel Sikes had gone out to the amphibious ready group Marine expeditionary unit (ARG-MEU) offshore for a JTF briefing. I was just lying down around 2200 when Staff Sergeant Issac came from the TOC. He said that some NGO was here claiming that her partner

279

had been kidnapped and was being held hostage. Intrigued, I went to the TOC. There an elderly Korean lady told me that her partner was being held in Brava (of all places). They were members of a Korean aid group who had gotten off the plane and gone forth to dispense aid without coordinating with anyone. They had managed to get to Brava with the help of their "bodyguards." Now one of them was being held in Brava for ransom.

I was suspicious about the whole thing, but I sent two platoons—one antitank and one infantry—down to Brava, with this woman as a guide. I told them to find out what was going on and get back to me as soon as possible. I mentally started the process of organizing a company team to go down to Brava and rip the Brava SNA chief a new asshole. I gave Gordy Flowers the warning order and told Van Hoesen to spot the trucks for rapid upload just in case. I told the TOC to call me the second they heard from our Brava element, then I went back to bed. I had the feeling it was going to be a long night.

Unfortunately, someone in the TOC had reported the "hostage situation" to the JTF, and we were flooded with a storm of inquiries. What group were the hostage takers from? How many hostages? Where were they? Were they injured? What were the demands? The JTF was asking if we needed to send the Marine ARG-MEU special operations hostage rescue team to Brava.

I went from being mildly annoyed to scared. The last thing we needed was a hostage rescue team trying to shoot its way into Brava; it was a small village to be sure, but it still had more than a hundred buildings, any of which might hold a hostage. It was the middle of the night, and the team would have no idea where to look. The only maps of Brava were those that our scouts had hand drawn. The Marines blasting into there in the middle of the night and kicking down doors would be sure to get into a fight with somebody that would probably be unnecessary. There just wasn't enough information available for this sort of thing. I worked frantically to call off the hostage rescue team, telling JTF that we already had forces en route and we'd let JTF know if we needed any help.

As it turned out, the whole thing boiled down to a kind of labor-management dispute. The hired guards had held the other Korean aid worker because she refused to give them the agreed-to amount for their services (or so they claimed). She in turn was sputtering mad in her broken English—"Bad men, velly bad men"—which set off the Somalis yelling about payment again. One of the lieutenants told me later that it was like watching an argument in a mental institution. Finally, Lieutenant Criswell lost patience with everyone. He told the gunmen to hand over the hostage posthaste and told the NGO to shut up and follow his troops back to Marka. The gunmen were unhappy, but faced with fifty soldiers and four gun humvees they got his point. I was happy to report to JTF that the hostage was "rescued," and Criswell and the boys got back around 0400.

Next we were alerted to go back to Kismayu (again). It was reported that the Jess faction might be getting reinforcements from Mogadishu to assist them in ejecting Morgan from the city. We were directed to send a company to a blocking position astride the road near Mundun outside Brava. We were also directed to establish an observation post on top of the ridgeline overlooking the ocean in case the gunmen tried to sneak by us in boats. In reading the order, I thought that someone in UNITAF headquarters had finally lost it. Overlook sea traffic? What would we do if we saw anything? How would we know it was a bad guy? The navy and our allies had ships so crowded off Mogadishu they were almost ramming one another and UNITAF wanted us to monitor coastal traffic. Silly, just silly. We sent Geoff Hammil's company to do the blocking position. They manned it for a total of four days; then the whole operation was called off as precipitously as it had begun. It was a success in that no Jess forces tried to come south while we were there. Because no ships had been sighted, our inadequacy as a naval coast-watching station was never put to the test.

Three weeks before we left, the scout platoon from the 2-87 finally was allowed to deploy to Somalia to replace the scouts from the 1-87, who were needed by their parent battalion for the preparatory training for a JRTC deployment. This to me was another example of peacetime requirements impacting upon combat-deployed forces. However, there wasn't anything we could do about it, so we said a reluctant goodbye to Lieutenant Harvey and his people. I took a walk through their platoon bay before they left and thanked them for the good work they had done. They had been part of my little independent command in Brava and had killed the bandits there. They had been in the thick of things ever since. I remembered Sergeant Zimmerman's excitement and enthusiasm when they'd gotten the bandits in Kismayu, and I got to see them in action as even more bandits blundered into us for another flurry of shooting. They were good troops and I was sorry to see them go. The only upside was that 2-87 would finally get its own battalion scouts. I was concerned that our battalion would be divided between the men who went to Somalia and those who didn't go. As much as I respected Geoff Hammil's company, I kept hoping we'd get Charlie Company out to augment or replace them. Lieutenant Colonel Sikes and Colonel Ward fought for it. Division would not support the cost of shipping out another company, though, so Geoff's guys were destined to stay with us to the end.

There were periodic incidents of robbery on the main highway between the K-50 airstrip and Afgoi. Because the last Brava mission was such a bust, Sikes allowed Geoff Hammil to conduct counterbandit sweeps of the nearby woods. We received intelligence that the bandits operated from a base camp not far from the K-50 airfield in the cover of the forest. I was skeptical of the intelligence, but it was all we had to go on. As it was, my skepticism was well founded. Geoff's people swept the forest for three days, finding no sign of a bandit base camp or any base camp. It reinforced our belief that hunting bandits in the woods was a waste of time. Bandits didn't live in the woods; bandits lived in the towns.

Leaving (April 1993)

Task Force 1-22 and its attachments came in over the next three days. Unit leaders were taken on patrols in Marka and on familiarization patrols of the key areas in the valley. Each staff section tried to impart as much knowledge as it could to its replacement counterpart. Sergeant First Class Hardcastle and I were especially heartbroken because the buildup shelters for the TOC humvees he had conceived and helped construct in the summer of 1992 would be left with the rest of our vehicles. I assured him that we would start on a new one when we returned to Fort Drum. Everywhere in the battalion, people were doing all they could to ensure that the men who replaced them made the best possible start.

Lieutenant Colonel Sikes and Walt Wojtas took Lieutenant Colonel Martinez down to meet the Marka town council. It was to prove a temporary acquaintance. Task Force 1-22 already was designated to go to Mogadishu to replace the outgoing Marines. HRS Marka would be turned over to the Pakistanis. We had mixed emotions about this. The Pakistanis were professionals, so we had no doubt that they would do a good job, but we felt a proprietary interest in Marka. It would have been nice to leave it with Task Force 1-22.

Lieutenant Colonel Martinez's battalion gave us a big sendoff. We had a massed formation inside the perimeter of Condor Base. There Sikes saluted Martinez as the two battalions faced each other. Then the 1-22 broke ranks and formed a single file on either side of the road, and the 2-87 marched out to the waiting trucks, with the soldiers of the 1-22 clapping and cheering us as we left. It was a nice touch.

Lieutenant Colonel Sikes and I stayed a few hours after the trucks left, going over details and answering any last questions that might be raised. It was more worry on our part than necessity; Task Force 1-22 was up to the job. They had the reins now and they'd do fine. At last we walked down to the helipad. I looked around and saw the new battalion settling in as though it was already at home, and I felt a real sense of accomplishment. Task Force 2-87 built this, I thought. Not a bad feeling at the end of the day. The Black Hawk came in and Sikes and I climbed on board. It lifted off, dusting Lieutenant Colonel Martinez, who waved and then turned to the matters at hand. We flew low along the shoreline, over the newly wrecked ship and the pristine beach. I looked down at the town of Marka for the last time with mixed emotions. The streets were crowded (but not with derelict cars), and life looked as much like normal as I thought it would ever get. Even then I felt an uneasiness. How long will it last? I wondered. As we flew high along the coastline ridge, I could see into the valley and was struck again by how green it was. I looked down into the woods below and wondered at the last, futile operations we'd spent there. Chasing ghosts. We'd have done better sending Geoff Hammil for one more night sweep up and down the road between Marka and Afgoi or Marka and Brava. Oh well, it was all one now. I saw K-50 airfield and remembered the cordon we'd done there. We'd had some good operations. It was time to go home.

Mogadishu loomed—big, sprawling, and ugly. We landed at the U.S. embassy compound; the difference in the place was astonishing. It looked like a modern mining camp, all trailers and generators and antennas, with glass back in some of the buildings and the grounds cleaned up of debris. I scarcely recognized the place.

We spent two days in Mogadishu waiting to leave. It was strange having nothing to do. I'd check in with Hardcastle and the guys, then go and check on the arrangements to get us to the airport. Everything was fine. There was a little souvenir stand on the compound where we were staying, and I bought a Somali wooden pillow. The Kuwaitis were next to our compound, so I walked over and tried some of my pidgin Arabic on them. It passed the time. Most of the men slept, but I was too wired.

After two days, it was time to go. I put on my last clean uniform and packed everything else. Finally we boarded trucks and drove through Mogadishu toward the airport. The sheer size of the place was daunting. The rabbit warren of streets seemed endless. It brought home to me just how small

Kismayu, Marka, and Afgoi really were. I was glad we had done our time in the valley as opposed to Mogadishu. This place could swallow a battalion and not even burp, I thought.

The airport was its usual beehive of activity. We were brought into a big hangar and given the usual customs brief and opportunity to use the amnesty box to get rid of anything that wasn't authorized to bring home, such as captured weapons. Then we were manifested—our names called out, checked off, and annotated on what seemed to be five different lists. Our aircraft, a Tower Air 747, was parked and waiting for us. It looked completely out of place in the ramshackle airport with its military aircraft and Russian MiG derelicts pushed to the side—like a big, peaceful dairy cow in a dog pound. We boarded slowly, because it takes time to stow weapons in the overhead compartments. I went on next to last followed by Lieutenant Colonel Sikes. The interior of the plane was so bright and new looking that it assaulted the senses. The feeling of unreality only grew as the plane taxied and I looked out at Mogadishu airport with its tent cities, supply depots, aircraft from a dozen countries, and derelicts. We built up speed and seemed to take forever getting off the ground. White-knuckle flyer that I am, I started to get apprehensive. Finally, with what seemed to be only a hundred feet of runway left, we lifted off and were instantly over the water. A deafening cheer went up throughout the airplane. We turned north, and I got my last look at Somalia as we gained altitude. It was green and tan and nondescript. Mogadishu was already behind us. We continued to climb, and the first movie of the flight started: *Airplane*, with Leslie Nielsen. Cool.

We must have amazed the cabin crew. By the time we reached Ireland, we had drunk every can of soda and eaten every meal and snack available. One stewardess remarked to me that it was the first time she'd ever seen people eat every bit of an airline meal. Lieutenant Colonel Sikes, as ever, was buried in his laptop, no doubt starting on his after-action report. He'd get up occasionally when his carpal tunnel syndrome set in to go around and talk to people. Joe Occhuzzio and most of the guys slept. I couldn't. So I just walked around the plane and visited. After a while there wasn't anyone left awake to talk to, so I just sat and listened to music, enjoying the civilization of it all.

We arrived in Shannon, Ireland, around 0300. Colonel Ward let us off the plane into the terminal, but there was no drinking, because we were still officially deployed. The Irish must have thought it odd that dozens of soldiers were lining up for ice cream and no one was going into the bar. I bought Irish scarves for Donna and my mother and sister. We were objects of curiosity in the sparsely populated airport, but the terminal workers couldn't have been friendlier. The feeling of a return to civilization was becoming more palpable. We took off just at dawn, the Irish countryside looking incredibly green as we banked to head out over the Atlantic.

I don't remember much of the rest of the trip, because I slept most of the way. Before I knew it, we were over Canada and less than an hour from Griffiths Air Force Base. Everyone put their boots back on and got their stuff collected. I wondered about Donna and John, especially John. I realized I'd been deployed for about 20 percent of his entire life. Would he even know me? Everyone was quiet, so I'm sure they were having many of the same thoughts. Coming home has an apprehension all its own, and I was tasting it in full as we landed.

As opposed to our outload in December, everything was well organized. The division band was there to meet us. Colonel Ward and Lieutenant Colonel Sikes answered a few brief questions from the local press. Duffel bags were uploaded on trucks, and Sergeant Major Key and the first sergeants got the battalion onto the buses. Kelly Jordan met us with a van and took Sikes, Joe Occhuzzio, Steve Michaels, Mike Klein, and me back to the battalion. On the way there he briefed us on all that had been done in preparing for the upcoming training cycle, what ranges had been laid on, what training areas, et cetera. He told us about Charlie Company's adventures at the JRTC and in Panama. The training exercises he described sounded remote and unimportant. I confess I had trouble listening as we drove behind the troop buses through rural upstate New York. There was still some snow on the ground. The everyday American normality of it was striking. Nothing had changed (no reason for it to), but we had changed. The anticipation was building, and with a curious feeling of light-hearted tension, we arrived at Fort Drum.

Lieutenant Colonel Sikes wanted to have a proper formation with companies and staff assembled and dismiss the men. Apparently, however, some prior arrangement was made and we all formed into one big mass in the gym: 2-87, 2d Brigade, and attachments all lumped together, with Colonel Ward and Lieutenant Colonel Sikes in front. The families were in the bleachers, and their cheers made it hard to hear. I was in one of the back ranks and strained to see Donna and John, but I couldn't find them. Major General Arnold was there, but he left the speaking to Colonel Ward, who talked for less than two minutes, thanking everyone present in a mercifully terse but heartfelt speech. Perhaps he could sense the families wanting to rush out to their loved ones. He shouted "dismissed," and there was a roar as the troops came forward and the families surged down. I walked forward slowly, looking for Donna and John. There was Hardcastle with his wife, Staff Sergeant Brown and the unsinkable Mrs. Brown, who'd continued to help and organize throughout the deployment. All sorts of little private moments were happening all around me. But I couldn't find Donna and John.

I heard a voice yelling my name, and there was Ruth Anne Sikes and next to her Donna and John. They were still standing in the bleachers and I climbed to meet them. Donna was beautiful in a blue dress. She was laughing and holding a camcorder. The battery had run out just as the ceremony began. John was shy at first and tried to hide behind his mother. We sat down and I let him look at my rifle, which seemed to break the ice. I sat and held them close and felt giddy and strange.

Collecting everyone for weapons turn-in took some doing, but we managed. Family members sat in the headquarters and barracks while weapons and sensitive items were cleaned and turned in. Inventories were made in record time and the companies were released. One by one I watched the S3 section depart. Dusty Hardcastle, Magnant, Brown, Slaughter, Jackson, Issac, Terry Henry, Higgenbotham, Hugley, and Labonte. Donna, John, and I walked down to the command group. Joe Occhuzzio was just pulling out of the parking lot with his family, and Sikes was in his office with Ruth Anne. "Anything else, sir?" I asked Sikes. Old habits die hard. "If not, I'm going the hell home." Jim Sikes shook his head and said, "No, Marty. Have a good weekend. See you Monday." We bid our good-byes, and Donna, John, and I went home. It was over.

Sixteen

The Big Picture: Operation RESTORE HOPE
April 1993–March 1995

When Task Force 2-87 and 2d Brigade left Somalia in April 1993, UNITAF was still in charge. However, the transition to UN command was well under way. UNISOM II officially took the reins from UNITAF in May. A most immediate consequence of this turnover was the departure of Task Force 1-22 infantry from Marka. The cantonment area we had built at the old police barracks was turned over to a Pakistani battalion and HRS Marka along with it. The Belgians departed Kismayu, replaced by troops from the Indian army. Task Force 1-22 would become the UNISOM II reaction force, based out of the university compound at Mogadishu. The last Marine battalion withdrew with UNITAF. Task Force 1-22, 1st Brigade headquarters, and some attack aviation assets were the only American combat units left in Somalia. In addition, we had a large logistical support contingent on the ground, and there was a sizable number of American officers in the UNISOM II headquarters. The deputy commander was also an American: Maj. Gen. Thomas Montgomery. The commander of UNISOM II was Turkish general Cevik Bir. Significantly, Ambassador Oakley also departed and was replaced by Adm. Jonathan Howe, a man whose methods and temperament were very different.

The situation in Mogadishu deteriorated rapidly after the UNISOM II transition. Several major riots took place, and in retaliation for the casualties inflicted in one of them, the forces of Mohammed Farah Adieed ambushed and decimated a Pakistani company in late June 1993. Task Force 1-22 was instrumental in the rescue of the survivors of this unit. Adieed became public enemy number one, and the war was on. Several large operations to capture Adieed and neutralize his forces ended in bloody fighting. Task Force 1-22, with a tireless Ahmed Omer still acting as chief interpreter, was in the thick of it, losing a number of soldiers wounded (but none killed, thank God). Other units were not as fortunate. An MP humvee was blown up by a command-detonated mine, with all four soldiers aboard killed. A helicopter was shot down by an RPG, and two crewmen died. Other soldiers were wounded in exchanges of fire. Other nation's units lost people—the Pakistanis, as previously mentioned, but also the Italians, Nigerians, and Botswanans. Several hundred Somalis also died in these fights. Most were actual gunmen or active supporters, but a few were unfortunate bystanders. Adieed proved elusive, and the special operations community was called in to capture or kill him.

Task Force 1-22 rotated back in August and was replaced by Task Force 2-14 infantry, our sister battalion from down the street at Fort Drum and the same unit that was alerted (but not deployed) at Christmas. Lieutenant Colonel David had realized then that eventually his unit would go to Somalia and had spent the year training at a fever pitch. At the same time, Rangers and other special operations soldiers went into Somalia to turn up the heat in the hunt for Adieed. These forces kept a constant pressure on the Adieed organization in a series of operations that culminated in the battle on 3 October 1993.

I won't go into detail about what happened that day. I wasn't there, and pundits have already picked the battle to death. If you want to read good accounts of that battle, read *Blackhawk Down* by Mark Bowden or *Savage Peace* by Dan Bolger. Suffice it to say that Adieed was not captured, but eighteen Americans and several other coalition soldiers (and hundreds of Somalis) died and almost a thousand other people were wounded. Task Force 2-14, along with Malaysian and Pakistani troops, fought its way into the surrounded Rangers and special operations troops and lost people doing it. The casualties and images of our dead being dragged through the streets shocked America. Other casualties quickly followed in mortar attacks on the Ranger camp at Mogadishu airport.

The Somalis were also shocked by the casualties. Nothing like the battle in the market had ever happened in their long civil war. The Adieed camp watched in fear as American reinforcements arrived—Task Force 2-22 infantry from Fort Drum, Task Force 1-64 armor from Fort Stewart (the armor badly needed on 3 October but denied to our forces by Secretary of Defense Aspin), a Marine battalion offshore on amphibious ships, more attack helicopters, AC-130 gunships, another company of Rangers, and other special operations augmentation. Plans were made to conduct a deliberate sweep of the whole city and destroy Adieed forces in detail. Everyone on the ground who had seen the videos of our dead being dragged around seethed with anger. The American forces poised outside of Mogadishu were like an attack dog straining at the leash.

But nothing came of it. The Clinton administration, shocked by the casualties, decided that Somalia wasn't worth it. The United States told Adieed that it was pulling out in March 1994. Fighting continued at a low level for the next few weeks but eventually died out. Before the new year, Adieed was flying to meetings in Ethiopia in U.S. military aircraft, a move that made the soldiers who had fought on 3 October cringe with disgust. Force protection became the name of the game. Don't make waves and don't do anything that might be risky to American life. We basically withdrew into our armed camps and waited for March to come.

We left UNISOM II in March 1994, and the soldiers of all of the countries we had talked into contributing troops were stuck in Somalia. We abandoned them like a pet at Yellowstone Park. It was explained away by some ludicrous rhetoric about a new phase of UNISOM II. No one believed it. The USA was running. It was a shameful episode.

If we weren't going to stick it out and do the hard stuff, why should anyone else? UNISOM II basically went into force protection mode and stayed there. The UN troops hunkered onto their own defensive perimeters and predictable local patrol routes. They didn't hassle the Somalis, and the Somalis generally left them alone. The civil war swirled and eddied around the UN soldiers. They resembled nothing so much as infield spectators in a NASCAR race, located right there, able to see all the action but powerless to affect it.

It was recognized (belatedly) that we had a moral obligation to help UN forces depart Somalia. I was stationed in U.S. Central Command Headquarters at McDill Air Force Base by this time and had a minor part in planning the withdrawal operation. Several of my friends made repeated trips to coordinate the withdrawal of the UNISOM II forces. Finally, Marine general Anthony Zinni, the future Central Command (CENTCOM) commander, went to personally talk to Adieed. Zinni's message was simple: let everyone go unmolested or there will be hell to pay. Adieed cheerfully complied with this. He didn't want to waste his forces in attacks on withdrawing UNISOM II when he needed them for the ongoing civil war with Ali Mahdi. Besides, he wanted to loot the UN compounds when the withdrawal was complete.

The UNISOM II withdrawal was done in stages. First the troops from the outlying posts were brought in: Belet Uyene, Baidoa, Bardera, Oddur, Gialassi, Baledogle, and Marka. I often think of crowds of Somalis streaming in to the pleasant base camp we built, tearing off the roofs and stripping the whole compound like locusts. It's a sad thought. We'd tried hard to bring a measure of stability to the place. Oh well, nothing lasts forever I suppose.

With the hinterlands evacuated, Kismayu was abandoned by the Indians. Finally the remainder of the UNISOM II forces left Mogadishu. The withdrawal of the last UNISOM soldiers was covered by the U.S. Marines and army special operations troops in Operation United Shield. This last withdrawal went generally unmolested, although the Marines did have a few firefights, killing a number of overenthusiastic

Adieed supporters who apparently hadn't gotten the word not to challenge the withdrawal. In March 1995 it was all over. The last UNISOM II troops were gone. Somalia degenerated into what it had been before the arrival of UNITAF.

The next five years were just more of the same: status quo stalemate followed by periods of intense but useless fighting. Mohammed Farah Adieed was killed in 1997 and was replaced by his son (a U.S. Marine reservist; hooray for life's little ironies). As of September 2000, Somalia had had several more floods and famines. A few dedicated (or masochistic) aid workers still soldiered on. Khat was still smuggled in and still bought by Somali banknotes that had no value (but a lot of faith) behind them. A barter economy existed under the benevolent eye of a half-dozen warlords. The world, however, has pretty much forgotten Somalia. This is probably just as well. Somalia always has been a no-account kind of place.

Epilogue

Where Are They Now?

The 2-87 Infantry still exists in the 10th Mountain Division at Fort Drum, but few if any of the soldiers in it are veterans of the battalion's deployment to Somalia in 1992–93. Transfer, discharge, and retirement have seen to that. Lieutenant Colonel Sikes put in eleven soldiers for bronze stars (Lieutenant Harvey and ten enlisted men), but these were turned down by the Department of the Army because Somalia wasn't a "combat zone." Ironically, the Combat Infantryman Badge and a right shoulder patch designating combat service were authorized to all members of the battalion. Crazy. Nor is there a campaign streamer on the Army flag for Somalia, in spite of the fact that more soldiers were killed and wounded there than in Grenada or Panama. Many of the soldiers have since left the army and successfully reentered civilian life without any idea of how extraordinary they really were. Others stayed in and maintained successful careers in the service.

Major General Arnold went on to get his third star and retired in 1998. Brigadier General Magruder went on to command the 10th Mountain Division and is currently a three star stationed in Atlanta, Georgia. Colonel Ward went on to two stars and is currently commanding the 25th Division in Hawaii.

Lieutenant Colonel Jim Sikes made full colonel and commanded a brigade in the 25th. He was the rarest of creatures, never selected below the zone, nobody's golden boy brigade commander, and he continued to do well by his troops. He is currently assigned to the Pentagon. He is no doubt cursing his luck and scheming to get back to troops.

Joe Occhuzzio made lieutenant colonel and was on the alternate list to battalion command twice but was never picked up. I guess brilliant performance in stressful situations wasn't what the army was looking for. He retired in 1997. Captain Mike Klein was another gem the army let go. In spite of serving in Desert Storm, Hurricane Andrew, Somalia, and Haiti, Mike Klein was not selected for major and left active duty. Military Intelligence branch told him he had "too much troop time" and his promotion file had a "bad picture" in it. Thus Mike Klein, the best tactical intelligence officer I have ever served with, left active duty. The National Guard snapped him right up and he is now a major. Military Intelligence branch once again proved that its name is indeed an oxymoron.

Captain Steve Michaels and Lieutenant Bill Haas both went on to other jobs in the army, and I lost track of them. Steve published an excellent article in *Infantry* magazine about support operations in Somalia. Captain Gordy Flowers is a major and a brigade S3 in Alaska. Captain Wes Bickford got out of the army and also lives in Alaska. Captain Tom Wilk is a major and lives at Fort Dix, New Jersey. Captain Geoff Hammil stayed in and was still in the division when I left in 1993. I have since lost track of him. Captain Kirk Haschak became a Russian linguist and a foreign area officer and is currently a major stationed in Byelorussia.

Of the lieutenants, the giant Bob Van Hoesen got out and planned to go to work in the fire and rescue department of the little upstate New York town he lived in. His coworkers will find him funny and a thoroughly dependable man in a crisis. George Harvey, the scout platoon leader, is a major on full-time duty in the Florida National Guard. Stan Genega left the battalion to become a lieutenant in the Ranger battalion. About half the others are still in the army and are all by now captains with four or five years in grade, or new majors. Time flies.

Sergeant Major Key stayed the perennial battalion command sergeant major. He was transferred to Fort Benning and became the command sergeant major of a mechanized battalion that made several unscheduled trips to Kuwait in response to Iraqi threats over the years. Sadly, he lost his son in 1998, but he continues to soldier on. He is one of the many truly admirable people I have met in the army.

Sergeant First Class Hardcastle was promoted to master sergeant and was sent to Fort Benning. He and Mrs. Hardcastle both beat cancer and as of this writing are doing fine. He retired from the army in 1998 and was hired immediately by a company developing the next generation of command posts for the army. He is still employed at Fort Benning and is training NCOs and officers on command post operations. It's comforting to know that a whole generation of new guys is learning how to do it the right way from Scott Hardcastle.

Magnant was promoted to sergeant first class and is stationed in Florida. Brown retired as a staff sergeant (a crime in my mind; he'd have been a hell of a platoon sergeant and first sergeant). Terry Henry was promoted to sergeant and as far as I know is still in the army. I had the honor of being invited to his wedding soon after our return from Somalia, and I wish he and Mrs. Henry all the best. Labonte and Hugley got out and returned to civilian life. I have no doubt they're doing well. The last I saw of Higgenbotham was the day I left the battalion. He was talking with Hardcastle about rebuilding the hardtop shelters on our new humvees to replace the ones we'd left in Somalia. Never a guy to rest on his laurels, Hig was already looking ahead to the next job. As long as the army has such soldiers, we'll be in good shape.

Me? I stayed in. Not that I'm that great (I frankly blush whenever I think of some of the mistakes I made in Somalia), but I do okay. Besides, where else in the world do you get to work with people like this?

Appendices

**Rules of Engagement to TF Mountain OPLAN 93-2
(Operation RESTORE HOPE)**
1. Situation. Basic OPLAN/OPORD
2. Mission. Basic OPLAN/OPORD
3. Execution.
   a. Concept of the Operation
   (1) If you are operating as a unit, squad, or other formation, follow the orders of your leaders.
   (2) Nothing in these rules infringes upon the right to use reasonable force to defend yourself or others against dangerous personal attack.
   (3) The rules of self-protection and the rules of engagement are not intended to infringe upon your right of self-defense. These rules are intended to prevent indiscriminate use of force or other violations of law or regulation.
   (4) Commanders will instruct their personnel on their mission. This includes the proper conduct and regard for the local population and the need to respect private property and public facilities. The Posse Comitatus Act does not apply in an overseas area. Expect that all missions will have the inherent task of force security and protection.
   (5) ROE cards will be published and distributed to each deploying soldier. (See Appendix II.)
   b. Rules of Self-protection for All Soldiers
   (1) U.S. forces will protect themselves from threats of death or serious bodily harm. Deadly force may be used to

defend your life, the life of another soldier, or the life of an innocent civilian. You are authorized to use deadly force in self-defense or to defend others when:

(a) you are fired upon

(b) armed elements, mobs, and/or rioters threaten human life

(c) there is clear evidence of hostile intent

1. Hostile intent of opposing forces can be determined by unit leaders or individual soldiers if their leaders are not present. Hostile intent is the threat of imminent use of force against U.S. forces or other persons in those areas under the control of U.S. forces. Factors to consider include:

a. Weapons: Are they present? What type?

b. Size of the opposing force

c. If weapons are present, in what manner are they displayed? That is, are they being aimed? Are the weapons part of a firing position? Are mortar/crew-served weapons crews active?

d. How did the opposing force react to the U.S. forces?

e. How does the opposing force act toward other unarmed civilians?

f. Other aggressive actions

2. You may detain persons threatening or using force that would cause death or serious bodily harm or interfere with mission accomplishment. Detainees should be given to the military police as soon as possible for evacuation to central collection points (see paragraph d below).

c. Rules of Engagement. The relief property, foodstuffs, medical supplies, building materials, and other end items belong to the United Nations until they are actually distributed to the populace. Your mission includes safe transit of these materials to the populace.

(1) Deadly force may be used only when:

(a) fired upon

(b) clear evidence of hostile intent exists (see above for factors to consider to determine hostile intent)

(c) armed elements, mobs, and/or rioters threaten:

1. human life
2. sensitive equipment and aircraft
3. open and free passage of relief supplies

(2) In situations where deadly force is not appropriate, use the minimum force necessary to accomplish the mission.

(3) Patrols are authorized to protect relief supplies and U.S. forces. Patrols may use deadly force if fired upon or if they encounter opposing forces that evidence a hostile intent. Nondeadly force or a show of force should be used if the security of U.S. forces is not compromised by doing so. A graduated show of force includes:

(a) an order to disband or disburse

(b) show of force/threat of force by U.S. forces that is greater than the force threatened by the opposing force

(c) warning shots aimed to prevent harm to either innocent civilians or the opposing force

(d) other means of nondeadly force

(e) If this show of force does not cause the opposing force to abandon its hostile intent, consider if deadly force is appropriate.

(4) Use of barbed-wire fences is authorized.

(5) Unattended means of force (such as unobserved mines, booby traps, trip guns) are not authorized.

(6) If U.S. forces are attacked or threatened by unarmed hostile elements, mobs, and/or rioters, U.S. forces will use the minimum force necessary to overcome the threat. A graduated response to hostile unarmed elements includes:

(a) warnings to demonstrators in their native language

(b) show of force, including the use of riot control formations (see below for rules about using riot control agents)

(c) warning shots fired over the heads of the hostile elements

(d) other reasonable uses of force, to include deadly force when the element demonstrates a hostile intent, which are necessary and proportional to the threat

(7) All weapons systems may be employed throughout the area of operations unless otherwise prohibited. The use of weapons systems must be appropriate and proportional to the threat. For example, an attack helicopter or a tank may be used in circumstances that warrant a show of force. In appropriate situations they may be used to fire warning shots.

(8) U.S. forces will not endanger or exploit the property of the local population without their specific approval. Use of civilian property will usually be compensated by contract or other form of payment. Property that has been used for the purpose of hindering our mission will be confiscated. Weapons may be confiscated and demilitarized if they are used to interfere with the mission of U.S. forces (see rule 10 below).

(9) Operations will not be conducted outside of the landmass, airspace, and territorial seas of Somalia.

(10) Crew-served weapons and armed individuals are considered a threat to U.S. forces and the relief effort whether they demonstrate hostile intentions or not. U.S. forces may use force to confiscate and demilitarize all weapons used to interfere with their mission. Leaders will exercise their discretion to determine if weapons they encounter are interfering with the mission, and will confiscate only those weapons that are interfering with the accomplishment of the mission. In the absence of a hostile or criminal act, personnel from whom weapons have been confiscated and their vehicles will be released after the weapon is confiscated/demilitarized.

(a) If an armed individual or weapons crew demonstrates hostile intentions, they may be engaged with deadly force.

(b) If an armed individual or weapons crew commits criminal acts but does not demonstrate hostile intentions, U.S. forces will use the minimum amount of force necessary to detain them (see paragraph e below).

(c) Crew-served weapons are any weapons system that requires more than one individual to operate. Crew-served systems include but are not limited to tanks, artillery pieces, antiaircraft guns, mortars, and machine guns.

    d. Use of Riot Control Agents (RCAs). Use of RCAs requires the approval of CJTF [combined joint task force]. When authorized, RCAs may be used for the following purposes:

        (1) Riot control in the division area of operations, including the dispersal of civilians who obstruct roadways or otherwise impede distribution operations after lesser means have failed to result in dispersal.

        (2) Riot control in detainee holding areas or camps in and around material distribution or storage areas.

        (3) To protect convoys from civil disturbances, terrorists, or paramilitary groups.

    e. Detention of Personnel. Personnel who interfere with the accomplishment of the mission or who use or threaten use of deadly force against U.S. forces, material distribution sites, or convoys may be detained and evacuated to a central location.

        (1) Detained personnel will be treated with respect and dignity. These people will be afforded the rights due to a captured enemy prisoner of war under the Geneva and Hague Conventions.

        (2) Detained personnel will be processed through designated UN personnel only. These personnel will not be sent to established refugee camps.

4. Service Support. Basic OPLAN/OPORD

5. Command and Signal. Basic OPLAN/OPORD

Acknowledge
Arnold
MG
OFFICIAL

SMITH
Staff judge advocate

Appendix II

10th Mountain Division
Rules of Engagement Card A

Nothing in these rules of engagement limits your right to take appropriate action to defend yourself and your unit.

    A. If you are operating as a unit, squad, or other formation, follow the orders of your leaders.

    B. You have the right to use force to defend yourself against attacks or threats of attack.

    C. Hostile fire may be returned effectively and promptly to stop a hostile act.

    D. When U.S. forces are attacked by unarmed hostile elements, mobs, and/or rioters, U.S. forces should use the minimum force necessary under the circumstances and proportional to the threat.

    E. You may not seize the property of others to accomplish your mission. You may use civilian property if the owner gives his permission. You may confiscate weapons or civilian property that interferes with the accomplishment of your mission.

    F. Detention of civilians is authorized for security reasons or in self-defense.

REMEMBER
    1. The United States is not at war.
    2. Treat all persons with dignity and respect.
    3. Use minimum force to carry out the mission.
    4. Always be prepared to act in self-defense.

Operations Summary, Marka

DTG [Date Time Group] 11 March 1993

PER ARFOR CDR'S GUIDANCE REQUEST THIS OP-
SUM BE FORWARDED COMPLETE AS IT IS ROLLED
UP AS A SEPARATE HUMANITARIAN RELIEF SEC-
TOR (HRS MARKA).

1. Enemy Activity: No significant enemy activity reported in
   the last 24 hours
2. Mission: No change
3. FLOT/COM: No change
4. Subunit Locations: B/2-87 TACON to Belgian Para in
   Kismayu
5. Summary of Operations
   A. Past 24 hours
      1. ADA platoon escorted a food convoy to Quorleey
         (MG 4896).
      2. The TF conducted normal security operations in Marka
         (MG 7490).
      3. Scout platoon conducted night patrols in Marka (MG
         7490).
      4. S5, S2, CI, and CA reps went to Mogadishu for the
         UNISOM HRS meeting.
      5. Support platoon went to Baledogle and picked up
         small-arms ammunition from the 210th ASP [Am-
         munition Supply Point].
   B. Next 48 hours
      1. ADA platoon will conduct morning patrols in Marka
         (MG 7490).
      2. AT platoon with a section from the mortar platoon will
         escort a food convoy to Brava on Saturday, 13 March.
      3. A/1-87 and scout platoon will conduct saturation pa-
         trols south of Afgoi.

6. Logistics: The main logistic concerns at Marka (MG 7490) are as follows:

   a. Given the vision for Condor Base, a complete electrical grid, fluorescent lights, washers and dryers, etc., TF 2-87 now needs three each thirty-kilowatt generators to assist in power requirements (recommendation by engineers). We understand that the request has been approved for purchase by Brown and Root and is scheduled to arrive by April. Current generators will deploy with TF 2-87 if we are reassigned within Somalia.

   b. SSSC [Self Service Supply Center] supplies are still a concern, the lack of which is affecting our mission capability. We are tasking soldiers to bring supplies to Somalia hand carried from Fort Drum. In addition we will attempt to purchase some of these supplies in Mombassa, Kenya.

   c. Need to know the status of the 25,000 feet of canvas roofing material for the Sister Anna TB clinic in Marka (MG 7490). CG interest on 9 March 1993.

2406 Status

Bumper #	Nomenclature	Reason NMC [non mission capable]
HQ 41	M923	Left rear brakes
HQ 75	M998	Run flat tire
HQ 42	M923	Oil pressure gauge
HQ 27	M998	Power steering hose
HQ 20	M998	Class III leak
204	M923A2 (57th Trans)	Air warning buzzer
207	M923A2 (57th Trans)	Flat tire

Supply status follows:

CL I: Green
   3 DOS bottled water, MREs, and T rations
   10,000 gallons bulk water

CL II: Amber (SSSC)

CL III: Green

2,000 gallons JP5, 700 gallons Mogas

CL IV: Amber

Require 200 sheets of plywood

CL V: Green

CL VI: Green

CL VII: Green

CL VIII: Amber

Refrigerator and VELOSEF

7. The following is the civil affairs summary for the past 24 hours:

   a. Major Wojtas, Captain Klein, and Lieutenant Lavellie attended the JTF provost marshal briefing in Mogadishu concerning the initial startup of the auxiliary security force. Among the topics discussed were payment of security force members ($103.00/month) and the disbursal of newly arrived equipment to the areas with now operational security forces. Marka received an initial allotment of sixty-five uniforms and police whistles. A six-passenger Toyota vehicle will be ready for pickup on Monday and will be outfitted with a Motorola radio. The police headquarters is due to receive a base station radio and a small amount of hand-held radios. Items that are awaiting arrival in country are such things as a five-kilowatt generator per police station and a supply of handcuffs, boots, blue berets, tables and chairs, and office supplies. Most of these supplies are on the ground in Nairobi awaiting transportation to Mogadishu. The JTF has a $4.6 million budget in which approximately $3.5 million will be used for wages. The World Food Program is also coming on-line with a work-for-food program to assist in payment of security force policemen.

   b. The ICRC expressed a positive attitude reference the Marka security force that is currently operating in the port. These policemen are under the command of Mohammed Omar Mohammed. His credentials were verified in Mogadishu by the JTF provost marshal and were found to be exemplary. The ICRC reported that things were operating much more smoothly as of late and the police in the port were being cooperative with the ICRC. They also noted that the police were being strict with anyone attempting to loot. It should be noted that the current police chief (Colonel Abdi) tried to order Mohammed O. Mohammed out of the port in order to continue suspected looting operations. Mohammed refused to leave, stating that Major Wojtas had left him to guard the port and he would not leave his post until Major Wojtas relieved him. It appears we may have found a good candidate for the new police chief.

c. Lieutenant Colonel Sikes visited the elders in Quorleey today. He is concerned about the lack of security forces in the town and outlying areas. The guidelines passed down from JTF-PMO [provost marshal office] today will help in establishing further security forces in the towns of the lower Shabele valley. Request information on how smaller communities can start a police force when none existed before.

8. PSYOPS

  a. Last 24 hours:

    The PSYOPS element in Marka is currently changing over its personnel with a new team.

  b. Next 24 hours:

    Continue changeover operations.

9. Commander's Summary

  a. Dragon trackers will be sent back with phase II redeployment shipping. Due to lack of available missile maintenance, no verification of sights/systems was possible on this deployment. Sights will have to be recalibrated upon arrival at Fort Drum.

  b. Debriefing by visitors of our soldiers/leaders continues.

  c. Require hair clippers. The battalion is down to two sets; all others are broken.

  d. Request engineer survey of Shalamboot FLS [flight landing strip] (MG 6487) to estimate the work required to restore it to operational status and increase its capacity to accommodate C-130s.

e. We continue to monitor looting and bandit activities along MSR [main supply route] Pickett north of Marka to determine pattern analysis for future operations.

f. Marka town council members request that UNITAF plan to make Marka safer and put weapons into the hands of the business owners. They want all weapons collected and registered only to Marka businessmen and others who are unanimously voted upon by the town council. They maintain that this will help prevent further looting in Marka and further bandit activity along MSR Pickett. I request guidance on the authority to initiate this program. Security in Marka is stable. The Marka town council requests this action to continue stability in Marka after we are gone.

g. Personnel concerns: 2-87 Infantry communications platoon is extremely short of soldiers and NCOs. At present they lack one E-7, one E-6, one E-5, and two EM [enlisted men]. In addition, two supply sergeants (76Y30) are ninety-day losses.

h. Security for B/2-87 attached to Belgians in Kismayu is a concern. Request rotation of forces if permanent presence is required.

i. Urgently request at least a coalition company be attached to TF 2-87 to take over security mission in Marka and provide TF 2-87 as the JTF RRF [ready reaction force] greater freedom of action.

Glossary

AAR after-action review

ADA Air Defense Artillery

ADVON advanced detachment

AFB air force base

AK-47 7.62mm Russian assault rifle

ALOC Administrative Logistics Operations Center

amtrac Marine Corps term for an AAV-7 amphibious armored personnel carrier

AN/TPQ-36 and -37 counterfire radars

AO area of operations

AOR area of responsibility

ARFOR army forces component of a joint task force. The other components can be MARFOR (Marine forces), AFFOR (air forces), NAFFOR (naval forces), and SOF (special operations forces)

ARG-MEU amphibious ready group Marine expeditionary unit. A USMC organization of reinforced battalion strength

AT antitank

ATK-AVN attack aviation (helicopter gunships)

BCTP Battle Command Training Program

BFV Bradley fighting vehicle

BLUEFOR friendly forces units in field exercises

BN battalion

BNOC Basic Noncommissioned Officers' Course

C-12 twin-engine Piper Cherokee used for flying general officers and VIPs

C-130 four-engine turboprop air force cargo plane capable of landing on short, unimproved airstrips

C-141 four-engine jet transport aircraft used for intercontinental movement of troops and equipment

C2 command and control

CA civil affairs

CH-46 very old USMC medium lift helicopter

CH-47 U.S. Army heavy lift transport helicopter

CH-53 USMC heavy lift transport helicopter

CIB Combat Infantryman Badge

class 1 rations and water

class 2 expendable supply items

class 3 petroleum, oil, and lubricants

class 4 construction and barrier material

class 5 ammunition

class 6 personal comfort items

class 7 major end items (that is, a new truck)

class 8 medical supplies

class 9 spare parts

commo communications

CP command post

CS tear gas riot control agent (when used in describing a weapon); combat support—engineers, signal, ordnance, MP, aviation units (when used in describing a type of unit)

CSS Combat Service Support: finance, adjutant general, quartermaster, transportation units

DISCOM division support command

DIVARTY Division Artillery

Dragon M47 guided missile surface attack. Man portable antitank guided missile

DRB division ready brigade, the first brigade from a division to deploy

DRF-1 Division Ready Force-1. The first battalion task force from the first brigade to deploy

E-5 sergeant

E-6 staff sergeant

E-7 sergeant first class

E-8 master sergeant or first sergeant

E-9 command sergeant major

EFMB Expert Field Medical Badge. A difficult award to achieve

EOD explosive ordnance disposal

ETS end time of service. When a soldier is honorably discharged from the army

FA field artillery

FARRP forward area refuel and rearm point. Used by aviation units

FDC Fire Direction Center

FIST field artillery forward observer team

FORSCOM Forces Command, the headquarters that controls all army forces in the continental United States

FSB forward support battalion. Normally one dedicated to each infantry brigade from DISCOM

FSCOORD fire support coordinator

FSE fire support element. Artillerymen attached to brigade headquarters to coordinate and control the fires of the artillery battalion

FSO fire support officer

GPS global positioning system

GSR ground surveillance radar

HEAT high-explosive antitank

HHC Headquarters and Headquarters Company

HQ headquarters

HRS humanitarian relief sector

HUMINT human intelligence from scouts, agents, or interrogation

humvee 1¼-ton truck commonly used by the army and Marine Corps.

ICRC International Committee of the Red Cross

ILLUM illumination

IR infrared. An older type of night vision device

JRTC Joint Readiness Training Center

JTF joint task force

KM kilometer

LBE load-bearing equipment. Individual soldier's equipment harness

LIC low-intensity combat. Term used for low-level guerrilla war such as Northern Ireland or Somalia

LRSU long-range surveillance unit. Descendents of the Vietnam-era long-range recon patrols (LRRPs)

M1A1 U.S. main battle tank

M113 Vietnam-era armored personnel carrier, replaced by the Bradley fighting vehicle in its primary role but still used as a support vehicle

M16A2 standard 5.56mm rifle of the army and Marine Corps

M203 40mm grenade launcher (individual weapon)

M249 5.56mm squad automatic weapon (SAW)

MAC Military Airlift Command

Mark-19 40mm automatic grenade launcher (crew-served weapon)

MEDCAP Medical Civil Affairs Program. Free medical treatment of the local populace to win their hearts and minds

medevac medical evacuation. Normally done by helicopter

MEF Marine expeditionary force

METT-T mission equipment terrain troops-time

MILES multiple integrated laser engagement system. Laser training device that allows soldiers to engage in realistic training war games

MILPERCEN U.S. Army's Personnel Management Division

MILVAN military designation for a large tractor-trailer-sized container

MOUT military operations in urban terrain

MP military police

MRE meal ready to eat

MSF Médecins Sans Frontières (doctors without borders, an NGO group)

MSR main supply route

NBC nuclear biological chemical warfare

NCO noncommissioned officer

NCOIC noncommissioned officer in charge; senior NCO in an organization (Sergeant First Class Hardcastle was the NCOIC of the S3 shop)

NGO nongovernmental organization

NTC National Training Center (Fort Irwin, California)

O-1 second lieutenant

O-2 first lieutenant

O-3 captain

O-4 major

O-5 lieutenant colonel

O-6 full colonel

O-9 lieutenant general (three-star general)

OC observer controller

OE254 antenna used to increase the range of radios

OH-58 small, two-man observation helicopter

OOTW operations other than war

OPORD operations order

OPSUM operations summary

PAC Personnel Action Center

PGM precision guided munition

PLDC Primary Leadership Development Course

PRC-77 primary backpack radio used by the 10th Mountain Division in Somalia

PRC-126 squad radio

PVO private volunteer organization

PX post exchange

QRF quick reaction force

RAOC Rear Area Operations Center

RETRANS retransmission site. A system that allows radio communications to extend beyond the range of a single transmitting radio

ROE rules of engagement

ROWPU reverse osmosis water purification unit

RPG-7 Russian antitank rocket launcher

RTO radiotelephone operator

S1 personnel and administration staff section

S2 intelligence staff section

S3 plans, operations, and training staff section

S4 logistics staff section

S5 civil affairs staff section

SASO stability and support operations

SAW squad automatic weapon

SICPS standard integrated command post system

SINCGARS single channel ground airborne radio system

SLGR satellite location ground receiver (also called PLGR position location ground receiver)

SNA Somali National Alliance

SNF Somali National Front

SNM Somali National Movement

SOF special operations forces

SOP standard operating procedure

SPM Somali Patriotic Movement

SSDM Somali Salvation Democratic Movement

TAC-1, TAC-2 Task Force 2-87 had two humvees configured for command and control. TAC-1 was Lieutenant Colonel Sikes's vehicle; TAC-2 was the S3 vehicle

TAC-AIR high-performance fighter aircraft in ground support role

TAC-CP tactical command post. Normally made up of a few vehicles or even men on foot with radios. Used by a battalion or brigade commander for forward control of the battle

TACON tactical control. A command relationship in which a unit TACON to another unit follows its orders but does not fall under the unit of attachment for such mundane things as personnel administration

TACP Tactical Air Control Party

TACSAT tactical satellite radio (man portable)

TALCE tactical airlift control element

TAOR tactical area of responsibility

TC truck (or track) commander

TF task force

TOC Tactical Operations Center

TO+E Table of Organization and Equipment

TOW tube-launched optically tracked wire-guided missile. Heavy antitank weapon carried by a humvee

UH-60 U.S. Army Black Hawk medium lift helicopter

UNISOM I United Nations mission before U.S. intervention

UNISOM II United Nations mission after U.S. intervention

UNITAF United Nations intervention task force

USMC United States Marine Corps

UTM universal transverse mercator
WD-1 communications wire for field telephones
XO executive officer
ZSU-23-2 Russian twin 23mm antiaircraft gun

Acknowledgments

This book was made possible by the support and cooperation of a lot of people. I would like to thank MSgt. Scott Hardcastle, USA (Ret.), who provided me with the duty logs of the 2-87 Infantry operations center during Operation Restore Hope. I would like to thank Col. James E. Sikes Jr., USA, for his help and recollections. I would also like to thank all the members of Task Force 2-87 whom I have conversed with over the years. They added their pieces of the story and their perspectives. I would like to thank Col. Dan Bolger, USA, who offered me encouragement to write the book; Brig. Gen. David Petraeus, USA, who helped me edit it; Lt. Col. Ralph Peters, USA (Ret.), who helped me find a publisher; and Mr. E. J. McCarthy of Presidio Press, who adroitly walked me through the publication process. Above all, I must thank my wife, Donna, who has patiently endured my obsession with this project.

Don't miss this absorbing book by
Martin Stanton

THE ROAD
TO BAGHDAD

Behind Enemy Lines: The Adventures of
an American Soldier in the Gulf War

In 1990, U.S. Army Major Martin Stanton was a
military advisor stationed in Saudi Arabia.
Encouraged by the Army to broaden his cultural
horizons, and assured by the U.S. embassy that
Kuwait was perfectly safe, Stanton took off for a
long weekend there. Roused by gunshots his first
night in Kuwait City, Stanton looked out the window and discovered he was in the middle of a full-
scale invasion. This book chronicles his incredible
true story. . . .

Published by Presidio Press
www.presidiopress.com
Available in hardcover wherever books are sold